SHLOMO AVINERI is a renowned Israeli political theorist and public intellectual. He is Professor of Political Science at the Hebrew University of Jerusalem and member of the Israel Academy of Sciences and Humanities. He served as Director-General of Israel's Ministry of Foreign Affairs under Prime Minister Yitzhak Rabin. His books, which have been translated into many languages, include *The Social and Political Thought of Karl Marx*, *Hegel's Theory of the Modern State*, *Moses Hess: Prophet of Communism and Zionism* and *The Making of Modern Zionism*. He has held visiting appointments at, among others, Yale, Cornell, University of California, Oxford, the Central European University in Budapest as well as the Brookings Institution and the Carnegie Endowment for International Peace. He is the recipient of the Israel Prize, the country's highest civilian decoration. He translated *Marx's Early Writings* into Hebrew and wrote the historical Introduction to the three-volume Hebrew edition of Herzl's *Diaries*.

HAIM WATZMAN has translated and edited many important Israeli books by some of the country's leading journalists, scholars and writers – among them David Grossman, Tom Segev and Amos Oz. His fiction and essays appear regularly in his 'Necessary Stories' column in *The Jerusalem Report*. He is also the author of two books of his own, *Company C: An American's Life as a Citizen-Soldier in Israel* and *A Crack in the Earth: A Journey Up Israel's Rift Valley*.

Herzl

Theodor Herzl
and the Foundation of the Jewish State

SHLOMO AVINERI

PHOENIX

A PHOENIX PAPERBACK

First published in Israel in 2008
by Zalman Shazar Center
First published in Great Britain in 2013
by Weidenfeld & Nicolson

This paperback edition published in 2014
by Phoenix,
an imprint of Orion Books Ltd,
Orion House, 5 Upper St Martin's Lane,
London WC2H 9EA

An Hachette UK company

3 5 7 9 10 8 6 4 2

Original text © Shlomo Avineri 2008
English translation © Haim Watzman 2013

A CIP catalogue record for this book is available
from the British Library.

ISBN: 978-1-7802-2455-8

Typeset by Input Data Services Ltd, Bridgwater, Somerset

Printed and bound by CPI Group (UK) Ltd, Croydon, CR0 4YY

The Orion Publishing Group's policy is to use papers that
are natural, renewable and recyclable products and
made from wood grown in sustainable forests. The logging
and manufacturing processes are expected to conform to
the environmental regulations of the country of origin.

www.orionbooks.co.uk

CONTENTS

ILLUSTRATIONS

Plaque on the site of the house in Budapest where Herzl was born *(Ian Pitchford)*

Herzl as a young man *(Central Zionist Archives)*

The title pages of eight different translations of *The Jewish State* *(Reproduced with permission from* Inyan ha-Yehudim (The Jewish Cause): Diaries 1895–1904, *published by The Bialik Institute and the World Zionist Organization, 1997)*

Herzl and Zionist delegation en route to Palestine, 1898 *(Central Zionist Archives)*

Herzl and Zionist delegation in Jerusalem, 1898 *(Central Zionist Archives)*

Kaiser Wilhelm II in Jerusalem, 1898 *(akg-images/Imagno)*

Herzl at the Second Zionist Congress in Basel, 1898 *(Central Zionist Archives)*

Joseph Chamberlain *(Illustrated London News/Mary Evans)*

Vyacheslav von Plehve *(Topfoto)*

Pope Pius X *(akg-images)*

King Victor Emmanuel III *(Alinari/Topfoto)*

Herzl's funeral in Vienna, 1904 *(Central Zionist Archives)*

Herzl Street, Tel Aviv, c.1914 *(Courtesy of Kedem Auctions, Jerusalem)*

The Haganah ship *Theodor Herzl* in Haifa harbour, 1947 *(Associated Press)*

It is impossible, I think, to name
All the countries where I've been.
The only one for which I yearn
I never find: my homeland.

RICHARD WAGNER, *The Flying Dutchman*

No one has ever thought to look for the
Promised Land where it actually is, and it
is so near – within ourselves.

THEODOR HERZL, *Diaries*

PREFACE

THEODOR HERZL was not the first to call for the establishment of
a Jewish nation-state. He was preceded, most notably, by the socialist Moses Hess in his *Rome and Jerusalem* (1862) and by the Russian
intellectual and physician Leo Pinsker in his *Auto-Emancipation*
(1882); and the Odessa-based Hovevei Zion ('Lovers of Zion') movement had been instrumental since the early 1880s in helping to set up
Jewish villages in Palestine. But Herzl's activity was crucial in creating
the institutional and organizational structure which helped to bring
the idea of a Jewish state to the attention of world leaders and international public opinion. This process eventually made possible the
establishment of Israel in 1948.

There is no dearth of detailed biographies of Herzl, some adulatory
and others more critical. Some mistakenly focus on the Dreyfus trial
as the trigger that caused Herzl to despair of the promise of Jewish
emancipation in Europe: as I will try to show, it was developments in
the Austro-Hungarian Empire that led him to the search for a Jewish
homeland. On another level, many accounts of Herzl's vision fail to
mention his insistence that in the future Jewish commonwealth, the
Arab population of Palestine should enjoy equal rights and participate
in the political life of the country. It is not easy to present an adequate
picture of his intellectual development and to transform the canonical image of a larger-than-life person – the 'Visionary of the State' in
common Israeli parlance – into a real, living human being and thus

extricate him from the mythological qualities connected with his name. This is basically the aim of this book.

Herzl was a relatively young man of 35 when he entered public life, promoting what he called 'the Jewish cause' (*die Judensache*). Being a private person with no organizational tools at his disposal, he could easily have failed, and his name would have been relegated to obscurity. Yet within less than nine years he had transformed Jewish public discourse and made the idea of a Return to Zion into a reality, albeit still a weak one, in world politics. But it was not inevitable that Herzl's project would succeed, that it would not become just another of history's lost causes.

This volume tries to focus mainly on Herzl's intellectual and spiritual odyssey and to bring out his own doubts, false starts, and wrong turns, as well as his evident achievements. It is this route that turned Herzl from a private and marginal individual into a Jewish political leader, and transformed Zionism from an esoteric, if not cranky, idea into a player on the international scene. For Herzl, this was also a process of self-discovery and self-education.

It is for this reason that Herzl's diaries serve as a major source for this book's narrative. With some notable exceptions, their entries, covering 1,500 pages, have been underutilized in describing how complex, and far from pre-determined, were Herzl's efforts. As in any other case of reverting to the diaries of a public figure who is also a gifted writer, one should obviously take the diary entries with a grain of salt: but they provide a fascinating picture of the incredible social network Herzl succeeded in weaving among various strands of *fin de siècle* European society. And because in many cases they describe Herzl's own internal turbulence and failures, they can be seen as a credible reflection of how unsure he was of what he was trying to achieve and how he learned from his mistakes. The diaries are his true 'novel of formation' (*Bildungsroman*), and it is this inner development, coupled with his unceasing activity against all odds, which I try to describe in this book.

I owe my interest in Herzl's intellectual development to the editors of the full Hebrew translation of Herzl's *Diaries* – Josef Wenkert and the late Michael Heymann of the Central Zionist Archive in

Jerusalem. Without their invitation to write the historical Introduction to the three-volume edition they were preparing, this book could not have been written. It was then that I realized that my own acquaintance with Herzl had actually been quite limited and inadequate, based as it was mainly on his published canonical writings – *The Jewish State* and *Altneuland*. I thus found myself plowing through the hundreds of pages of Herzl's entries, which vividly described his contacts and meetings with hundreds of people, Jews and non-Jews – a true tableau of Europe's Yesterday's World *(Die Welt von Gestern)*. Yet unlike Stefan Zweig's memorable book, Herzl's entries were written in what we would now call real time, and not in retrospect: so they are free not only from hindsight, but also from the kind of understandable nostalgia which sometimes mars Zweig's evocation of a lost world. Reading the diaries from cover to cover – which I dare say even some of Herzl's biographers did not really do – presented to me the incredibly wide scope of Herzl's tireless efforts as set against the tremendous odds facing him.

I would like to thank Zvi Yekutiel, Director of the Zalman Shazar Center for Jewish History in Jerusalem, who suggested I write an intellectual biography of Herzl to be included in their series of Jewish Thinkers. I am indebted to Yehiel Leket, Chairman of the Jewish National Fund History Institute, for research support. I learned a lot from my translator, Haim Watzman, a gifted writer in his own right, who was of great help in making my text more accessible to the general reader not versed in Jewish history. I owe a special gratitude to my research assistant, Eyal Tsur, for locating and identifying the quotes in the various English translations of Herzl's writings, including the *Diaries*. Cathie Arrington, Lucinda McNeile as well as Anat Banin and Rochelle Rubinstein from the CZA helped with identifying and locating the pictures for the photographic section.

As always, my wife Dvora served as my most critical reader, and my thanks to her can only give a glimpse of how much I owe her for her patience and wisdom.

Finally, I would like to dedicate this volume to my grandchildren, Eynat, Noa and Ido, living proof that Herzl's vision was not a dream.

CHAPTER ONE

JERUSCHOLAJIM

AT THE END OF OCTOBER 1898 the small steamer *Rossiya* made its way from Alexandria in Egypt, via Port Said, to Jaffa. Its passengers included Theodor Herzl and four other members of a Zionist delegation on their way to Jerusalem, where they planned to meet Kaiser Wilhelm II of Germany during his tour of the Holy Land. Herzl wrote in his diary that the five men shared a single narrow berth on the boat. The heat was stultifying, so they decided to spend the last night of their voyage on deck.

Just two years previously, Herzl had been a successful Viennese journalist and a less successful playwright with no political ambitions and no independent public standing. That changed in 1896, when he published a pamphlet entitled *The Jewish State* that called for a political-territorial solution to the Jewish question. The following year he convened a Zionist Congress in Basel. The Congress founded the Zionist Organization in order to establish a national home for the Jewish people in Palestine, recognized and guaranteed by public international law. The founding of the Zionist movement made a small splash in the Jewish public and in the international press, but during its first two years the Zionist Organization achieved very little of political or public significance. True, Herzl had done all he could to make connections with European statesmen and national leaders, but had been largely unsuccessful. Now, less than 15 months following the convention in Basel, Herzl was making his way to Jerusalem for a public audience with one of the world's most important and powerful leaders. Herzl had, in fact, already met Wilhelm in secret in Constantinople. At that preliminary meeting, the Kaiser had voiced his enthusiastic support for the Zionist idea and stated his willingness for Germany to play the role of extending a protectorate over Jewish settlement in Palestine.

Unsurprisingly, then, Herzl was rapturous when he landed in Jaffa. He had never visited Palestine and he knew as little about it as he knew about other Jewish subjects. But his feelings are evident in the diary entry he recorded just a few days later:

> At night and in the morning the sea was wonderfully still and shimmered in its multi-colored luminosity. When it grew light, we began to see the Jewish coast [*die jüdische Küste*] ... We approached the land of our fathers with mixed feelings. Strange what emotions this desolate country stirs up in most people: in the old German pastor from South Africa, in the Russian *muzhik* in the foul-smelling steerage, in the Arabs who had been traveling with us from Constantinople, in us Zionists, in the poor Romanian Jewess who wanted to join her sick daughter in Jeruscholajim.

That's no error – he wrote 'Jeruscholajim,' a German transcription of the city's name in Hebrew, rather than the standard 'Jerusalem.' And this from the pen of a man who had his doubts about whether Hebrew could be revived to serve as the language of the Jewish state. 'Who amongst us has a sufficient *acquaintance* with Hebrew to ask for a railway-ticket in that language?' Herzl asks in *The Jewish State*. But Herzl was also well aware of Jerusalem's universal significance. It was, after all, a city of profound historical and religious importance not just to the Jews but to all the world's nations, the Arabs included. This ambivalence between the universal and the Jewish Jerusalem accompanied Herzl during his entire charged and tense visit to Palestine.

But how did Herzl and his delegation get to the point of making their way to Palestine to meet the Kaiser? After all, the Zionist Organization had yet to achieve anything like a breakthrough in putting the Zionist plan on the world's political and diplomatic agenda. Indeed,

Herzl had been taken by surprise when he was unexpectedly presented with the opportunity of meeting the German Emperor in Jerusalem. Skeptical at first, he became persuaded that it was an extraordinary opportunity. So extraordinary, in fact, that he feared that, were the Turkish authorities to comprehend the political import of this event, they would refuse to allow him to come ashore in Jaffa. Once safely landed, he feared that he would be deported or slapped in prison. He even feared for his life, although this concern had little basis in fact and was more a product of his journalistic instincts for narrative embellishment and over-dramatization.

The initiative for Herzl's visit to Palestine and his meeting with Wilhelm in Jerusalem came from the German Ambassador in Vienna, Prince Philip von Eulenburg. Herzl had cultivated this diplomat, seeking to persuade him to arrange him an audience with his sovereign. Relations between Germany and Turkey were getting closer, in part as a result of a plan to build a rail line that would connect Berlin, through Constantinople, with Baghdad. The Baghdad Railway project was an element of Germany's imperial game against Britain, which through its control of the Suez Canal reigned supreme over trade with India and the Far East. Herzl understood that German support for his project was essential, especially after the failure of his attempts at direct contacts with the Sultan's court. Herzl heard that, as part of his Oriental policy, the Kaiser resolved to make a pilgrimage to Jerusalem, ostensibly to dedicate the new Lutheran Church of the Redeemer. When Herzl also learned that the German Emperor planned to stop first in Constantinople, he redoubled his efforts. During a visit to Vienna by the German Foreign Minister, Bernhard von Bülow, Ambassador von Eulenburg arranged an appointment at which Herzl presented the Zionist program and asked to be received by the Kaiser. Herzl's impression was that the Foreign Minister listened closely and with a certain amount of sympathy. But weeks went by without word from Berlin. Herzl had a tendency to misinterpret diplomatic *politesse* as consent.

Then, on October 2, while in Amsterdam to speak to Zionist activists and bankers regarding the proposal to establish a Zionist bank, Herzl received a message telling him to proceed immediately to the

German consulate. At the consulate he received an urgent communiqué from von Eulenburg that had arrived in the diplomatic bag. He opened the letter and found himself overwhelmed – it appeared that, for the first time, his diplomatic efforts seemed to be bearing fruit. The German Ambassador in Vienna wrote that Kaiser Wilhelm II was prepared to present the Zionist program to the Sultan during his visit to Constantinople and to lend the program his personal support. Furthermore, the Kaiser was prepared to establish a German protectorate for the Zionist enterprise – an admittedly vague concept, but one with obvious political implications. Finally, he agreed to receive a Zionist delegation in Jerusalem. If Herzl headed the delegation, von Eulenburg wrote, the Emperor would be willing to allow Herzl to explain the Zionist position to him at an official audience. Von Eulenburg enclosed the Emperor's itinerary, including the dates of his stays in Constantinople and Jerusalem. In the meantime, Herzl was to proceed forthwith to Berlin to meet the Ambassador and discuss the next steps.

Von Eulenburg painted Herzl an optimistic picture – one that would later prove to be overly sanguine. But for Herzl it was enough that he had, for the first time, been invited to appear before the leader of a world power. Not only that, the power in question was at present the closest ally of the Ottoman Empire, which ruled Palestine, and the audience would take place in Jerusalem. Nevertheless, Herzl was well aware of the complexities. True, he was a senior editor at Vienna's most powerful newspaper, the *Neue Freie Presse*, but he held no public office. He was, in diplomatic terms, no more than a private individual. He would have to ask the newspaper for leave. As he wrote in his diary, he was a 'wage slave' and the publishers were not great fans of the Zionist cause. Yet a request from the Emperor was tantamount to a command – in fact, von Eulenburg had written explicitly, Herzl noted in his diary, that 'the Kaiser would be disappointed if he did not get to see me in Jerusalem.'

During a dinner in The Hague on the evening after he received the summons, Herzl revealed, in confidence, the contents of the letter to the other members of the Zionist Executive. He personally believed that the matter was still 'not ripe.' During the meeting in Berlin he would, he resolved, seek to persuade von Eulenburg that it would be better for the Kaiser to receive him secretly in Berlin rather than officially in Jerusalem. From The Hague he proceeded to London for previously scheduled consultations regarding the Zionist bank and for a large public meeting in Whitechapel that was attended, Herzl wrote in his diary, by some 10,000 people. The optimistic tone of the speech he gave there, which was published the next day in London's Jewish newspapers, was undoubtedly influenced by the encouragement he felt coming from Berlin.

Then Herzl changed his travel plans. He had originally planned to return to Vienna from London, but instead he traveled straight to Berlin. During two intense days he spent in the German capital he participated in a number of meetings in Potsdam, the imperial residence just outside Berlin, but his mood swung precipitously from sky-high to profoundly melancholic. Exposed for the first time to high diplomacy, he discovered to his chagrin that it was replete with sleight of hand and deceit.

When he arrived in Berlin on the evening of October 6, Herzl expected that a message from von Eulenburg would be waiting for him. But there was no letter. He exchanged cables with the Ambassador and finally received instructions to take a train the next morning to von Eulenburg's estate in Brandenburg. This was Herzl's first encounter with the vast northern German plain, so different from the dramatic and romantic mountain landscapes he knew from Austria and southern Germany. He was astonished to discover that the Brandenburg region offered beautiful green vistas and was 'by no means a sandy desert as people say it is.' And when he took in the Prussian countryside from his train window, he could not refrain from writing in his diary: 'So we too shall convert the sandy deserts of our country into beautiful meadows.'

Herzl's arrival at von Eulenburg's estate coincided with the height of the shooting season – the Prince received him in hunting garb. He keenly felt the disparity between the aristocratic milieu he had landed in, combining high politics with pheasant shooting, and his own status as a bourgeois Viennese Jew. True, he was a well-known journalist, author, and playwright, but he had no previous exposure to the opulence of a princely estate. He knew very well that his social background placed him light years distant from the gentile military tradition and love of the hunt evinced by the suits of armor on display in the mansion and the spears and swords hanging on the walls.

Yet all this faded away when he sat down to discuss business with his host. Von Eulenburg told him that his letter had been written at the behest of the Emperor, who had personally approved its contents. He told Herzl that, in several meetings, he had managed to infuse the Emperor with enthusiasm for the Zionist idea and that, as a result, 'The Kaiser is very warmly inclined toward the project.' He added that Foreign Minister von Bülow had also been persuaded, despite the reservations he had expressed to Herzl during their meeting in Vienna. 'One restrains oneself – which is understandable at a first meeting. One is cautious, does not let oneself go immediately. However, the main thing is not what he said to you, but what he said to me when I tried to persuade him. I convinced him.'

When Herzl expressed his doubts about the wisdom of an audience in Jerusalem, von Eulenburg responded that this was the Emperor's wish. Wilhelm wished to receive not only Herzl but an entire Zionist delegation, and that 'he had already got quite used to the idea of a protectorate.' That being the case, there was no point in a secret meeting. The diplomatic program would come to light in any case, so it was best to make a public show of it from the start. Given the warming relations between Germany and Russia, von Eulenburg was confident that the latter country would be favorably disposed to the idea of a German protectorate. 'If worst comes to worst, our Kaiser could write a letter [to the Czar] and win him over to Zionism.' In von Eulenburg's view, the Kaiser had no doubts that the Sultan would respond positively to his proposal. The Ambassador proposed that Herzl meet von Bülow to lay out the protocol of the audience. Furthermore, the Emperor's uncle, the Grand Duke of Baden, who already supported Herzl's ideas, happened to be in Potsdam. The two would have an opportunity to meet again.

Herzl was encouraged:

A protectorate! Many will shake their heads over it. But I believe the only right course is to accept it gratefully, now that it has been

offered. For surely no one among us has dreams of a monarchy
... Also, at one stroke we would obtain a completely formal in-
ternal and external legal status. The Porte's suzerainty along with
Germany's protectorate would certainly be sufficient legal pillars.

Egypt's semi-autonomous status at the time provided Herzl with an
appropriate administrative model for the Zionist entity to be established in Palestine.

In fact, his spirits were so high that he saw the matter as almost a
fait accompli. As soon as a protectorate was established, he thought to
himself, he would resign from the leadership of the Zionist movement,
so as to fend off charges that he was seeking personal benefit or political
power. He would submit his resignation at the movement's climactic
moment, 'and this would be the last service I would perform for the
Jews.' Yet he also remarked to himself that perhaps this would not be
possible, '[f]or the German government, which is making agreements
with me, will want me to remain so I can keep them!'

But these castles in the air dissolved into mist the very next day.
Yes, the Grand Duke of Baden seconded von Eulenburg's assertions
that the Kaiser 'has taken to your idea quite warmly. He speaks of it
in the liveliest terms,' and that the Sultan would support it. But his
meeting with the Foreign Minister was like a cold shower: von Bülow
was anything but enthusiastic. Herzl had managed to gain access to
the highest levels of European politics, but what he heard from the
Foreign Minister was not encouraging. His mood swung again. In his
diary, he described his arrival for his meeting with von Bülow at the
imperial palace – he was led by impeccably uniformed officers and
obsequious courtiers into an ornate rococo set of rooms. 'One cannot
get higher than this,' he wrote. Von Bülow was waiting for him in his
elegant chamber, along with 'a short, crooked old gentleman, bedecked
with decorations, a yellow grand-cordon across his court dress': Herzl
found himself being introduced to the Chancellor of the German
Reich, Prince Chlodwig von Hohenlohe-Schillingsfürst.

Herzl was thrilled – the presence of the Chancellor was an indication of how seriously the German government took the subject. But he
was taken aback by the Chancellor's first remark: 'Do you think that

the Jews are going to give up and leave their stock exchange and follow you? The Jews, who are comfortably installed here in Berlin?' Herzl offered the clinching Zionist argument – perhaps the stock market's Jews would not go with him, but the common Jews, including those in Berlin, certainly would.

Following this unpromising beginning, the Chancellor asked several practical questions. How much territory were the Zionists asking for? Up to Beirut or perhaps beyond? Herzl's response was: 'We will ask for what we need – the more immigrants, the more land.' From whom would they buy the land? Herzl said: 'Arabs, Greeks – the whole mixed multitude of the Orient.' Was it his intention to establish a state? Herzl replied: 'We want autonomy and self-protection.' The conversation then touched on other subjects. What would Turkey's position be? Who would fund the migration of the Jews? Herzl divulged that he had at his disposal tens of millions of pounds sterling, although in fact these funds did not exist anywhere outside his fertile imagination. Von Bülow commented: 'That's a lot! . . . The money might do the trick. With it one can swing the matter.' He added ironically: 'In any case it would be the first eastward migration of the Israelites. Until now they have always moved westward.'

Herzl had understood from von Eulenburg that his audience with the Emperor would take place in Jerusalem. He was thus surprised when von Bülow bid him farewell with 'See you in Constantinople, Herr Doktor!' Herzl asked, 'In Constantinople and in Jerusalem?' The Foreign Minister replied coolly: 'In any case, only once!' Herzl managed to extract from von Bülow an affirmative answer to his question: 'Shall I, then, submit at Constantinople the address which I am to deliver in Jerusalem?'

The conversation was cut short because the Germans had to hurry to a state dinner. Herzl was left with a sour taste in his mouth. It was now clear to him that the two most important statesmen in the German Reich were cool to the Zionist project and that they adhered to anti-Semitic stereotypes. He had no way of knowing whether the Emperor thought differently. Or perhaps, being experienced diplomats, they were simply speaking with extreme caution so as to avoid entering into any commitments? If nothing else, the two days in Potsdam were an education for Herzl on the complexity and uncertainty he would encounter in Constantinople and Jerusalem.

Herzl returned to Vienna on October 9 and commenced making personal and political arrangements for his voyage. First he had to ask for leave from his newspaper. While publishers and editors of the *Neue Freie Presse* were not enthusiastic, they could not deny the import of the occasion – after all, Herzl was to meet with the German Emperor. Still, Herzl's two hats, as an editor at the paper and as the leader of a small political movement who had managed to insinuate himself into high-level politics, made life difficult for them.

In parallel, Herzl convened his colleagues from the Zionist Executive. Its members all wanted to be included in the delegation and, of course, those who were not chosen felt insulted. After a series of meetings and fevered exchanges of telegrams, it was decided that the delegation would consist of five members: Herzl, chairman of the Zionist Executive and president of the Zionist congresses; Moritz Schnirer, vice-chairman of the Zionist Executive; Max Bodenheimer, president of the Zionist Federation of Germany; David Wolffsohn, chairman of the planning committee of the Zionist bank and later to be Herzl's successor as president of the Zionist Organization; and Joseph Seidener, a Russian-born engineer and the only member of the delegation to have visited Palestine before, as a representative of the Hovevei Zion movement in 1891. It would be just one of the ironies of Herzl's life and of Zionist history that this sole visit to the ancestral Jewish homeland by the founder of the Zionist movement was initiated by the Emperor of Germany.

The delegation boarded the train for Constantinople on October 14, less than two weeks after Herzl first learned of the Emperor's desire to meet him in Palestine. At the last minute, before setting out, Herzl met with the Turkish Ambassador in Vienna, Mohammed Nadim Bey. Herzl hoped to obtain personal letters of introduction to Turkish leaders, but the Ambassador demurred, offering a convoluted Arabic parable as an explanation. Just before leaving, Herzl gave a reading to the actors of his newest play, *Unser Kätchen* (*Our Cathy*), slated for production at the Burgtheater in Vienna. His parents came to his house to bid him farewell, apprehensive about the dangers of the Orient. Their fears were reinforced by a warning relayed to him from Jerusalem – Eliezer Ben-Yehuda, the Hebrew lexicographer and journalist, warned Herzl of plots to assassinate him.

The Turkish Ambassadors to Vienna and Berlin, both of whom Herzl knew from his newspaper work, rode on the same train as the Zionists. Herzl took the opportunity to chat with them, but without revealing the purpose of his trip. They presumably thought that he was traveling to Constantinople as a journalist to cover Wilhelm's visit.

Herzl had been to Constantinople before on unsuccessful Zionist missions. This time he found himself groping through the same fog of uncertainty that he had felt during his brief sojourn in Potsdam. He was told that the Emperor would receive him, but not when or where the audience would take place. His attempts to see the German Ambassador in the Ottoman capital were rebuffed. The Turkish chief of protocol avoided having any contact with the delegation. Tensely expecting to be summoned to the Emperor, Herzl and his colleagues went to see a play presented by a visiting Yiddish theater troupe. The production was pathetic, Herzl wrote. Beyond that, they spent their time discussing the political program they would present to the Emperor. After four days of fruitless anticipation, a despairing Herzl dispatched letters to Foreign Minister von Bülow and the Imperial Lord Chamberlain. He noted the tight schedule – to reach Jerusalem on time to meet the Emperor, the delegation would have to sail for Alexandria the next day, October 19. Might it be possible to receive some word from his benevolent Majesty?

Herzl inserted a personal note to the Emperor into the envelope bearing the letter sent to the Lord Chamberlain. Since he had no way of knowing whether the Emperor would indeed receive him, he laid out the substantive points he wished to convey. He hoped that Germany would indeed consent to take it upon itself to establish a protectorate over the Jewish settlement in Palestine, as Herzl had been given to understand it would. He noted that France, which had clear interests in the Middle East, was likely to object. But France's international position was weak. Russia would certainly view the Zionist solution to the Jewish question as 'an enormous relief.' Herzl recommended that the Emperor explain to the Sultan, his ally, 'what aid the

Zionists would bring to his impoverished, bankrupt state.' The way to achieve this would be to grant his consent for the establishment, under German sponsorship, of a 'Jewish Land Society for Syria and Palestine' (*Jüdische Landgesellschaft für Syrien und Palästina*). Herzl concluded his letter with a plea to the Emperor to receive him for a confidential audience prior to the departure of the last available passenger ship to Alexandria. The Emperor and his entourage would sail on the German imperial yacht *Hohenzollern* and as such were not dependent on passenger ship timetables. Herzl stressed that he wished to personally convey an overview of the plan he would present at their upcoming meeting in the Land of Israel (*im Lande Israels* – here he did not use 'Palestine,' the standard geographical designation).

Herzl wrote all these letters, including his detailed memo, in his own hand (twice he made mistakes in his first fair copy). He and the delegation lacked the services of an office or assistants in Constantinople. Wolffsohn was sent in a hired carriage to deliver the letters, in the hopes that he would be able to get through the Turkish and German barriers at the entrance to Yildiz Palace, where the Emperor and his entourage were staying.

Almost at the last moment, at 3:30 in the afternoon, an unsigned note arrived from the Germans: Dr. Herzl was requested to appear before the Emperor at 4:30. Herzl, accompanied by Wolffsohn, rushed off to the palace. Before leaving, he stretched out his hand before the other members of the delegation to show them how it was shaking. He told them that his pulse was up to 108, 'which is very fast for me.' One of his associates asked him if he would like a dose of bromide to calm his nerves, but when Herzl was told that the drug would take half an hour to work, he decided against it. Herzl did not neglect to note in his diary that he dressed meticulously: 'The color of my gloves was particularly becoming: a delicate grey.' When he arrived at the palace at the designated time it turned out that, of course, the Emperor was delayed at a visit to the German Embassy and at a German school. The courtiers graciously but firmly asked Dr. Herzl to wait and not to leave the anteroom. At 5:30, an hour late, the Emperor arrived and the Lord Chamberlain led Herzl and Foreign Minister von Bülow into the imperial chamber.

The account of the audience that Herzl recorded in his diary combines the precise reporting of a journalist with the awe he felt on this, the most important political meeting he had had thus far in the Zionist cause. Today, knowing as we do the events of World War I, we find it hard to credit Herzl's admiration for the Emperor as a person. His description of Wilhelm's eyes is not easy to stomach: 'A remarkable, bold, inquisitive soul shows in them.' But Wilhelm II was still relatively young at this point, quite popular in Europe and an enthusiast for modern ideas. The brutal side of his personality, which cast a shadow over Europe in the period leading up to and during the Great War, had not yet become apparent. Nevertheless, Herzl tempered his wonder by noting that the Emperor, dressed in an impeccable hussar uniform, was notably uneasy about his prominent physical defect – one arm was shorter than the other.

Despite Herzl's understandable nervousness, the meeting went well. There were no preliminaries – the Emperor asked him to go straight into his presentation. After a moment of bewilderment ('Where shall I begin, Your Imperial Majesty?'), Herzl recovered and launched into a cogent presentation, focusing on the issues he had included in the memo – the establishment of a Land Company under German protection. Herzl wrote in his diary that the Emperor nodded in agreement, reaffirming that he was favorably disposed to the Zionist movement. He asked Herzl to tell him explicitly what he should request from the Sultan. Herzl replied, 'A Chartered Company under German sponsorship.' The Emperor replied, 'Good, a Chartered Company.'

Everything seemed to be going well, even better than expected. But Herzl was bothered by two matters. First, despite the Emperor's seeming willingness to take the Zionist enterprise under his protection as part of Germany's policy in the Levant, Herzl discerned an unsympathetic tone in Wilhelm's references to the Jews themselves. He used the expression '*Ihre Landsleute,*' 'your people,' adding: 'There are elements among your people whom it would be quite a good thing to settle in Palestine. I am thinking of Hesse, for example, where there are usurers at work among the rural population.' However, the Emperor noted that anti-Semitism was strongest in France, 'for there the

Church is behind it,' adding immediately that 'Herr von Rothschild seems to know this too, for he is having his art collection shipped to London.' It was very unpleasant.

Von Bülow also lent a distasteful atmosphere to the conversation. He commented that German Jews ought to be but were not hugely grateful to the Hohenzollern dynasty for their emancipation and economic prosperity following the unification of Germany. Yet, he said, 'now the Jews were to be seen among all the opposition parties, even the anti-monarchical ones.' The Emperor muttered the name of Paul Singer, a leader of the Social Democrats. Herzl saw, as he had many times previously, that European leaders, consciously or not, often accompanied their expressions of support for the idea of a Jewish state with typical anti-Jewish prejudices.

The conversation continued with an intelligent exchange of views about European politics. Herzl felt comfortable during this part of the audience because, as the political editor of an influential newspaper and the leader of the Zionist movement, he was well versed in the issues. Even if the tone was not always friendly, Herzl wrote in his diary, it was an impressive achievement. After three years of intensive labor, 'the obscure word "Zionism"' had become familiar currency in the courts of emperors and kings, no mean achievement.

Following the audience, which lasted for more than an hour, von Bülow accompanied Herzl to his carriage. The faces of the courtiers they passed on the way displayed astonishment at the gesture. Von Bülow summed up the details of the coming public audience in Jerusalem and asked Herzl to convey, urgently, before leaving Constantinople, to the German Ambassador, a copy of the speech he would make before the Emperor in Jerusalem. The two men agreed that von Bülow would read through the speech and approve it. Herzl would of course not include anything that had not received prior approval.

Elated by the congenial atmosphere of his audience with the Kaiser, but fully understanding the limits of German support, Herzl proceeded to draft his speech. Uncertain as to whether they were indeed proceeding to Palestine, the members of the delegation had not yet made arrangements for their journey. At the last minute they managed to secure tickets on the Russian ship *Imperator Nicholas II*.

The ship made stops at Piraeus and Izmir. At the first stop, the delegation made a visit to the Acropolis in Athens, but Herzl was not in the mood for sightseeing. He was focused solely on the trip to Palestine, an unknown realm of Jewish longing but also the site of what seemed to him like a prophetic vision. He would be received there by a potentate who seemed, more than any other statesman he had thus far met, to favor the Zionist cause. It was so surprising, so unexpected, and the future remained shrouded in mystery. Herzl must not have been unaware of the irony in the ship's name – the Russian Czar, cousin to Wilhelm II, headed an oppressive regime that bore much responsibility for the greatest sufferings the Jewish people had endured in modern times. It was the oppression the Jews suffered under the Czar that had given birth to the proto-Zionist Hovevei Zion movement. Another irony that also goes unmentioned in Herzl's diary was the name of the smaller boat that took them from Alexandria to Jaffa – the *Rossiya*.

On October 26, 1898, Herzl set foot on the Jaffa shore. He and his delegation spent just short of ten days in Palestine, most of them in Jerusalem. It was a tense time, full of notable experiences, and Herzl's diary entries bear witness to his turbulent emotional state. There were three causes. The first was his electric encounter with the Land of Israel, the Jewish people's ancient homeland, with all the associations it brought up, including his visits to the first new Jewish settlements. The second was the concrete reality of the country, Jerusalem in particular, as it looked to an educated man of the world who was aware of historical forces but found himself repelled by the neglect and decrepitude he saw everywhere. The third were his expectations and nervousness about how his upcoming audience with the Emperor would turn out and what it would mean for the future of the Zionist movement. It is hardly surprising, then, that his diary entries display ambiguity and contradiction regarding both Jerusalem and the entire visit. 'When I remember thee in days to come, O Jerusalem,' he wrote, 'it will not be with pleasure.' Yet he also waxed poetic: 'Jerusalem is spread before me in all its glory. Even in its present decay it is a beautiful city, and, if we come here, can become one of the most beautiful cities in the world again.'

The jumble, noise, and clutter of Jaffa and its port struck Herzl in full force, just as it did other visitors at that time. 'Again poverty and misery and heat in gay colors,' he wrote. His stay on the coast was spent largely visiting Jewish agricultural settlements, the *moshavot* established by Hovevei Zion and the first wave of modern Jewish immigration to Palestine, the First Aliyah. He also visited the Mikveh Israel agricultural school just east of Jaffa. He was impressed but also reserved – Mikveh Israel was excellent, he thought, but its management, drawn from the French Alliance Israélite Universelle, looked askance on Herzl and his delegation. 'Fear of Monsieur le Baron [Edmond de Rothschild, who provided financial backing for Jewish settlement] hovers over everything,' he wrote. Rothschild was apprehensive about any contact with the Zionist Organization because of its political orientation, the result being, Herzl wrote, that 'The poor colonists have swapped one fear for another.' Herzl felt similar misgivings when he visited the *moshava* Rishon LeZion, despite the polite reception he received there. The welcoming speech made by one of the settlers sought 'to harmonize their obligations towards the Baron and their love for me.' The Rothschild-appointed administrator 'received us with a frightened air.' Neither did the faces of the settlers make a good impression. 'Again, row upon row of faces such as I have seen in London, Berlin and Brünn, everywhere,' he wrote.

His visit to another agricultural community, Rehovot, offered a more encouraging picture, perhaps because this *moshava* was not run by the Rothschild administration. As the delegation approached, a posse of about twenty young people mounted on horses came out to greet the visitors and conducted a 'fantasia' in which they sang Hebrew songs and chanted the Hebrew cheer '*heidad!*'. He and his colleagues, Herzl admitted, 'had tears in our eyes when we saw those nimble, daring horsemen into whom our young trouser-salesmen can be transformed.' The implication was clear – here, in Rehovot, Herzl saw the answer to the malicious incitement of the anti-Semitic German historian Heinrich von Treitschke, who had warned against the immigration to Germany of poor Jews from the east, the 'trouser-hawking Jewish boys' whose descendants were taking control of the German press and economy. Here, in Palestine, a new kind of Jew, free and self-confident, could grow up, emancipated from degenerating occupations and from bourgeois acquisitiveness. No wonder Herzl was so impressed by this visit: 'Such great results with such meager means.'

The next day Herzl conducted a public relations stunt, only partially successful. Learning that the Emperor, who had in the meantime landed in Jaffa, would be riding on horseback to Jerusalem on a route that passed by Mikveh Israel, Herzl stationed himself on the road so as to stage an unplanned encounter. The school's administrators had not asked him to do so, and sent out its students to receive the imperial entourage. Herzl suggested to the headmaster, Joseph Niego, whom he had met the previous day, to present him to the Kaiser, 'should the latter recognize me and speak to me.' Niego 'begged me to refrain from doing this, because it might be regarded as a Zionist demonstration and could harm him.' It was not the only hostile response Herzl and his Zionist delegation received from members of the Yishuv, the Jewish community in Palestine.

When the German caravan, led by the Emperor, reached the Mikveh Israel junction, the student choir sang out the German imperial anthem, 'Heil Dir im Siegerkranz.' Herzl positioned himself next to one of the school's plows and raised his pith helmet in deference. He was happy to see that Wilhelm recognized him ('at a distance'), pulled his horse around to face him, 'and when he leaned down over the neck of the horse,' extended his hand down in greeting. The Lord Chamberlain also offered Herzl a friendly salute from high up on his horse. Herzl offered a polite reply and asked the Emperor how his trip had been. 'Very hot! But the country has a future,' he replied. 'Water is what it needs, a lot of water!' Herzl concurred and the Emperor repeated: 'It is a land of the future,' before heading off. The student choir again sang the German anthem and the imperial party went on its way.

It's hard to imagine a less important conversation, but the image of Herzl, hat in hand, standing before the mounted Emperor has become a Zionist icon. It was no mean fact that Wilhelm stopped to speak with Herzl. 'The spectators at Mikveh Israel were quite dumbfounded,' he wrote. 'The Rothschild clerks looked frightened and out of sorts.' But the two photographs taken by Bodenheimer did not come out well. In fact, the familiar image of Herzl holding his hat before the mounted

Kaiser is a photomontage. Yet the encounter is firmly ensconced in Zionist legend.

During most of the visit, Herzl was indisposed – he had not been feeling well since he disembarked at Jaffa. Struck with fever, he felt weak during his entire stay in Palestine. It may have been a real illness, perhaps malaria, or simply overexcitement. Schnirer, a physician, recommended quinine, but when Herzl tried it he vomited; alcohol and camphor rubdowns did not help either. Whatever the case, Herzl's understandable agitation was accompanied by physical weakness, and the effects on his conduct were evident throughout his visit.

Later that day, a Friday, Herzl and his party boarded the Jaffa–Jerusalem train. It set out a full hour behind schedule, and the cramped and narrow car was infernally hot, turning Herzl's rising fever into a 'real torture.' The delay meant that the train would arrive in Jerusalem after sunset and the onset of the Sabbath. They were to lodge at a hotel half an hour's walk from the train station but it was not clear whether Herzl, in his condition, could manage that. The delegation conferred and decided that it was inconceivable that they ride by carriage from the train station to the hotel – Jewish religious law forbids traveling by vehicle on the holy day. As a result, Herzl wrote, 'I had to resign myself to walking to the city, weak with fever though I was. I tottered all over the place on my cane; with my other arm I braced myself alternately against [two companions].' That was not how he had envisioned his entry into Jerusalem. But, once they were settled, Herzl's condition did not prevent him and his colleagues from taking in the city's sights, as they waited for official word about the audience with the Emperor.

On the walk from the train station to the hotel, with his fever raging, the city made a potent impression on him. 'In spite of my weariness, Jerusalem by moon-light with its grand outlines made a powerful impression on me. Magnificent the silhouette of the fortress of Zion, the Citadel of David. The streets were crowded with bunches of Jews [*Judenscharen*] strolling in the moonlight.'* He spent the

---

* This description of the Sabbath eve in Jerusalem remained etched in Herzl's memory – and would later serve as a foil to his description of the onset of the Sabbath in Jerusalem, under very different conditions, in his *Altneuland*.

Saturday in his hotel room, too weak to go out, but on Sunday he and his colleagues went for a walk. The romantic Friday night image had dissipated – now he saw the neglect, the decay, and the simmering hostility between the city's different faiths. Herzl, a secular man of culture, well aware of the city's history and its implications, was shocked by the filth and the beggars who swarmed in the holy places. But in addition to this, he recorded in his diary a vision of how to plan a modern Jerusalem:

> The rotting deposits of two thousand years of inhumanity, intolerance, and uncleanliness lie in the foul-smelling alleys. The one man who has been present here all this time, the amiable dreamer of Nazareth, has only contributed to exacerbating the hatred.
>
> If we ever get Jerusalem and if I am still able to do anything actively at that time, I would begin by cleaning it up. I would clear out everything that is not sacred, build homes for workers outside the city, empty the nests of filth and tear them down, burn the secular ruins, and transfer the bazaars elsewhere. Then, retaining the old architectural style as much as possible, I would build around the holy sites a comfortable, airy new city with proper sanitation.

Further on he wrote:

> From the gallery of an ancient synagogue [Tif'eret Israel] we enjoyed a view of the Temple area, the Mount of Olives, and the whole legendary landscape in the morning sunshine. I am quite firmly convinced that a magnificent New Jerusalem could be built outside the old city walls.
>
> The Old Jerusalem would still remain Lourdes and Mecca and Jeruscholajim. A very pretty, elegant town would be quite possible beside it.

Two days later he wrote:

> In the afternoon we were on the Mount of Olives.
> Great moments. What couldn't be made of this countryside! A

city like Rome, and the Mount of Olives would furnish a panorama like the Janiculum [hill in Rome].

I would isolate the Old City with its relics and pull out all the regular traffic; only houses of worship and philanthropic institutions would be allowed to remain inside the old walls, and the wide ring of hillsides all around, which would turn green under our hands, would be the location of a glorious New Jerusalem. The most discriminating visitors from every part of the world would travel the road up to the Mount of Olives. Tender care can turn Jerusalem into a jewel. Include everything sacred within the old walls, spread everything new around it.

We climbed the Russian Tower [of the Church of Ascension] . . . Incomparable view of the Jordan Valley with its mountain slopes, the Dead Sea, the Mountains of Moab, the eternal city of Jerusalem.

It would require time and a clear head to sort out all these impressions.

He found the Western Wall, the holiest Jewish site in the city, repulsive: 'We have been to the Wailing Wall. A deeper emotion refuses to come, because the place is pervaded by a hideous, wretched, speculative beggary. At least, this is the way it was when we were there, yesterday evening and this morning.' He was now more certain than ever that the city needed a fundamental makeover.

But they also encountered other problems in their tour of the Old City. When they came to the Via Dolorosa they walked 'rather quickly . . . because it is said to be an ill-omened place for Jews.' The delegation refrained from visiting the mosques on the Temple Mount, because of 'a rabbinical ban of excommunication.' Presumably Herzl, as a private individual and a man of culture with an interest in history, would very much have liked to visit both the Church of the Holy Sepulcher and the Dome of the Rock, but he realized that an official Zionist delegation, no matter how secular its members might be, had to respect the sensitivities of religious Jews in its public actions.

Herzl also found himself in conflict with members of the Old Yishuv – the traditional Jerusalem community, both Ashkenazim and Sephardim, who were hostile to Zionism and wanted nothing to do with the delegation. Yet the worst suspense was over the question of whether the audience with the Emperor would indeed take place. Urgent letters flew back and forth and the Zionists again and again inquired at the magnificent encampment next to the Russian Compound that served as the Kaiser's headquarters. It was a humiliating experience – repeated petitions to the German staff went unanswered. Herzl feared that his personal standing and the future of the Zionist movement would be undermined if there were no imperial audience.

He and his colleagues had not seen a newspaper for two weeks. We have 'no news of what has been happening in the world,' he wrote in his diary. Suddenly, on October 31, at three in the afternoon (the fact that he recorded the precise time is an indication of how anxious he was), they heard from one of Herzl's contacts in the Emperor's court about a confrontation between the British and French at the Sudanese town of Fashoda. The two countries' forces had stopped just short of shooting, but Herzl's source said that France had declared war on England. Herzl wrote that 'The whole thing seems incredible to me,' but a Jewish official at the Russian consulate confirmed the rumor. The Zionist delegation now feared that Europe would turn into a battlefield, leaving them stranded in Palestine. A few hours later they learned that the war alarm was a false one, but the Anglo-French confrontation was very real and the word in Jerusalem was that the Emperor would cut short his visit and head straight for Beirut. Herzl again sent emissaries to the imperial tent camp. They returned with a promise that the audience would indeed take place, 'Tomorrow or the day after.'

On November 1, Herzl was summoned – alone – to the office of the German Consul-General. Upon arriving at the consulate, he was told that he was to proceed to the encampment and meet a diplomat named Kemeth, whom Herzl had never heard of. He rushed over to the tent camp and discovered that the name had been mispronounced – it was Klemeth, a low-level Foreign Ministry official. Klemeth gave Herzl – somewhat condescendingly, Herzl noted – the edited and censored version of the speech he was to make in the Kaiser's presence. The German asked Herzl to send him a new, clean version of the speech, without the passages that had been struck out. This demand and the humiliating nature of the meeting were infuriating, but at least it was a clear indication that the audience would indeed be taking place. That evening, after providing the undistinguished German with an updated version of the speech, Herzl was informed that he would be received by the Emperor the next day. The delegation was ordered not to publicize the event, even after it took place, despite the fact that 'your representative, Dr. Herzl, spoke about publicity.'

The delegation began feverish preparations for the meeting. Herzl, nervous as always, asked his colleagues 'if their clothes, linen, cravats, shoes, hats are in order' (Bodenheimer's top hat was 'grotesque' and his cufflinks did not match, setting off a search for replacements). After serious consideration, it was decided that the men would not take a dose of bromide to calm their nerves. All were intensely aware of the signal importance of the moment. As Herzl wrote afterward: 'The brief audience will be preserved forever in the annals of Jewish history, and it is not beyond possibility that it will have historic consequences as well.' Herzl was only half right – the occasion was memorable, but it had no effect on history.

The audience was disappointing, not at all up to the expectations raised by the meeting with the Emperor in Constantinople. Herzl had concluded on that occasion that the Emperor would adopt the idea of a German protectorate. Documents from the German Foreign Ministry and internal German correspondence would later show that von Bülow and his diplomats had cooled the young Emperor's somewhat romantic enthusiasm. But Herzl, of course, did not know this at the time. Then, Wilhelm was easily fired up about many subjects and his advisers frequently had to douse his fervor. Later, after maturing, he shook free of these professional statesmen and replaced them with people more in tune with his character. That change led Germany to throw caution to the wind and enter into sweeping treaty obligations – commitments that in the end dragged Germany and all of Europe into a catastrophic war.

'In the burning noonday sun and the white dust' the delegation arrived at the imperial tent. Herzl was permitted to present the members of the delegation. Von Bülow stood beside the Emperor, 'dressed in a dusty gray lounge-suit' (apparently not only the Zionists were affected by the Orient) and holding a copy of Herzl's corrected speech. Herzl read his address from the pages he held; out of the corner of his eye he saw the Foreign Minister following the words on his copy with his finger. At the end, the Emperor responded courteously: 'I thank you for this communication which has interested me greatly. The matter, in any case, still requires thorough study and further discussion.' He applauded the European settlements in Palestine, both those of the German Templers and those of 'your people' (again using the German word '*Landsleute*'). 'The work of the colonists will also serve as a stimulating example to the native population.' He added: 'The land needs, above all, water and shade.' Furthermore, 'Your movement, with which I am thoroughly acquainted, contains a sound idea.'

The subject turned to the weather (the Emperor remarked that in Ramleh, on the way to Jerusalem, the temperature had reached 31 degrees Celsius in the shade, 45 in the sun). He returned to the subject of water. Herzl noted that the development of water resources would cost a great deal. Then the Emperor, leader of Europe's greatest industrial power, remarked: 'Well, money you have plenty . . . More money than any of us.' Von Bülow seconded him: 'Yes, this money which is such a problem for us you have in abundance.' In this tone, following a few more technical comments on the various uses of water (electricity production, hygiene, elimination of eye diseases), the audience ended.

What an anti-climax. There had been no political discussion, no mention of a land purchase society or German protectorate or chartered company. Herzl sought to paper over his disappointment by blurting out to his colleagues as they left the tent: 'He said neither yes nor no.' He immediately sent a cable to the Emperor's uncle, the Grand Duke of Baden, who had previously been of such great assistance. Herzl laconically thanked him 'for all his kindness' without mentioning the substance of the audience. There was really nothing to mention.

The next day, November 3, the delegation boarded the train to Jaffa. The lack of certainty over when they would be seeing the Emperor had made it impossible for them to schedule their return sea trip in advance, so they had to scramble to find berths on a ship. They finally, with much difficulty, were able to obtain passage on a British freighter, the *Dundee*, carrying a cargo of citrus fruit. Herzl was in a hurry to leave Palestine in part because he believed that anti-Zionist Jews in Jaffa were spreading malicious rumors, for example that the delegation was connected to Christian missionaries. He wrote in his diary that he now feared being arrested by the Ottoman authorities, who might by this time have learned of the political nature of the delegation's petition to the German Emperor. Herzl's diary contains no further detailed report, evaluation, or summary of the audience with the Emperor, even though he and his colleagues must have discussed this in the days that followed. Once again they fled the oppressive heat of their cabins and spent their time on deck. Herzl reassured himself that 'in spite of this bad passage I feel fine when I consider that this venture of a pretender's [that is, the Zionist movement's] journey to Palestine has, up to now, come off successfully.'

The futility of the audience was not the only reason for the Zionists to feel dejected – they were not even allowed to publicize the fact that a meeting with the Emperor had taken place. Herzl, as a journalist, knew very well the importance of public relations, and was profoundly frustrated by the embargo imposed on them by the German court. He was even more upset when, upon arriving in Vienna with the other members of the delegation, he found a news service item in one of the papers:

> Kaiser Wilhelm has received a Jewish deputation, which presented him an album of pictures of the Jewish colonies established in Palestine. Replying to an address by the leader of the deputation, Kaiser Wilhelm said that all those endeavors were assured of his benevolent interest that aimed at the improvement of agriculture in Palestine, thus furthering the welfare of the Turkish Empire, with complete respect for the sovereignty of the Sultan.

There was not a word about a Zionist delegation nor any mention of Herzl's name. The subject was restricted to agriculture development, with a pronounced nod toward the Sultan's sovereignty, so as not to offend him. It would have been hard to imagine a paler or less meaningful statement. The delegation was bound by its agreement with the court not to offer the press its own version of the audience – but even had they been allowed it, it would not have demonstrated any real diplomatic achievement.

Herzl slowly began to comprehend that the trip had been useless. He laid out his disappointments in a long letter to the Grand Duke, who had encouraged Herzl from the start. His greatest frustration was the Emperor's failure to accept the idea of a protectorate. Herzl believed correctly that 'difficulties seem to have arisen' between the audiences in Constantinople and Jerusalem, most likely in German-Turkish relations. But this was cold comfort. 'It was only external difficulties and not a change of mind on the part of His Majesty that have for the time being postponed the expected declaration of a German protectorate,' he wrote. Even if that were the case, it hardly mattered – Herzl had not secured a diplomatic breakthrough. Yet he found something good in that, despite it all:

> The fact that the Emperor did not assume the protectorate in Jerusalem is, of course, an advantage for the future development of our cause.
>
> My companions, it is true, were quite disappointed. For the protectorate would have been a clear immediate benefit. But not so in the long run. We would subsequently have had to pay the most usurious interest for this protectorate.

Herzl sounds here like the fox and the sour grapes. But when he returned to Vienna to 'tempestuous welcome' from his fellow Zionists (after all, the delegation had been received by the German Emperor!), he pleaded with them to cancel plans for a huge ball that they had planned in his honor in one of the city's luxurious halls. It wasn't a time for celebration, he said.

It was a whimper that ended one of the most fascinating political initiatives that Herzl pursued in the few years between the First Zionist Congress and his death in 1904. But was it merely a failure? Yes, it was, if the measure is the high hopes that Herzl had entertained for his encounter with the Emperor in Jerusalem – which, it should be recalled, was a German initiative, not his. Throughout the series of events leading up to the official audience – in Potsdam, Constantinople, and Jerusalem – Herzl had viewed himself as a statesman making his entrance onto the stage of international diplomacy, on the verge of a dramatic historical breakthrough that would once again make the Jewish nation a player in the world of international politics. He saw himself as a figure in a historical tableau set in Jerusalem. The city had almost been placed in his hands so that he could turn it from a Levantine backwater into a jewel. Presumably, had he not thought that he was on the verge of a turning point in history, he would not have built castles in the air. Now, instead of turning his dreams to reality, of building a nation through statesmanship, he discovered that he was little more than a run-of-the-mill supplicant who had been outmaneuvered in a world of court intrigues over which he had no control and in which he had no understanding of the forces in play.

Yet the failure carried within it the kernel of an unprecedented achievement. Never before had a Jewish leader met with a powerful emperor to plead the cause of Jewish political independence; never before had a world leader lent his ear to a plan for a Jewish commonwealth so openly and directly; never before in the modern age had the idea of the establishment of a Jewish homeland in the Jews' historical territory been placed on the international political agenda; never before had the Zionist cause been discussed at such high levels – by Kaiser and Sultan, at the level of heads of government and foreign ministers, by the top diplomats of the world's most powerful countries. Even if the idea was rejected, this was the first time the world's major movers and shakers had considered it and taken a stand about it – even if to negate it. The Zionist idea was on the world's map and would from this point onward be a factor in international relations.

Herzl's audience with the Emperor in Jerusalem was in a way emblematic of all his political activity – his diplomatic efforts in other venues did not come out well, either. The Zionist Organization, bringing together at Herzl's initiative a number of hitherto disjointed associations and individuals, created the institutional structure that would in time serve as the foundation for the State of Israel. But during Herzl's lifetime it was weak, marginal, and lacking in any real influence. Yet Herzl transformed the notion of a political solution to the Jewish question from an idea debated by a handful of Jewish intellectuals sitting in cafés and writing in Jewish journals to a challenge for the international community. This was his phenomenal achievement.

Herzl's failure with the German Emperor, as with other world leaders, was an inseparable part of the Zionist idea's entry into the world arena. In time it would lead, through the Balfour Declaration and the League of Nations Mandate, to the United Nations' partition decision, on November 29, 1947, and finally to the establishment of the State of Israel. It was a glorious failure that produced impressive results. This book tells the story of how Theodor Herzl, combining a visionary idea with practical action, fashioned the policies and institutions that paved the way for the Jewish state.

CHAPTER TWO

EMANCIPATION
AND ITS DISCONTENTS

HERZL'S ERA, the second half of the nineteenth century, was one of the most peaceful that Europe had known for many centuries. It was also one of the best times ever for European Jews. True, the Franco-Prussian war of 1870–71 had briefly interrupted the tranquility of the age, but peace quickly returned, along with unprecedented prosperity. A Russian-Turkish war broke out at the continent's margins, in the Balkans, in 1877, but it was far away and barely disturbed the lives of the inhabitants of Vienna, Budapest, Berlin, Paris, and London and looked as if it would have no serious implications for their future. When, in the wake of the war, the Berlin Congress convened in 1878 to redraw the map of the Balkans, Europe's statesmen, under the direction of Germany's Chancellor Otto von Bismarck and British Prime Minister Benjamin Disraeli, demonstrated how sophisticated diplomacy, based on the preservation of a balance of power and give and take of interests could produce compromises, long-range understandings, and peaceful coexistence.

The circumstances of this half-century were completely unlike those of the revolutionary era of 1789–1814, when the French Revolution and the Napoleonic Wars had shaken Europe as it had never been shaken before. Dynasties were toppled and the heads of kings and princes rolled; borders were dissolved and redrawn nearly overnight. Some countries vanished and new ones appeared. Tens of myriads of men were conscripted into armies that traversed Europe north and south, east and west, killing, pillaging, and destroying, being killed themselves in unprecedented numbers. It ended in 1815 with Napoleon defeated and the Bourbons restored to the French throne, but the peace and stability the new settlement brought with it was short-lived. In 1848 a new wave of radical revolutionary fervor swept through Europe. In the German-speaking lands and the Italian peninsula, in Austria, Hungary, and Poland, insurgents combined social revolutionary fervor with radical demands for national sovereignty. The doctrine of national self-determination threatened to bury kingdoms and dismantle empires. The mid-century revolutions served as a reminder that the forces that set off the French Revolution, while suppressed, continued to churn under Europe's superficially placid surface.

Yet, as the century's second half proceeded, the thirst for revolutionary social and political transformation reflected in *The Communist Manifesto* of 1848 seemed to yield to liberal and social democratic movements that sought to reform rather than overthrow regimes. These forces worked to improve the lot of the working class and to enable it to participate in the political process. Conservatives like Bismarck, Disraeli, and Napoleon III responded with social legislation aimed at dulling the allure of insurgency by seeking to ameliorate the economic and social inequality that had deepened as a result of the Industrial Revolution. The gradual expansion of suffrage integrated the lower middle classes and a portion of the proletariat into the fabric of the parliamentary system. True, the unification of Germany and Italy during the 1860s and 1870s was accompanied by war, but the confrontations were relatively brief. It looked as if these two new nation-states were set to become anchors of stability in the heart of Europe. The *Ausgleich*, the Compromise of 1867 between the Austrian and the Hungarian parts of the Habsburg Empire, establishing the Dual Monarchy, seemed to create a fair balance between Vienna and Budapest and to solve, to a certain extent, the national problem in that vast and diverse empire.

Franz Joseph, the Austrian Emperor and now also the King of Hungary, had ascended to the throne in 1848. Queen Victoria of Britain had been crowned in 1837. The long reigns of both these rulers gave the age a sense that monarchies could be stable and monarchs beloved by their subjects. When the end of the nineteenth century, the *fin de siècle*, was celebrated in 1900, British grandparents had lived all or nearly all their lives under a single Queen and Austria's elders had known only one Emperor. Victoria and Franz Joseph seemed like Europe's strict but loving mother and father (or perhaps its benevolent grandmother and grandfather), symbols not only of continuity and stability but even more so of an eternal order. Who any longer remembered that in France, just a century before, an angry populace had guillotined royalty and aristocrats and Europe's monarchs had quaked in their boots?

This applied to the Jews as well. The nineteenth century had been good to them, better than any other era since the pagan Roman Empire had morphed into a Christian realm. True, the century's tranquility was more a phenomenon of Europe's west and center than of its east, but even in the latter the century's progress toward enlightenment could be felt, in particular by the millions of Jews who lived under the Russian Czar. Russia, too, was being swept forward by the tide of social progress, even if it moved slowly and hesitantly. The best measure of the nineteenth century's landmark and liberating significance for the Jews of Europe, especially during its second half, was their move into Europe's geographical and social fabric in a wide variety of areas of life.

At the century's start, most Jews had lived on the margins of urban life, and were hardly a presence in Europe's metropolitan centers. Only a handful of Jews lived in Paris and London. Berlin was practically *Judenrein* – just a few decades previously an internationally known Jewish philosopher, Moses Mendelssohn, had needed to obtain a special royal permit to live there. There was no Jewish community in Vienna – only a small number of 'court Jews' and army suppliers were allowed to reside in the Habsburg capital. Hardly any Jews lived either in Buda or in Pest, then still two separate cities. A small number lived in Warsaw and there were none at all in St. Petersburg or Moscow. The only exception – in relative terms – was Prague, where special historical circumstances prevailed, but that city had declined from the days when, centuries previously, it had served as the Habsburg capital.

At the century's dawn, most of Europe's Jews lived in villages and small market towns – in the French province of Alsace and the German province of Hessen, in Moravia, Galicia, and the provincial cities of Hungary, and of course in Russia's Jewish Pale of Settlement, in what is today eastern Poland, Lithuania, Belorussia and Ukraine – then the most densely populated Jewish area in Europe. These market-town and village Jews served, for the most part, as intermediaries, both economically and socially, between the peasantry on the one hand and the nobility and urban elites on the other.

The marginality of the Jews in European cities had many causes. One of the most prominent was that, at the end of the Middle Ages and the beginning of the modern era, the rising European urban burgher class succeeded in pushing their commercial and economic competitors, the Jews, out of the cities. As the urban bourgeoisie gained strength at the expense of feudal lords and kings, it acquired a legal privilege to exclude Jews from the cities – the so-called *privilegium de non tolerandis Iudaeis*. Cities founded in the Polish-Lithuanian Commonwealth adopted these laws, creating a situation in which most of the Jews of Eastern Europe lived in small towns and villages, under the jurisdiction of the aristocracy, rather than in the major cities. As a consequence, Jews had nearly no foothold in European metropolitan centers until the French Revolution.

By the end of the nineteenth century, this picture had been completely redrawn. Within two to three generations, Jews were notable and numerous among the inhabitants of Europe's capitals and large cities. By 1890 they constituted around 10 per cent of the populations of Berlin, Vienna, and Budapest; in Warsaw they were nearly 30 per cent of the population. In Paris and London their proportion was smaller, but still significant given their near total absence just a century previously. Similar changes had occurred in other large cities – Breslau and Leipzig, Krakow and Pressburg (Bratislava), Brünn (Brno) and Lemberg (Lwów). In the Russian Pale, many Jews moved from towns and villages to provincial urban centers. A European who traveled among Europe's great cities in 1790 would have met almost no Jews. A century later a similar traveler would have found them to be a salient feature of the urban and metropolitan landscape. Vienna was a prominent example of this transformation. The parents and grandparents of most of the Jews living in the city in 1890 had moved to the vibrant Austrian capital from Moravia, Bohemia, Galicia, and Bukovina, from the Hungarian plains and the marches of 'Upper Hungary' (now Slovakia), or from the Banat and Vojvodina regions of what later became Yugoslavia.

Not surprisingly, the move from country to city brought on social and economic transformations as well. A gradual change in the legal status of the Jews made their geographical and social mobility possible. In keeping with the progressive principles of the Enlightenment, France's Jews won full and equal rights in 1791. While France was home to less than 40,000 Jews at the time, the Revolution and Napoleon's conquests spread the principle of equal rights over much of the continent's west. Following the Congress of Vienna in 1815, some of these rights were revoked in parts of Germany, but some of them, like the opening of schools and some free professions to the Jews, were to a certain extent retained. The changes in the Habsburg Empire were more gradual and less radical, but, beginning with Emperor Joseph II's 1781 *Toleranzpatent*, most prohibitions against the entry of Jews into the professions were gradually lifted, as were restrictions on their residence in the cities. Similar processes began in the German states following the revolutions of 1848. In the wake of the unification of Germany in 1871, Jews were finally granted full legal equality. By the end of the century, in Germany, Austria-Hungary, and Western Europe, there were no longer any legal barriers as to where Jews could live, what economic activities and professions they could engage in, and what schools – from elementary schools to universities – they could attend. That does not mean, however, that it was easy for a Jew to gain a senior civil service appointment, and in particular officer rank in European armies. But in Austria-Hungary the aristocracy was even opened to the Jews – the Rothschild family's first title of nobility was an Austrian one. The palaces of wealthy and ennobled Jews graced the avenues and boulevards of Vienna and Budapest. Franz Joseph's empire then included not only today's Austria and Hungary, but also what is now the Czech Republic, Slovakia, southern Poland (Galicia and Silesia), Bukovina, Transylvania, Croatia, Bosnia, and parts of today's Serbia. As a result, the rights he extended to the Jews affected almost two million of them – the largest Jewish population of any country outside Russia.

The Jews' attitudes toward the societies that opened up before them also changed. The French revolutionary armies, which brought emancipation to the Jews in all the lands they conquered, were welcomed by Jewish communities. Emancipation was sometimes greeted by the Jews as akin to the end of days, and Jews who wrote about Napoleon often did so in terms that contained messianic references, as in special prayers composed in response to events of his reign. The new Jewish Reform movement, especially in Germany and Hungary, internalized the values of liberalism and equality, seeing the grant of equal rights not only as the end of persecution but also as an almost cosmic event that transformed the Jewish Diaspora. 'We are no longer living in exile,' they argued, 'rather, we are Germans (or Hungarians) of the Mosaic faith.' Reform communities omitted all mention of Zion and Jerusalem from their prayers – but not because they wanted to assimilate or blur the differences between Jews and non-Jews. It was, rather, testimony to the Jewish victory over discrimination and maltreatment and proof that it was possible to live as Jews with equal rights in gentile society. The new modern Orthodoxy in Germany and Hungary did not give up the doctrine of a messianic redemption, but also reflected an accommodation with the normality of life among the gentiles.

The architectural expression of this phenomenon was the construction of magnificent synagogues in Europe's major cities. Previously synagogues had been modest buildings located in Jewish neighborhoods, even in places where there were no ghettos, as Christian theology opposed the construction of prominent synagogue buildings. The result was that Jewish places of worship had been plain and in many cases hardly distinguishable from a standard home (as was the case, for example, in Venice). That changed in the nineteenth century. Large and beautiful synagogues were built in the cities. More often than not, their architecture displayed oriental-like elements so as to distinguish them from the Romanesque and Gothic styles identified with churches. These buildings were designed by the best architects, both Jewish and non-Jewish, in Budapest, Vienna, Warsaw, Florence, Bucharest, Berlin, and dozens of other cities. They were located in the cities' centers and became part of the urban fabric, symbols of the new social status and growing wealth of the Jewish population.

In 1800, the history of Central and Western European culture could have been written without reference to the Jews or to any specific Jewish person. European literature, poetry, and philosophy could have been chronicled adequately without including any Jewish names save perhaps Mendelssohn's (who was widely seen as an exception). Nor had there been a single Jewish figure in European politics, intellectual life, research, or science. Even an account of European economics over the centuries could have made do with reference to a handful of Jews, like the Rothschilds and a few 'court Jews' (keeping in mind that the latter had lost much of their importance by the end of the eighteenth century). Yet even these represented at best a marginal phenomenon. In short: in 1800 Jews were insignificant in every area of European society.

As 1900 approached, the picture was entirely different. Jews, or people of Jewish origin, now played critical roles in economics, politics, science, and the arts. Key figures on both the political left and the right had been born Jews or were the children of parents who had been born Jews. The Jewish backgrounds of Karl Marx and Benjamin Disraeli were apparent to all, as was also the case with figures whose names are less recognized today, like the German socialist leaders Ferdinand Lassalle, Eduard Bernstein, and Paul Singer. European science – be it physics, chemistry, mathematics, or psychology – was replete with Jewish names. The same was true of European literature, music, and philosophy. The only cultural arena into which Jews had not yet made significant inroads seemed to be painting and sculpture, most likely because of the traditional Jewish taboo against pictorial representation. Jews entered all the major professions – law, journalism, medicine, teaching, research, banking, and entrepreneurship. Jews owned and worked in shipping companies and industrial concerns. In just one century the Jews had moved in many fields from the margins of Western and Central European society to its center – even to its peak. The same thing was happening, if more slowly, in Russia, and certainly in the territory of Poland that was ruled by Russia and which was more open to Western influences than was Russia itself. In Austria-Hungary, Jews were the promoters of the empire's dominant culture in its peripheral areas – they were among the prominent Germanizers in the Austrian-ruled regions of Bohemia, Galicia, and Bukovina, and the disseminators of Magyarization in the Hungarian-ruled regions of Slovakia and Transylvania. They were thus identified with the regime and enjoyed its demonstrative sympathy. It was hardly surprising that Jews referred to Franz Joseph with the Hebrew acronym 'HaKiReH' (the Glorious Kaiser), or even Yiddishized his name, privately and half-jokingly referring to him as 'Fraim-Yossel'.

Stefan Zweig, perhaps the best exemplar of this Judeo-European cultural melding, was certainly exaggerating when he wrote in his autobiography, *The World of Yesterday*, that everything Vienna had to offer in terms of culture, literature, art, and society had been created by the Jews. On the other hand, it is hardly surprising that many people, both Jews and non-Jews, believed this. And it was precisely this impression of Jewish influence that was the fly in the ointment.

Had the Jews of the nineteenth century, a century that seemed to be going well for them, taken a more careful look at the processes that led to their emancipation and to the public reaction to it, they might well, even then, have noticed signs that something more problematic was lurking in the wings. Jewish spokesmen in all fields – rabbis, intellectuals, public figures, politicians – focused on the battle for equal rights and for the guarantee of their civil status. They were so intent on trying to convince governments and the public that they quite naturally tended to dismiss the dissonant voices they heard as unimportant squeaks in an otherwise well-functioning mechanism. The remaining manifestations of hatred of the Jews was, they were certain, no more than a relic of ancient and dying superstitions.

The example of revolutionary France, the cradle of equal rights for Jews, established by the Declaration of the Rights of Man and the Citizen, is telling. Few of those who argued in favor of equal rights for Jews in the National Assembly in the summer of 1789 came from the Third Estate, the commoners who were the Revolution's main leaders. The Jews' champions came, rather, from the Church and aristocracy. One of the most vocal advocates of equal rights for Jews was Abbé Henri Grégoire, who had, prior to the Revolution, published a pamphlet calling for the elimination of all the legal restrictions on the Jews. As a delegate to the Assembly, he called again and again on his colleagues to lift all legal bars that affected the Jews. His colleagues preferred to issue a general declaration of human rights, which would guarantee the status of the Jews without mentioning them specifically. Another enthusiastic promoter of equal rights for the Jews was Count Stanislas de Clermont-Tonnerre, who, on December 23, 1789, made a powerful speech in the National Assembly defending equal rights for the Jews. At the same time, the bourgeois representatives of the Third Estate often spoke disparagingly about the Jews, especially those of Alsace, whom they viewed as exploitative usurers and the adherents of a sinister religion. Their attitude toward the Jews was determined much more by their class interests than by liberal and universal principles.

But those with acute hearing would have noticed the ambiguity in Clermont-Tonnerre's speech. The count rejected the claim made by the opponents of emancipation that the Jews, with their community structure, constituted a state-within-the-state with its own judicial system and religious legislation. This, the detractors charged, made the Jews incapable of being true citizens of a community based on universal principles. Clermont-Tonnerre maintained that the Jews had gone into money-lending because gentile society had forbidden them to buy land and had excluded them from most professions. Yet his speech also included a sentence that would become a symbol of the complexities of emancipation: 'To the Jews as individuals – everything; to the Jews as a nation – nothing.'

Implicit in this statement was the assumption, going back to Jean-Jacques Rousseau's radical republicanism, that the only legitimate and permissible attachment in a well-ordered commonwealth is to the general good. Any particularist loyalty – to a guild, a professional association, a political party, or a religion – infringes on the citizen's ability to identify with the general good that is the only proper guide in public affairs. For this reason, the Republic, in its radical stages, did indeed outlaw labor unions. This aspect of the French Revolution, which some observers eventually saw, not without reason, as totalitarian in nature, signaled a willingness to grant equal rights to the Jews but not legitimacy to their separate identity, their special customs, or their tradition. They would be accepted only one by one, as individuals, and only if they were willing to fall into line with the general public and its principles. Clermont-Tonnerre's fervent call for equal rights for the Jews contained within it a paradox. He was not willing to accept the Jews as they were and to see them as equals *despite* their differences. While he did not say so explicitly, the meaning is clear – the Jews would have to pay a price for emancipation. They would have to shed their Jewish identity and consciousness as they themselves understood it. In other words, the tension between equality and autonomy would accompany them into the new liberal state. It should be noted that Clermont-Tonnerre was consistent – he demanded a revocation of the Catholic Church's special legal status as well.

But a Jewish observer should have been more concerned about the social hostility that surrounded him than the theoretical debates in the National Assembly. The Jews of Alsace, who were a majority of France's Jews on the eve of the Revolution, were the victims of periodic pogroms that were a product of their social circumstances. In this region the Jews were scattered through villages and towns, and most of them were shopkeepers, wine merchants, and money-lenders. As a result, most Alsatian farmers felt as if they lived under the thumb of Jewish credit. When the Revolution broke out, many French commoners were thus inimical toward the Jews and even attacked them violently, and thus, of course, were also unsympathetic to the Jews' demand for equal rights. During the Revolution's first climax, in the second half of July 1789, when a Parisian mob stormed the Bastille, pogroms against the Jews broke out in Alsace. When throngs of Frenchmen torched the palaces of the nobility, they also plundered the homes of Jews in most Alsatian cities and burned their promissory notes. According to contemporary testimonies, nearly a thousand Jews had to flee their homes. Many of them found refuge in Basel, over the border in Switzerland. Similar acts of violence took place in neighboring Lorraine – Jews were expelled from their homes, which were then pillaged. The Revolution did not change social attitudes toward the Jews – quite the opposite. These disturbances did not alarm the French nor were they condemned by public figures. Abbé Grégoire was the only one to even bring it up in the National Assembly.

In short, the French Revolution's message to the Jews was not a simple matter of equality. Similar things happened in Germany after 1815, when the student fraternities (*Burschenschaften*) that led the fight against royal absolutism and for the unification of Germany expressed a particularly hostile attitude toward the Jews. They refused to accept Jews into their ranks on the grounds that they were aliens rather than true Germans. Ironically, Jewish membership into these clubs had not even been an issue until Jews were allowed to enroll in the universities at the beginning of the nineteenth century. The attitude of these German students was one of the first signs that the opening of a society in the name of enlightened liberal principles could end up producing new kinds of hostility. On top of this, the first German pogroms of the modern age, the so-called Hep-Hep riots, took place in 1819. Jews were attacked on the streets and Jewish stores were ransacked. It was a new and as yet unknown phenomenon in the German-speaking lands. The riots were led by students, ostensibly the anti-absolutist and progressive force in German society.

Two years earlier, in 1817, German students and intellectuals convened a massive event at Wartburg castle in Thuringia. It was held to celebrate the third centennial of the event that set off the Reformation – Martin Luther's nailing of his 95 theses on a church door to challenge Catholic doctrine. The students built a bonfire to burn books that they objected to, in particular the works of conservative thinkers. It was the first such event in the modern age. The very idea of a book burning – not by an incited crowd of illiterates, nor by the Catholic Inquisition, but by educated young people and intellectuals dedicated to the struggle against tyranny, would later bring the German-Jewish poet Heinrich Heine to voice his chilling prophecy: 'Where they burn books, they will end up burning people.' A radical himself, Heine understood that progress cast shadows no less than light.

The key speaker at the Wartburg festival was one of the prominent German philosophers of the time, Jakob Friedrich Fries of the University of Heidelberg. Fries, a follower of Immanuel Kant, was one of the most prominent liberal thinkers of his time. Not only did he support the book burning, but he also published an essay entitled 'On the Danger Posed by the Jews to German Well-Being and Character.' In this work, Fries proposed a number of practical ways to mitigate the threat presented by the Jews. Among these were the elimination of Jewish educational institutions, the promotion of Jewish emigration from Germany and the prohibition of Jewish immigration, a ban on marriages between Jews and Christians, and a law forbidding Jews to employ Christian servants (especially female servants). Last of all, he suggested that Jews be required to display a special badge on their clothing so that they could be distinguished from the rest of the population. Fries's essay appeared in a journal published by his university, the *Heidelberger Jahrbücher*, one of the most respected intellectual periodicals in Germany at that time.

Such phenomena were not common and could be dismissed as trivial. But they were persistent, from 'revolutionary' pogroms to French socialist thinkers accusing the Jews of being the agents of capitalism through their control of the banks and newspapers. The most prominent of the latter were the utopian socialists Charles Fourier and Pierre-Joseph Proudhon, but there were others as well. Still, these writings were not widely read, and many thinkers and writers of the left castigated such anti-Jewish rhetoric. For example, Karl Marx, who had no great love for his ancestral people, wrote that the first symptom of anti-revolutionary reaction was the attempt to revoke the Jews' recently acquired rights. Yet it is evident that the revolutions of 1848 brought on a real improvement in the status of the Jews, yet it was occasionally accompanied by populist anti-Jewish riots. But the political discourse on their rights, which was conducted largely by Jews and their supporters, rarely mentioned the outbursts of hostility. When they were referred to, they were portrayed as no more than the remnants of primitive medieval beliefs that would soon dissipate in the warmth of the sun of enlightenment and liberalism.

But this was wrong. The Jew-hatred of the modern age was a novel phenomenon, a product of the Enlightenment itself. The traditional European opposition to the Jews had grown out of the anti-Judaism that was built into Christianity. The new enmity toward the Jews had a different character, which would later be named by a new term – anti-Semitism. It stressed the ethnic and racial character of the Jews, not their religion. It came in reaction to the fact that the Jews were no longer a separate and oppressed religious community living on the margins of European Christian society. They were now a central component, an inseparable part of society. Precisely as such their difference – their success, the economic and intellectual talent that was seen as part of their nature – was seen as threatening. They were considered a menace because they were present, because of their influence over the societies they lived in, its values and structures. They were a peril because they seemed to be the most eager and flourishing members in the new elites that had emerged in modern industrial society. It was not their suffering and weakness that sparked the new hatred – it was their success and their power, whether real or imagined.

Such political and social phenomena, as expressed in the popular discourse and ideology, intensified over the nineteenth century. One product was Richard Wagner's essay 'Judaism in Music,' published in 1850. Wagner warned against the Jewish penetration of German and European cultural life, into which they were introducing foreign and inferior elements. Wagner's prime examples were Felix Mendelssohn and Jacques Offenbach. Paradoxically, Wagner was friendly with Heine and in his early days shared radical and revolutionary ideas with him. In fact, once Wagner became famous – with Jews making up a considerable portion of his most enthusiastic fans – he no longer repeated his charges about the depravity of Jewish influence in music, even if symbolic anti-Jewish elements appeared in his later works. Wagner was not simply envious of the success of Jewish composers. When he wrote his essay he was still affiliated with radical politics. Just a year previously he had joined Bakunin and Engels on the barricades of the Dresden uprising. It was the very same radicalism that led him to argue that the decadence and corruption of the rising bourgeoisie made it incapable of defending the glorious heritage of European culture. This created an opening for the Jews, who were themselves decadent, to take over. Wagner's anti-Jewish doctrine linked up later to the larger racial theories then in vogue. Houston Stewart Chamberlain, one of the fathers of modern racial theory, later married Wagner's daughter.

In fact, the more successfully the Jews integrated into Europe's culture and economy, the more they were condemned for being different. This was particularly the case in Germany, where openness to the Jews reached its peak following German unification in 1871. In

1879, Wilhelm Marr, a journalist and political activist from Hamburg, published his pamphlet *The Way for the Victory of Germanism over Judaism*. Like Wagner, Marr was at the start of his career a radical of anarchist leanings and took part in the 1848 uprisings. In this diatribe he coined the term 'anti-Semitism' to designate the new kind of anti-Judaism – not the traditional Christian critique of the Jewish religion, but a concept to rally Europe against the menace of the Jewish nation and race. This was the beginning of modern racial Jew-hatred, which claimed that the Jews' nefarious nature was a matter of scientific fact, solidly based in biology and anthropology. While the new anti-Semitism built on the foundation of deep-seated European religious and social hostility toward the Jews, its claims were new and constituted to a large extent a reaction to the Jews' success in entering non-Jewish society and the perceived threat they constituted in the economy, banking, culture, literature, and the press. Following the publication of his pamphlet, Marr founded the League of Anti-Semites. While the organization was short-lived, it had a lasting influence on German political discourse, helped along by Marr's ongoing publication of anti-Semitic material.

Eugen Dühring, economist, philosopher, and popular commentator on current events, in 1881 published an essay entitled 'The Jewish Question as a Racial, Moral, and Cultural Issue.' It was widely read by German and Austrian intellectuals and students. According to Dühring, who also hailed initially from the socialist movement, a deep and unbridgeable gap yawned between the Nordic 'Aryan' races and the Semitic race. The beginnings of the Jewish takeover of Europe, he argued, lay in the continent's acceptance of the teachings of Jesus the Jew. His radical background prompted Dühring to call on the European peoples to liberate themselves from the Jewish religious heritage contained in both the Old and New Testaments. To guard European culture against the Jews, he proclaimed, the Jews should once again be forced into ghettos.*

---

* Dühring's influence was so pervasive that Friedrich Engels called one of his most famous polemical works *Anti-Dühring*. The book's main target was Dühring's economic views, but Engels also warned against the perniciousness of his opponent's racial and anti-Semitic doctrine, which was especially popular in academic circles but also found an audience among the proletariat and among socialist intellectuals.

One of Germany's greatest historians, Heinrich von Treitschke, joined the anti-Semitic tide. As professor of history at the University of Berlin and a member of the Reichstag for the National Liberal Party, Treitschke was hugely influential. He published his first anti-Jewish work in 1879 in the prestigious journal he edited, the *Preussische Jahrbücher*.

Treitschke's conception of history reflected events in Germany following the country's unification. Liberals and democrats had tried to accomplish this during the revolution of 1848, but had failed. In the end it was Bismarck who accomplished the task, using force of arms to bring German-speaking lands under the rule of Prussia. The wars that Bismarck's Prussia fought against Denmark, Austria, and France fundamentally changed German historical discourse and amplified the militarist traits traditionally identified with Prussia. This militarism eclipsed the humanistic tradition of Germans who viewed their country as 'a nation of poets and thinkers,' in the spirit of Kant, Goethe, and Schiller. Treitschke accordingly highlighted the role of force in international relations. In his account, Rome's greatness derived from its conquests. The same was true of imperial Britain, and such was Germany's destiny as well. He maintained, however, that the German Reich's political and cultural hegemony were threatened by the Jews, whose penetration of all parts of the nation's economic and intellectual activity was weakening Germany from within. The Jews, who were migrating en masse into Germany from Eastern Europe, were a foreign, alien, 'Asiatic' element that constituted no less a danger to Germany than had the barbarians who had moved in to sap the strength and greatness of the Roman Empire. Germany, he proclaimed, had to defend itself against the Jewish threat with appropriate legislation and policies. Treitschke coined the slogan *'Die Juden sind unser Unglück,'* 'the Jews are our misfortune,' which would later appear at the top of the Nazi newspaper *Der Stürmer* and on the banners of the Nazi Party's mass rallies in Nuremberg. While Treitschke rejected Marr's crude racism, he denounced 'mongrel culture' and the 'mixing of blood' as mortal dangers for Germany. His writings inspired the establishment of an anti-Semitic political party that won seats in the Reichstag. While it was a small and marginal faction, its very existence marked anti-Semitism's entry into German political and parliamentary discourse and granted legitimacy to ideas that had at first seemed entirely foreign to the nineteenth century's spirit of progress and equality. Thus, the pall of the new anti-Semitism darkened the astounding social mobility experienced by the Jews of Germany and Austria-Hungary over a brief period of time. These Jews were doing well but found themselves face to face with a new and worrying phenomenon. But most Jews, like most of the liberal and socialist thinkers and writers of these two countries, dismissed the threat, certain that it represented the last gasp of ancient prejudices that would soon vanish.

Gezö Istóczy, a member of the Hungarian parliament, founded an anti-Semitic party along similar lines in 1883. After a number of parliamentary speeches warning about the Jewish threat failed to rouse much public interest, his new party campaigned to place legal constraints on the country's Jews, who were flourishing as a result of the rapid industrialization of Hungary that followed the Austro-Hungarian Compromise of 1867. Many Jews were among the prime movers of the industrialization process and founders of the country's new heavy industry. As they gained prominence, the blood libel against the Jews was revived, most infamously in the village of Tisza-Eszlár in 1882. The case became an international *cause célèbre* because it seemed to run entirely counter to the liberal and tolerant spirit of the times. Yet it, too, was seen as an exception, a holdover from the Middle Ages, a relic of superstition that would soon be extinguished by an enlightened Europe.

But the new racial anti-Semitism, aimed at the Jews' economic success and their integration into European culture, did not emerge from the unschooled masses. It became popular in many cases among European, and especially German, intellectuals, and was most widespread and prominent in the academy and among students. At times of revolution and upheaval, violence may be committed largely by ignorant mobs fired by sinister fanaticism. But that was not the case in the peaceful latter half of the nineteenth century. Racial anti-Semitism was from the start an intellectual movement, its claims grounded, according to its advocates, in the discoveries of biological and anthropological sciences in the wake of Darwin's doctrine of the survival of the fittest. The ostensibly scientific claim that humanity was divided into superior and inferior races transformed Jew-hatred into a legitimate scientific position, acceptable in polite society. Leading figures in the fields of economics and history, Dühring and Treitschke being only the most prominent examples, advocated the exclusion of the Jews from society. Under the circumstances, it was hardly a marginal view confined to the dregs of society. Anti-Semitism was a legitimate point of view in educated European society, which was what made it so ominous – had people only taken the trouble to notice.

*   *   *

Obviously, the picture was different to the east, in the lands of the czarist empire. The ideas of the Enlightenment and the French Revolution had yet to penetrate this region with anything like the same intensity and extent that they had in Western and Central Europe. Furthermore, the key role that Russia had played in the defeat of Napoleon, and therefore also of the vestigial ideas of emancipation that the French Revolution had bequeathed to the Bonapartist empire, injected new life into the czarist autocracy. But reason, freedom, and other revolutionary ideas did reach Russia eventually, mostly imported by members of the nobility who studied or traveled in Western Europe, and this had complex consequences for the Jewish population.

The seminal liberal event in Eastern Europe came in 1855, with the accession of Czar Alexander II. The Jews had good reason to be hopeful. Alexander freed the serfs in 1861 and radically reformed the czarist administration, courts, and political system. Some legal restrictions on the Jews were lifted and the gymnasia high schools and universities gradually opened up before them. Even the edicts restricting Jewish residence in the cities and outside the Pale of Settlement were loosened, at least for the well-off, and some of the restrictions that barred Jews from many professions were lifted. The result was the slow emergence of a Jewish bourgeoisie, both commercial and intellectual, in some Russian cities. Jews entered the timber and sugar trades, imported goods, and went into banking. At the same time, thousands of Jewish men and women received secular secondary and higher educations. These *maskilim*, as they called themselves, wrote works in Russian and a newly resurgent Hebrew language expressing their hopes that the Western ideals of freedom, equality, and human brotherhood had finally arrived in Russia. The Jews had a bright future in this new, more liberal and more open Russia, according to writers such as the Hebrew novelist Peretz Smolenskin and the Hebrew thinker and essayist Moshe Leib Lilienblum.

But this liberal era ended when Alexander II was assassinated in 1881 by revolutionaries from the *Narodnaya Volya* (People's Will) movement. Jews were among the conspirators, setting off a chain reaction of anti-Jewish events. While these incidents were largely spontaneous and local, rather than guided by a single group, they represented a sharp reversal of what had previously seemed like inexorable progress and emancipation. 'The Jews murdered our father the Czar just as they murdered Christ' became the battle cry of a wave of pogroms of hitherto unknown ferocity that swept through Russia in the months that followed. Russia's Jews had always suffered from legal discrimination and social hostility, but these riots, most of which took place in the southern part of the Pale of Settlement, in Ukraine, were a new phenomenon. These outbreaks of anti-Jewish violence were spontaneous, catching the local authorities unprepared and clueless as to how to respond to them. As time passed, local leaders and the central government began to view the pogroms favorably, as an outlet for popular violence that might otherwise be directed at the regime. Widespread rumors claimed that the Czar had been murdered by a Jewish conspiracy rather than by Russian revolutionaries. The local authorities looked the other way or sometimes even actively encouraged thugs who attacked Jews. Both Jews and non-Jews soon realized that the authorities actually supported the pogroms.

The assassination had far-reaching political and bureaucratic implications for Russia's reforms. The regime realized – rightly so, from its point of view – that its modest liberalization had not put a lid on dissent against the repressive nature of the government. On the contrary, the reforms encouraged and fed discontent. When the country became open to Western ideas, its people were exposed to dangerous notions. The lesson the regime drew was that the reforms had to be stopped and even reversed. State oversight of schools and universities was tightened, censorship was intensified, draconian new laws severely restricted freedoms of organization and assembly, and the secret police was beefed up. The conspirators against the Czar were tried and hanged, but the police did not stop there. Thousands of citizens, mostly from the educated classes, many of them Jews and members of the nobility, were also put on trial and exiled to Siberia.

As part of this retrenchment, most of the rights granted to the Jews as part of Alexander II's reforms were revoked. Tens of thousands of Jews who had left the Pale of Settlement for the cities, both legally and illegally, were now expelled from these areas and banished to the Pale. They lost not only their homes but also their livelihoods. They were also once again banned from the professions, and strict quotas – the *numerus clausus* – were imposed on the number of Jews allowed into the gymnasia high schools and universities.

All hopes for emancipation and equality within Russia were dashed. The new repressions and the pogroms set off a mass migration of Russian Jews to the West – to the United States, England, Canada, Argentina, South Africa, as well as to Romania, Germany, and Austria-Hungary. A small number organized themselves into the Hovevei Zion movement and established the first modern rural settlements in Palestine. The leading *maskilim*, Lilienblum and Smolenskin among them, lost faith in Russia and began also to explore the options of emigration and settlement in Palestine. A Russian physician who had served with distinction in the Czar's army also concluded that the Jews had no future in Russia. His name was Leo Pinsker and he published a pamphlet entitled *Auto-Emancipation*, arguing that the Jews should no longer wait for Europe to free them. The Jews, he said, had to emancipate themselves.

But these developments were part of a wider general context. As Europe's economy thrived and its industry took off in the early nineteenth century, not only class differences deepened – other cleavages developed as well. Some were public, others remained hidden. These cracks were the product of the clash between the universal values of the French Revolution, which emphasized the freedom of the individual, and the rising national consciousness of stateless peoples who sought to foster their national cultures and traditions.

The French Revolution itself had raised the flag of the popular sovereignty. On the face of it, it was meant to be a basis for the democratization of political life. But the dawn of the nineteenth century was also the dawn of the Romantic age. Romanticism, in its political incarnation, sanctified the particular history of nations. In parallel, secondary and higher education ceased to be the preserve of the nobility and the wealthy and more members of the middle and lower classes received schooling. This turned the attention of both scholars and commoners to the histories, traditions, and languages of ethnic groups that had heretofore been politically marginal. Furthermore, as a result of secularization, another product of the Enlightenment, people's identity with religious principles and institutions weakened and they began to search for other foci of identity. Until the beginning of the nineteenth century, most Europeans defined themselves in terms of their religion – they were first and foremost Christians, or, more precisely, Catholics, Protestants, or members of the Orthodox Church. Now many began to refer to themselves as German, French, Italian, Polish, Hungarian, Romanian, or Czech. Such national identities first centered on culture, but gradually led to political demands as well, based on the dual meaning of popular sovereignty. National consciousness, when added to the principle of political self-determination, produced the doctrine that every group that viewed itself as a nation or people could demand self-government, sovereignty, and independence. It was the appearance of these ideas that gave the name 'the springtime of nations' to the 1848 revolutions. In keeping with the *Zeitgeist*, Jews began to identify themselves, and be identified by others, not just as a religious group but also as an ethnic and national entity.

The prophet of Italian nationalism, Giuseppe Mazzini, was the theoretician who tied the universal principle of popular sovereignty to the principle of the nation-state. It is by realizing my right to be a citizen of my nation, he argued, that I make myself a citizen of the world. I cannot be a citizen of the world without first being a citizen of my country, and my nationality is the link, the mediating factor, between the individual and humankind as a whole. The cause of war, Mazzini argued, was that borders between states were established arbitrarily by dynastic rulers in accordance with their ambitions. If political borders follow national boundaries, the world will be peaceful and harmonious, he claimed. Italy's centuries-old divisions and conflicts would end when it was united into a single country rather than being divided between the Austrian Emperor, the Pope, and half a dozen other dynasties and city-states. The same was true of other regions. It sounded good, but the real world was more complicated. During the second half of the nineteenth century, it became evident that drawing borders that included all the members of a given national or linguistic group without including members of other groups was impossible. Populations overlapped too much. The creation of the nation-state inevitably created both national and ethnic minorities that did not identify with the ruling culture, as well as diasporas – members of the sovereign national group that lived in territories outside the borders of the nation-state. Discontent seemed guaranteed. Poles and Germans both lived in Silesia, Posen, and Galicia; Bohemia and Moravia were home to both Czechs and Germans, as Transylvania was to Hungarians and Romanians. Not only that, but pockets of speakers of Hungarian, Slovakian, Croatian, Slovenian, and German could be found scattered through all these regions. No matter how surgically one drew the border, it would motivate the continuation of conflict rather than its resolution. On top of that, Romanticism fostered claims of the rights of peoples to territories to which they had historical ties or over which they, or, more precisely, lords or kings who spoke their language, had once ruled – even if the areas in question were now inhabited partly or mostly by members of other nations.

But that was not the only problem. What criteria determined whether a given group of people was a nation or not? Were the Ukrainians a distinct ethnic and linguistic group, or was their language just a dialect of Russian, or should they be called 'Ruthenians'? Were the Macedonians a nation, or was their language merely a variety of Bulgarian (or perhaps Serbian)? The Serbians and Croatians understood each other's speech perfectly well but wrote it in different alphabets and went to different churches – were they a single nation or two distinct ones? What about the Hungarians, who demanded independence from German-speaking Austria, but who were not prepared to grant the same right of self-determination to the Slovakians, Croatians, and Romanians who lived in the territory they claimed as their own? It seemed obvious that the Greeks had a right to shake off Turkish rule and gain independence, but the establishment, in the 1820s, of a small Greek state in the south-east Balkans did not solve the Greek national problem. Large numbers of Greek speakers remained in other parts of the Ottoman Empire. And language was only one marker. To what nation did Turkish-speaking Greek Orthodox Christians living in Anatolia belong? Were they 'true' Greeks? Such questions have dogged Europe from then until the present day, as shown by the vicious wars that broke out when Yugoslavia fell apart in the 1990s.

These issues were particularly important political and cultural issues in the Austro-Hungarian Empire at the end of the century. This large realm, acquired over many centuries by the Habsburg dynasty through war, diplomacy, and marriage, encompassed a vast variety of ethnic and linguistic groups. The only link that united them was their historical allegiance to the Habsburgs. Speakers of German, Hungarian, Czech, Slovakian, Polish, Ukrainian, Romanian, Croatian, Serbian, Slovenian, and even Italian lived side by side under Habsburg rule. And Jews lived beside all these throughout the realm. There were two million of them, the second largest Jewish population in Europe, second only to the number of Jews subject to the Russian Czar.

During the nineteenth century, especially after Emperor Franz Joseph's accession to the throne and the failure of the 1848 revolutions, the Habsburg monarchy introduced more modern administrative and governmental methods and practices. The Compromise of 1867 between the Austrian German-speaking and the Hungarian-speaking parts of the realm created a two-headed, quasi-federal system. There were two capitals, Vienna and Budapest, two parliaments, two prime ministers, two cabinets, with a common government responsible for foreign affairs, the military and finances. Most provinces received their own provincial parliaments as well, and the elites of all the Empire's far-flung regions were impressively integrated into a common ruling class. A glance at the names of Habsburg prime ministers, cabinet members and diplomats during the second half of the century shows that not only German-Austrians and Hungarians held these offices. Many of the names are Polish, Czech, Croatian, or Italian. Some of these groups also had the right to an education in their own language. It looked as if this liberal and enlightened regime, in which imperial and bureaucratic authority when wielded alongside extensive if restricted representative government, had created a model of a tolerant, open multi-ethnic, multi-confessional society. No wonder that for the Jews it was the *goldeneh medineh*, the golden country. They had never enjoyed such benevolent tolerance anywhere in the world, together with such economic success and official defense of their rights. Russia's Jews viewed the Austrian-Hungarian Empire as an exemplar for their own – a liberal and tolerant multi-national and multi-religious empire in which they, too, could find their future.

But churning under the surface were forces that threatened to undermine this seemingly impressive arrangement. The Compromise had granted broad autonomy to the Hungarian part of the Empire, symbolized by the majestic neo-Gothic Hungarian Parliament building in Budapest, on the banks of the Danube. Now the seat of government for a modest country of 11 million inhabitants, it was, at its dedication in 1904, the largest such building in the world. Yet the Hungarians were not always satisfied. Each year, during the annual debate on the national budget in parliament, the Hungarians demanded a larger portion of the Empire's income. Another tense subject was the status of the Hungarian reserve forces in the imperial army. According to the Compromise, foreign policy was to be set by a joint ministry, but was often a subject of fierce contention between the two polities. Time and again controversies raged over the division of power and even over the status of the Emperor, whose title in Budapest was 'King of Hungary.'

Moreover, Hungary's part of the Empire included broad swaths of territory in which ethnic Hungarians were a minority, such as Slovakia, Croatia, Dalmatia, and Transylvania. Linguistic differences paralleled economic and social distinctions. The nobility spoke Hungarian; the peasantry spoke a variety of Slavic languages or Romanian; the cities were largely German and Jewish. Some of these ethnic groups demanded cultural and linguistic autonomy and sometimes even self-government. The Croatians, for example, demanded that the two-headed empire become a three-headed one – Austrian, Hungarian, and Croatian. The Hungarians, for their part, viewed this as a threat to their country and the integrity of their historical kingdom, the Lands of St. Stephen's Crown. When, under the Berlin Treaty of 1878, Austria-Hungary gained control of Bosnia-Herzegovina from Turkey, it found itself with new minority groups, Bosnian Muslims and Serbs.

The situation was no less complex in the German-speaking Austrian lands. The Czechs of Bohemia and Moravia demanded an end to the social and linguistic hegemony of German speakers. In this case the linguistic division largely coincided with a religious one – the German speakers were Catholics while the Czechs were mostly Protestants of various kinds. The latter still recalled the repression of the Hussites at the end of the Middle Ages and viewed its founder, the religious reformer Jan Huss, as the father of Czech nationalism. While there was little historical basis for viewing Huss in nationalistic terms, once it became imprinted on the consciousness of the Czech-speaking elite, it became a powerful political rallying cry. The Jews of Bohemia, who for the most part spoke German, found themselves in the crossfire between these rival national identities. When hundreds of thousands of Czech-speaking farmers migrated to Vienna at the end of the nineteenth century, attracted by the jobs offered by the city's rapidly developing industry, the battle of languages and identities migrated with them and became a feature of the city's municipal politics.

Similar tensions could be found in the cities of Galicia, the southern region of Poland that the Habsburgs acquired in the partitions of Poland at the end of the eighteenth century. Cities like Lemberg and Krakow became the scenes of cultural tensions between Polish and German speakers, with the Jews again in the middle. These tensions intensified as the right to vote for the Reichsrat in Vienna expanded. Czech, Polish, and Italian national parties, turning parliamentary sessions into public sparring rings over the national issue, paralyzed the functions of government. Democratization, as was demonstrated several times in the twentieth century, instead of mitigating ethnic conflicts, can paradoxically exacerbate them.

One response to the rise of nationalist and separatist groups within the Empire, especially in its Austrian half, was the emergence of German nationalist and racialist movements. These were especially powerful in Vienna and Prague. The ethnic Germans, who formed the traditional ruling elite, felt threatened by the increasingly restless Slavic minorities. To highlight their special status, the German speakers fashioned an extensive system of German symbols, sometimes of a pagan nature. Pan-Germanists also appeared in these two cities, advocating the dismantling of the Austro-Hungarian Empire and separation from the Hungarian- and Slavic-speaking regions, with the German areas uniting with the German Reich.

This was the first manifestation of the concept of the *Anschluss*, the absorption of German-speaking regions into a greater Germany. This concept was later invoked by the Nazis to justify their annexation of Austria and the Czechoslovak Sudetenland. Movements that stressed the 'Aryan' character of pan-Germanism also arose in Vienna. These viewed the Jews as a threat to the German nation. Even a Jew eager to adopt Christianity could not turn into an 'Aryan' – he remained biologically a 'Semite.' Student fraternities, press associations, and sports clubs declared themselves 'Aryan' and expelled their Jewish members, including those who had converted to Christianity. The preservation of the purity of the Aryan race became a political rallying cry. The imperial authorities viewed these groups as dangerous but marginal. Few Jews took the German racialists seriously.

The new anti-Slavic and anti-Jewish racist movements were headed by men such as Guido von List and Lanz von Liebenfels – figures who are quite rightly forgotten today. Some of these movements adopted new symbols, one of them the swastika, introducing powerful new visual elements into the political discourse. This ancient Hindu emblem thus migrated to Europe and became the symbol of an 'Aryan' racism, anti-Slavic and anti-Jewish in late nineteenth-century cosmopolitan and multi-ethnic Vienna.

CHAPTER THREE

BUDAPEST – VIENNA – PARIS

It was into this cauldron that Herzl was born. As he grew up, he imbibed its brew of hope and tension, which molded his personal and professional development and shaped his consciousness.

Theodor (or Tivadar, as he was called in Hungarian) Herzl was born in 1860 to a bourgeois Jewish family well ensconced in Budapest society and business. Like most of the Hungarian capital's Jews, the families of Herzl's parents moved from the provinces to Budapest in response to incentives the Industrial Revolution created for rural populations to migrate to urban centers. Herzl's father's family had originally lived in Zemlin (Zemun), today a suburb of Serbia's capital, Belgrade. In Budapest, Herzl first attended a Jewish grade school and then enrolled in a gymnasium, as academic high schools were called in Central European lands. The family moved to Vienna in Herzl's nineteenth year. Both Hungarian and German were spoken at home, although a bit of Hebrew and snatches of Judeo-German appear from time to time in his diaries and letters. In 1878 he enrolled in the University of Vienna's law school, receiving his degree in 1884.

As was common practice at that time and in the circles in which he moved, Herzl kept a reading journal. A portion, covering the period from January to May 1882, has survived. It contains his notes on 40 books he read during this five-month period. Some of the entries are quite brief, others somewhat longer. As a whole, the journal shows him to have been a voracious reader with a wide variety of interests. He read fiction, non-fiction, and poetry in German and French, including translations of foreign works into these languages (Dostoyevsky's *Crime and Punishment* was 'a first-rate psychological novel,' he wrote enthusiastically). Such journals were not meant to be simply private records of books read – they served as exercises in prose style and criticism. The young Herzl appears at times to be swept away by his own rhetoric. Clearly this law student had literary ambitions.

Only two books mentioned in the journal are on Jewish subjects, to which may be added his marginal notes on a book by Ferdinand Lassalle, the Jewish founder of the German labor movement – Herzl lauded the author and his socialist philosophy. One of the books on Jewish subjects was a historical novel by one of the most popular German-language authors of the nineteenth century, Wihelm Jensen. Herzl loved this genre, at which Jensen excelled. The book, *The Jews of Cologne*, published in 1869, tells of the persecution of the Jews during the Black Death of the mid-fourteenth century. Herzl marveled at Jensen's empathy for the Jews, accused unjustly of spreading the plague, and at his depiction of the Jews' dignified behavior when confronted with Christian ruffians and mobs. Jensen, Herzl noted, successfully and sympathetically portrayed life in the ghetto and depicted the Jews as a 'noble oriental tribe' that, despite its tribulations in exile, preserved its distinguished heritage.

Herzl added that medieval persecution of the Jews, caused by envy and resentment, could in his time be seen 'in Holy Russia not less than in today's Holy German Empire.' It is the first indication we have of his feelings about German anti-Semitism. His diagnosis was that the cause of any negative Jewish traits – if indeed there were such – was their enforced segregation from the general culture. These peculiarities would vanish if they were welcomed into society – a welcome that should include intermarriage. The ghetto, however, still persisted, not as a physical reality but as a conceptual one, 'in the narrow-minded consciousness of parts of the common people as well as among some of the "enlightened and educated" classes.' The passage foreshadows an issue that would trouble Herzl's thoughts in the future and which would find expression in his play *The New Ghetto*. In the modern age, he maintained, the Jews still lived in a spiritual ghetto.

But the book on a Jewish subject to which Herzl devoted most space in his reading journal was Eugen Dühring's book on the Jewish question, which had appeared the previous year. As already noted, Dühring, as a man of public and professional stature, granted an ostensibly scientific stamp of legitimacy to racial anti-Semitism. His writing on the Jews demonstrated that the new Jew-hatred had found a home in the German intelligentsia. Herzl's notes on the book (which he would later say had been his first encounter with the modern 'Jewish question') are fascinating. He wrote wrathfully, sometimes in ferocious terms, of the author's 'vileness.' Yet he admitted that the book was well written, clear, and captivating – which was precisely why it was so dangerous. The danger went further than that, however. Herzl acknowledged that a number of the book's premises were correct. The problem was that Dühring used them to reach warped and inflammatory conclusions. Readers were liable to be led from the author's largely accurate description of European Jewry to entirely false conclusions. 'This is a despicable book,' he wrote, but 'unfortunately written with great talent, as if it were not written with a poisoned pen full of base envy and personal seeking of vengeance.'

Herzl was most appalled by Dühring's contention that the Jews were an inferior race, from which he derived his claim that the Jews' evil qualities were inherent rather than the product of social and historical circumstances. Herzl also tried, like later critics of anti-Semitic racial theory, to overturn the claim of inferiority:

> How could such a low and untalented race survive in the world for fifteen hundred years of inhuman pressure if it did not possess something good? A false liberal hack like Dühring, who constantly blabbers about 'loyalty' – how does he not recognize the heroic loyalty of this wandering people to its God?

Herzl attacked Dühring's scientific pretense, pointing out his disregard of the historical circumstances that compelled Jews in the Middle Ages to engage in money-lending. They had little choice, he noted, because all other kinds of economic activity were forbidden to them. It was not the racial characteristics of the Jews that turned them into 'leeches' but, rather, their imperative to survive in an economic order that was imposed on them, restricting them to a narrow range of businesses. But 'did the Jews play this role out of their own free will?' he asked. Dühring, claiming that he was pursuing a scientific approach, describes 'the Jew precisely as he appeared in the dark Middle Ages, as concocted in the imagination of wicked witches.' Herzl went on to analyze Dühring's claim that Christian Europe had assigned the Jews the role of usurers because they were racially suited to it. The author, Herzl charged, had reversed effect and cause. Dühring replaced the fabrication of the murder of Christian children by Jews with a new libel – the Jews, Dühring claimed, now sought to undermine and appropriate Christian capital:

> Blood libels about murdered Christian children have been replaced, thanks to the invention of the printing press, by stories about the people's wealth and Christian property being robbed by Jewish capital ... Modern oil has been poured on the medieval stake ... Free-thinking liberals like Dühring are the true successors of the Dominicans who played that role in the malodorous Middle Ages. And after burning at the stake, robbery will follow (or the other way around), and gentlemen like Dühring will look around for booty.

In his book, Dühring advocated confiscation of the property of Jewish capitalists (on the grounds that it had been 'robbed' from the people) and expelling the Jews from their professions and businesses – just as the Nazis would do 50 years later. Herzl countered that the author's aim was

> to de-judaize [*Entjudung*] the court system, the legal profession, medicine, to cleanse the legislative institutions of Jews – in one word: 'Out! [*Raus!*]' But how will those wretches find a livelihood if they would not be allowed to engage in usury, to teach, heal the sick, serve as jurists and civil servants, write for newspapers, sell their books – in short, sell anything at all?

Herzl also mocked Dühring's provocative language. The latter referred to the German poet and thinker Gotthold Ephraim Lessing, author of the play *Nathan the Wise*, as a 'half-Jew.' In fact, he applied the word 'Jew' to pretty much everyone whose views he did not like, from Lassalle to the radical French statesman Léon Gambetta. Herzl's attention to the anti-Semites' use of language was prescient – it was a phenomenon that would reach its acme in Nazi propaganda.

Dühring's book clearly made a huge impression on Herzl. At a time when many Jews of his age, along with many liberals and socialists, dismissed Dühring and refused to take him seriously, Herzl recognized the menace.

Less than a year later, in March 1883, while writing his doctoral dissertation, Herzl took his first public stand against anti-Semitism. At this time Jew-hatred had begun percolating through Vienna's German nationalist student fraternities, including Albia, the one into which Herzl had been inducted two years previously. On March 5, 1883, these clubs held a ceremony in memory of the composer Richard Wagner, at which a member of Albia made an anti-Semitic speech. Herzl was not present, but after reading about the speech, and others like it, in the press, he wrote an angry letter to his fraternity, notifying them of his resignation. The letter was sharply worded, presumably because he realized, after reading Dühring's book, that this was not an isolated phenomenon but, rather, a manifestation of a growing political anti-Semitic trend in the German-speaking lands and elsewhere. Despite the furious tone of the letter, it opens with all the formal niceties that were considered proper by the German fraternities. But, the formalities dispensed with, Herzl got to his point:

During that celebration, matters developed into an anti-Semitic demonstration. It would not occur to me to pick an argument against this benighted tendency which has now become fashionable. I would only like to remark that from the standpoint of liberty, non-Jews should also denounce this tendency, since if you do not protest forcefully against these developments, you are actually identifying with them ('*Qui tacet, censentire videtur*,' silence implies consent). I have not seen in the newspapers which reported about the event any statement from the academic fraternity Albia distancing itself from what happened; nor do I – regretfully – accept one in the wake of my letter to you. There is no doubt that I myself, burdened with the defect of Semitism [*belastet mit dem Hindernis des Semitismus*] – a word yet unknown at the time of my entry into the fraternity – would not have now applied to the Albia fraternity, nor would I have been accepted today. Under these circumstances, it is clear to any honest person that I would not like to remain a member of the fraternity. I therefore ask you to release me from my membership . . .

Herzl signed with his name and with the name he took when he had joined the fraternity, Tancred. His choice of the latter moniker is telling. Most of his fraternity brothers chose names from German history or from the Nibelungen saga. Herzl instead chose the name of one of the leaders of the First Crusade who set out for Jerusalem and the Holy Land to liberate it from the Muslims. When the Crusader Kingdom was established, Tancred was named Prince of the Galilee. Herzl, as a graduate of a gymnasium with a liberal arts education, almost certainly knew the story from reading *Gerusalemme Liberata*, a verse epic by the Italian Renaissance poet Torquato Tasso. But there was more – Tancred was also the name of one of the best-known novels of Benjamin Disraeli, later Queen Victoria's Prime Minister. Telling the story of a young contemporary British nobleman who takes a journey to Palestine, the novel includes detailed descriptions of Jerusalem, including an account of the view of the Old City from the Mount of Olives. Disraeli used his novel to convey his romantic view of the Jewish nation's nobility. We have no evidence that the young Herzl knew about *Tancred* the novel, but after the establishment of the Zionist Organization he cited Disraeli, together with George Eliot and Moses Hess, as writers 'who supported Zionism.' Whatever the case, Herzl's choice of name is at least ironic, if not prophetic – the name Herzl used in the fraternity he walked out of because of its incipient anti-Semitism was one with powerful connections to the ancient Jewish homeland.

After completing his legal studies, Herzl followed the usual path of clerking in a court for a year. But it was clear that his heart was in writing, not the law. His genre was the *feuilleton*: the chatty, pointed, literary-opinion section that was very popular in Europe at the time.

Herzl published such pieces in a number of Vienna's newspapers. He also wrote a play that he tried, unsuccessfully, to get produced in a Berlin theater. In the end one of that city's leading newspapers, the liberal *Berliner Tageblatt*, took him on as a regular contributor. To collect material for his articles, Herzl traveled extensively, to Berlin, Prague, Italy, the Rhineland, Belgium, France, and England, producing popular travel pieces. He also published a book of short stories. He finally made his way into the theater when, in 1888–9, three of his plays were staged in Prague, Berlin, and in the prestigious Burgtheater in Vienna. In 1889 Herzl married Julie Naschauer. A year later their daughter Paulina was born.

Despite what seemed like a promising start in the literary and theatrical worlds, Herzl never took off as a playwright. Neither did his marriage go well. In May 1891, he notified his father-in-law that he intended to divorce Julie, even though she was pregnant at the time (a pregnancy that would produce Herzl's son, Hans). While the underlying causes of the marital crisis can only be speculated on, one difference between them was clearly that Julie had little interest in the intellectual subjects that her husband found so fascinating. At about this time Herzl's best friend from his student days, Heinrich Kana, killed himself. Kana was a Jew of Romanian birth, and Herzl viewed him as a tragic educated Jew who had been unable to find a place for himself in European society. In the end Theodor and Julie remained married, but Herzl set out on a long journey to France and Spain, intending never to return home, nor to Vienna. His crisis, both professional and personal, was profound. Then, traveling in the South of France, he received an offer from the influential liberal Viennese daily the *Neue Freie Presse*, to serve as its correspondent in Paris. He jumped at the opportunity – it gave him a prominent journalistic perch while also providing a good reason not to return to his wife in Vienna. He remained in Paris for four years, from 1891 to 1895. Despite the fact that he seldom saw his wife during this period, his third child, his daughter Margaritha (Trude), was born in 1893.

The *Neue Freie Presse*'s owners and editors were Jews or Jews who converted to Christianity. A large portion of its readership, both in Vienna and in the Habsburg Empire as a whole, were educated upper-middle-class Jews who viewed themselves as well integrated into the Empire's culture and economy. It was to this class that Herzl himself and the social world in which he circulated also belonged. During his time in Paris, he sent the newspaper hundreds of articles, many of them brief reports on current events, politics, and social issues. Others were longer analytical pieces in which he tried to convey to his readers France's ambience and bring them into the political milieu.

That racial anti-Semitism was gaining strength in Germany and Austria was not news to Herzl. He corresponded from Paris with a number of Austrian public figures who sought to combat this trend through moral persuasion. His letters convey his skepticism about whether this approach was effective, but he had no alternative to offer. Consequently, when he encountered similar currents in France it was hardly an eye-opener for him, even if they were situated in a different political and cultural context.

France at the beginning of the 1890s was a wounded and divided country that had yet to recover from its humiliating defeat in the Franco-Prussian war of 1870–71. It had lost Alsace-Lorraine and staggered under the crippling burden of the reparations it owed Germany. Emperor Napoleon III abdicated following the surrender of his person and his army to the Prussian king, who led the German forces. Revolt broke out in Paris, where socialist and anarchist forces took control and formed the short-lived Paris Commune, which was violently suppressed by the Prussian army and the newly established French Third Republic. Etched now on the French collective consciousness was not only its military defeat but also the fact that it had contributed to the unification of Germany and the establishment of the German Empire. To add insult to injury, the victors, led by Chancellor Bismarck, crowned the new German Emperor in the magnificent Hall of Mirrors in France's royal Versailles Palace.

While France's liberal forces declared the establishment of the Third Republic, many, both on the right and the left, viewed the new regime as illegitimate. The Catholic, royalist, and conservative right saw the new republic as a rerun of the hated French Revolution, while the radical and anarchist left claimed it was no more than a bourgeois tyranny with parliamentary window-dressing. Not long before Herzl's arrival in Paris the republican regime faced a severe crisis. Minister of War General Georges Boulanger was dismissed in 1887 after seeking to provoke a war of revenge against Germany. In 1889 his followers tried to stage a *coup d'état*. It failed, and two years later Boulanger committed suicide. Yet the affair ripped one more seam in the already tattered French political fabric. Government followed government in quick succession, with none able to gain the confidence of the French public. In June 1894, France's President Carnot was assassinated by an anarchist.

This political instability and ferment provided a gold mine of material for journalists, and offered Herzl an opportunity to develop a precise and fluent style. His articles demonstrated the talent for description and narrative that would so characterize his diaries and political writing. While his dialogue for the theater remained at best somewhat wooden, contemporary readers thoroughly enjoyed his cultured way of writing about public affairs.

Events, of course, dictated what Herzl wrote about. He focused his coverage on the French Republic's central institution, the National Assembly. The sense of national humiliation and the lack of any broad consensus on the legitimacy of the regime created a situation in which every dispute over policy turned into a constitutional crisis. It proved a fertile breeding ground for populist demagogues and for transforming every police investigation into a political scandal. The scandals, inflated by the press and a gossip-loving public far beyond their real significance, toppled governments. In his Austrian homeland, Herzl was an advocate of the expansion of suffrage and increased powers for elected officials. The liberal circles from which he came believed that democratic institutions could cure all modern society's ills. But French parliamentary life showed him that the democratic ideal had a darker side – it could produce chaos. He also gained some new insights on Jewish issues.

The most notorious of the affairs to rock French politics during Herzl's time in Paris was the Panama scandal. Centering on two dramatic court cases, it caused the fall of successive governments and the resignation of ministers. It involved the financing of a project, initiated by the famed Ferdinand de Lesseps, father of the Suez Canal, to dig a canal in Panama. The company that planned the project went bankrupt and de Lesseps was accused of bribing French officials and government ministers. Numerous members of parliament were accused of receiving bribes from the Panama Canal Company to prevent the public from learning about its financial problems. In the two trials, some of the members were convicted, while the charges against others remained unproved. It was such a financially and legally complex and tangled affair that the public found it difficult to understand the details. But it created an impression that corruption was rife in parliament and the cabinet. The benefit accrued to those who sought to undermine the legitimacy of republican rule.

Herzl covered the scandal and the trials, which attracted interest throughout Europe largely because of their connection with a second attempt, after the success of the Suez Canal, to use modern technology to shorten shipping routes. His detailed reports, especially from the courtroom, are a trove of information about the affair and the public atmosphere surrounding it.

But the Panama scandal had another aspect that, at first, remained in the background of Herzl's reports. Jews were prominently involved – including the two most important financiers who stood accused of speculation and corruption. The role of Jews in the scandal was a matter of public debate, so Herzl could hardly ignore it. In fact, the scandal was the main impetus for a wave of anti-Semitic incitement and provided ammunition for people like Édouard Drumont, an anti-Semitic polemicist and author of the book *La France juive*. French anti-Semitism was especially notable given the fact that France had been the first country to grant Jews equal rights, and because its Jewish population was minuscule. The two Jewish financiers were cast as the archetypical cosmopolitan Jews, speculating with the earnings of loyal and hard-working French citizens.

One of the financiers was Cornelius Herz, born in France to Jewish parents of German extraction. He went to school in Germany but volunteered for the French army in the Franco-Prussian war and was named to the Légion d'honneur. He later emigrated to the United States. He married an American woman, received US citizenship, and studied medicine. He then returned to France, where he opened an electronics store. His business flourished. When the Panama scandal broke, he was accused of serving as a middleman between the Panama Canal Company and the members of parliament that it had bribed. Furthermore, he claimed to have in his possession documents that incriminated the legislators. When the investigation against him began, Herz absconded to Italy, from where he made his way to Germany and then to England. The court sentenced him in absentia to five years in prison. His membership in the Légion d'honneur was rescinded and the French government sought his extradition, without success.

The second Jew embroiled in the affair was Baron Jacques de Reinach, also scion of a German-Jewish family, in this case a family that had produced a number of French political leaders and scholars of Jewish studies. His banking house had been involved in issuing the Panama Canal Company's stock certificates, and he served as a financial adviser to the company. Drumont accused de Reinach of having received 'three million francs' from the government for 'public relations,' which he then used to bribe politicians. De Reinach was subpoenaed by the National Assembly's investigatory committee and, when he failed to appear, an arrest warrant was issued against him. The next day, November 20, 1892, he was found lifeless in his bed, apparently a suicide. Another Jewish person whose name became mixed up in the scandal was a member of one of the most prominent Jewish families in French politics, Adolphe Crémieux.

Herzl covered all this extensively, reporting also on the atmosphere that the charges against the two Jewish suspects created. In an ironic piece entitled 'Anti-Semitism in France' that he published in the *Neue Freie Presse* on September 3, 1892, before the scandal reached its height, Herzl played down the possibility that anti-Semitism would grow in France. But as revelation followed revelation the dimensions of the scandal ballooned, providing grist for the anti-Jewish propaganda mills. The picture grew increasingly grim for the Jews and Herzl realized that the ugliest kind of anti-Semitism was deliberately being injected into French public life. A large portion of his articles from November 1892 to July 1893 were devoted to the scandal and its political repercussions, including the growing anti-Semitic tone surrounding the alleged involvement of Herz and de Reinach in the bribe operation. At the same time, he also reported extensively about the campaign of a group of socialist members of the National Assembly, led by Jean Jaurès, against the incitement that identified Jews as capitalists. In May 1893 he informed his readers in Vienna about a book published by the French historian Leroy-Beaulieu, *Israel among the Nations: A Study of the Jews and Antisemitism*. Leroy-Beaulieu condemned anti-Semitism, which he said 'is incompatible with our principles as well as with our national spirit.' Herzl stressed that the author was a French Christian and that the very fact that he had thought it necessary to write such a book underlined just how much traction anti-Semitism was gaining in France. Herzl also reported the author's comment that 'in antisem-itism you can find everything in the world – old and new, medieval elements and phantastical socialism, reactionary passions and rev-olutionary inspirations.' It was a description that would later apply perfectly to fascism.

Even though a large majority of socialist parliamentarians op-posed the anti-Semitic tenor of the public discourse about the Panama scandal, Herzl noted that anti-Semitic sentiments sometimes appeared also among socialists. The prominence of Jewish capitalists such as the Foulds and the Rothschilds in the Second Empire's world of finance had made them anathema to many socialists. A reference to this can be found in an article Herzl wrote for the *Neue Freie Presse* in August 1893 about socialist rallies, when new elections had been called after the fall of yet another government because of the scandal. In the piece, Herzl displayed a certain liking for the socialists and sympathy with their social critique, but he also expressed his profound disgust with Paul Lafargue, a socialist leader and Karl Marx's son-in-law. Herzl dis-liked Lafargue's demagogic style ('he cries, boasts, threatens, incites') and his blind deference to the 'principles of scientific socialism.' But the article reveals another aspect of Herzl's critique – with piercing irony he wrote: 'And then Marx's son-in-law starts his attack on the Jews: "Comrades," he says, "when you first elected me, it was against a bloodbath carried out by Jews and entrepreneurs."'

In another article about the election campaign, Herzl reported about a large rally attended by 'all the social classes, from the concierge to the landlord, along with some petty businessmen, a few workers in shirts, and half a dozen bourgeois with gold chains on their bellies.' The candidate who spoke painted the corruption of parliament in strong colors, shouting: 'They stole half a billion from you!' Shouts of 'Out with the Jews!' and 'Long live anarchy!' came from the crowd. The anti-Semitic tone of *La Libre Parole*, the newspaper Drumont had founded, grew so virulent that some Jewish members of parliament and the director of the Rothschild bank challenged Drumont and members of his staff to duels.

All this showed Herzl that even republican government could not guarantee the safety or civil rights of the Jews. In Vienna he had observed the rise of modern intellectual anti-Semitism among German thinkers and the political and social milieu of the conservative Austrian Empire. In France he now saw that democratic process and representative government were hardly a cure for these ills. The majority of Herzl's readers in Vienna were well-off middle-class Jews who supported liberal reforms. They avidly followed Herzl's reports on the French scandals in which Jews had been implicated. While he did not press the point, his coverage implied to his readers that the challenges facing the Jews were universal and anti-Semitic phenomena appear under all regimes, regardless of their political character.

Further evidence of Herzl's interest in the Jewish issue appears in a brief article about a seemingly marginal issue. In September 1893 a flotilla of Russian warships arrived in Toulon, the port city where the French navy had its most important base. The visit was meant to mark the growing ties between the two countries. Some French Jews voiced objections to this tightening Franco-Russian friendship, going so far as to call on Jews not to participate in the celebrations held to welcome the flotilla, because of Russia's anti-Semitic policies. Herzl informed his readers, without comment or an indication of his own opinion, that a French Jewish playwright had authored a public letter on the matter:

> The comic playwright Albin Valabrège has issued a manifesto to his
> Jewish co-religionists, demanding that, given the attacks on French
> Jews and the aspersions cast about the patriotic feelings of the

French Jews, they should increase their participation in the coming Franco-Russian celebrations, in order to prove that they love their country. France owes a debt of gratitude to Russia, and when patriotism is at issue, all other considerations should be set aside.

There can be no doubt that his readers in Vienna knew exactly what he meant. One of his comprehensive articles on the composition of the French parliament at the time of the Panama scandal, published on July 23, 1893, offered an account of a group of representatives who had switched from the republican to the monarchist-conservative camp. They were called the 'Ralliès,' meaning the 'joiners,' and Herzl offered a forecast of what they might be called in the future. 'Their role has been, and will continue to be, like that of those medieval Spanish Jews who were baptized for naught. They were no less persecuted under their new name than they had been before. They remained *Nuevos Christianos* [New Christians].' Obviously, only a Jew writing for what was in part a Jewish audience could have made such a comparison. Many non-Jews would not have understood the reference, and even for those who did it would not have resonated the way it did with educated Jewish readers.

But one should not be mistaken – most of Herzl's journalistic writing was not about Jewish issues. It focused on the violent reversals in French politics, exacerbated by the Panama scandal. Students rioted, and legislators shot at each other on the floor of the National Assembly. After President Carnot's assassination, his anarchist murderer was apprehended, tried, and executed. A series of bombs were set off by other anarchists in Parisian cafés and other public places. The perpetrators were also tried and executed. Herzl portrayed a broken, highly polarized, and brutal society, torn between the monarchists on the right and the republicans on the left, a country whose representative institutions seemed powerless to create a political framework that all factions would accept as legitimate.

The Panama scandal's repercussions lasted a long time. In May 1894, Herzl provided his readers with a detailed account of a financial settlement between Cornelius Herz, living as a fugitive in England, and the heirs of the late Baron de Reinach. That same month he also reported at length on a parliamentary debate about the demand that Herz be extradited from England and about another of the expatriate's legal entanglements. Herz's and de Reinach's names lingered on in the newspapers and continued to fire French politics.

*   *   *

It was against this background of entrenched corruption, violence, and anarchist terror that Captain Alfred Dreyfus was arrested and charged with espionage. It is important to remember that the arrest took place in a divided society in which many did not recognize the legitimacy of the republic. In the years to come, the Dreyfus Affair, which soon came to be called simply *l'Affaire*, would rend the French political fabric and widen the fissure between the republican left and the conservative-Catholic-monarchist right, the latter supported by the army. But all these events, including the virulent anti-Semitic polemics that the affair provoked over the years, would all take place *after* Herzl left Paris in 1895. In fact, *l'Affaire* would not reach its denouement until 1906, when Dreyfus was finally acquitted. During Herzl's time in Paris the trial had only begun and had not yet turned into a historic controversy, so it is hardly surprising that his initial reports were rather pedestrian. While the common wisdom is that the Dreyfus affair triggered Herzl's Zionism, there is in fact no evidence of this, not in Herzl's voluminous diaries nor in the many articles he sent from Paris to his newspaper in Vienna.

Herzl's first article on Dreyfus's arrest appeared in the *Neue Freie Presse* on November 1, 1894. He told his readers that his account was based on rumors and that it may well contain inaccuracies. An officer named Dreyfus, he wrote, had been accused of selling secrets to Italy. His guilt was not in doubt. He would be court-martialed and executed by firing squad. The next day Herzl offered further details, also inaccurate. Dreyfus, he wrote, was known as a card-player and had been sighted in Monte Carlo with a senior Italian officer. Herzl conjectured that the government's disclosure of the arrest and the fact that the Minister of War brought it up at a cabinet meeting 'seems to suggest that Dreyfus did indeed commit the shameful act.' Herzl provided further information on the officer's position on the French General Staff and the circumstances of his arrest. The accused, he reported, had been born in Mulhouse, in Alsace. Son of a well-off textile manufacturer, he married the daughter of a wealthy diamond trader. In this report, and in Herzl's further dispatches, the Jewish identity of Dreyfus is not mentioned, but the informed reader could deduce this from the comments about his industrialist father and diamond trader father-in-law; his readers would also have identified 'Dreyfus' as a Jewish name. Toward the end of his article, Herzl added a seemingly incidental but apparently not accidental remark: 'In the French army, there are now serving, in addition to the accused, another 39 officers with the name "Dreyfus."'

The rumors regarding Dreyfus's alleged Italian connections provided Herzl with material for several more items in the days that followed. On November 5 he wrote that 'new rumors surface all the time. Now they say that Dreyfus was entrapped by an Italian lady spy, who so infatuated him that in his mad passion he consented to do every incautious deed she asked for, and eventually divulged to her the country's defense secrets.' It was on November 7 that Herzl first revealed to his readers that the espionage charge was related to Germany, not Italy. Up to this point there had been no indication that Herzl had any doubts about Dreyfus's guilt, although he did report that the accused man continued to proclaim his innocence:

> Now it is clear that Dreyfus sold the secrets of homeland defense to Germany. In order to mislead him, some false secrets were conveyed to him, and he handed them over, as he did the previous ones, which definitely establishes his guilt. Huge losses at cards have led him down the path of crime.

A short while later, Herzl reported that 'in the last few days, a lot of imagined or real spies have been arrested.' He told of two German officers who had been arrested in Paris and expelled from the country on suspicion of espionage. On November 28 he revealed that the French press was demanding the expulsion of all foreign military attachés from France on the grounds that they all engaged in spying. He quoted, without reservation, the French Minister of War, General Auguste Mercier, to the effect that 'Captain Dreyfus's guilt is proven. For three years Dreyfus committed acts of espionage for a foreign power whose name can easily be guessed. What cannot be proved is that he did it for money.' The implication is that Dreyfus, as a native of Alsace, formerly belonging to France and since 1871 part of Germany, owed allegiance to the enemy, and therefore had not needed any payment to betray France. Herzl still voiced no doubts as to the truth of the charges against Dreyfus. His reports were relatively brief and largely summed up the hearsay he found in the French press and heard on the street. The subject did not fire him up at the time. During this period he devoted much more space to the corruption trials that continued to rock France, the tense debates about corruption in the National Assembly, the debate between the conservative government and the socialist opposition on municipal issues, the election of the National Assembly's speaker, a duel between the socialist leader Jaurès and Minister of Labor Barteau (after they traded insults on the floor of the National Assembly), on the huge funeral given to de Lesseps ('Today the funeral took place of the person who lost in Panama the glory he won in Suez'), and about Jaurès's temporary suspension from parliament. In short, French politics, tempestuous, conflicted, and violent, continued to provide Herzl with plenty of exciting material. Dreyfus was a marginal matter.

On December 1 Herzl informed his readers that the German Ambassador in Paris had handed the French Foreign Ministry a formal protest against what it called false reports regarding the role allegedly played by members of the German Embassy staff in the Dreyfus spy case. 'Embassy personnel have never engaged in espionage or any other scandal,' Herzl quoted the protests as stating. Furthermore, he wrote that the French Foreign Minister had confirmed 'the wholly impeccable behavior of the Ambassador and his staff.' But Herzl also wrote at length about how Dreyfus's arrest had undermined the standing of the French Minister of War, and that conservative supporters of the army and members of the republican left were debating in the pages of French newspapers about whether a military man or a citizen should head the Ministry of War. Herzl was much more interested in this debate than in Dreyfus's case. Evidently at this point he viewed it as a run-of-the-mill espionage case with no important public – or Jewish – implications.

It was only when Dreyfus's trial began on December 19 that Herzl began focusing on the affair. He produced three detailed accounts of the three days of hearings, using all the courtroom drama skills he had acquired in covering the Panama scandal trials. His readers were provided with detailed descriptions of the Court Martial hall ('an old, dilapidated palace, devoid of any of the regal glory of a hall of justice'), and leisurely, meticulous depictions of the atmosphere, the witnesses, and the spectators. His account was gripping, but it offered only his impressions as a dispassionate observer. He did not address the question of Dreyfus's guilt or innocence. The three articles mentioned the trial's implications for the political standing of the Minister of War, for if Dreyfus were found guilty, Herzl reported, the calls to replace him would grow, on the grounds that the spying took place on his watch. Readers in Vienna benefited from Herzl's detailed reports of the witnesses' testimony, both those given in the open courtroom and those offered behind closed doors. And he told of the passion the trial provoked among the French. On December 22, Herzl reported that Dreyfus had been found guilty of espionage. In the days that followed he recounted Dreyfus's appeal and the rejection of that appeal. He told his readers that Dreyfus would be stripped of his rank, 'an extremely unpleasant ceremony.'

But as the German Embassy continued to insist that Dreyfus had played no role in German espionage against France, the tone of Herzl's reports began to change. This was a time when people still granted at least some credence to official announcements of this sort – the Victorian code that 'gentlemen don't read other people's letters' was taken very seriously. It was only a few days later, on December 27, in an article in which Herzl again cited Dreyfus's wife claiming that her husband was innocent, that he mentioned to his readers for the first time that Dreyfus was Jewish. Even now he did so indirectly, writing that a story circulating in Paris related that 'Dreyfus has been saying in conversations with his prison guard: "You see I am a victim of a personal vendetta. I am being persecuted because I am a Jew."' Herzl also recounted the complexities faced by the Dreyfus family in Alsace. Dreyfus's brothers, it turned out, had stayed in Mulhouse after Alsace was annexed to Germany in 1871, but one of them continued to send his son to a French school over the border in the nearby French city of Belfort. Now that their brother had been convicted of spying for Germany, they had been 'unofficially asked to take the boy out of the school in that town.'

On December 30, the day after Dreyfus's appeal was rejected, the *Neue Freie Presse* published a long article of Herzl's under the headline 'France in 1894.' It had been a tumultuous year for the Third Republic, he wrote, set off by the assassination of President Carnot. Since then, he continued, tensions between right and left had only grown worse. With the government growing weaker by the day as one scandal after another shook it, the socialists, who were viewed as having clean hands, were gaining strength, Herzl reported. In the meantime, he continued, some right-wing circles were taking refuge behind declarations of patriotism, chauvinism, and Catholic piety. 'More than ever before, love of the homeland is being stressed and made into something that should not be questioned,' he wrote. For their part, the socialists were accusing the parties in power of making 'chauvinistic excuses for avoiding social reforms.' That he did not mention the Dreyfus trial in his summing up of the year 1894 clearly shows how little he viewed the case as being of major significance.

Herzl's most dramatic article on the Dreyfus affair appeared a week later, on January 6, 1895. In it, he depicted the ceremony in which the convicted spy was stripped of his rank and humiliated (*degradation*, in French legal military parlance). The ceremony had taken place the previous day in the courtyard of the École Militaire. Of all the reporting Herzl did from Paris, this is the article that Israelis know best, and it became almost part of the Zionist canon. He offered a vivid account of the ceremony in which Dreyfus was dishonorably discharged from the French army as a traitor. The ceremony was attended by a large number of officers and their wives, as well as by several journalists. Dreyfus was brought before a mounted general who declared: 'Alfred Dreyfus, you do not deserve to bear arms for France. In the name of the French nation, I hereby strip you of your officer's rank.' Dreyfus,

Herzl reported, 'raised his right hand and said in a loud voice: "I swear that you are demoting an innocent person. *Vive la France!*"'

At that moment a drum roll was sounded. An officer cut the buttons and insignia off Dreyfus's uniform and then broke his sword. Dreyfus, Herzl reported, stood erect and silent. 'Then they passed Dreyfus before the various contingents, Dreyfus marching as a person who feels he is innocent.' Herzl then wrote:

> He reached a line of officers who roared at him: 'Judas! Traitor!' Dreyfus shouted in their direction: 'I forbid you to sully my honor!' ... When he reached a group of journalists, he halted and said: 'You must tell all of France that I am innocent!' Some replied by vilifying him. The mob outside, which peered through the bars of the fence and saw the degradation, shouted from time to time: 'Death to the traitor!'

It's telling that in the Hebrew translation of the article that appears in nearly all the history textbooks used in Israeli schools and in most other Hebrew-language books about Herzl, the mob chants 'Death to the Jews!' But that is not what Herzl wrote, even if the epithet 'Judas' hurled at Dreyfus by his erstwhile fellow officers (but not by the crowd) certainly had anti-Semitic implications. So how did it come about that Israelis have grown up believing that the French public shouted 'Death to the Jews!' at Dreyfus?

It was Herzl's own doing. It comes from his essay 'On Zionism,' written in 1899 for the literary journal *North American Review*. The piece was later translated and published in German some years after the author's death, in one of many anthologies of his writings. Herzl wrote this article on Zionism and the nature of European anti-Semitism in order to promote the Zionist cause among non-Jewish Americans. It was the only piece of writing in which he highlighted the Dreyfus case, in a way he did not in any of his other works, letters, or diary entries. 'On Zionism' was written four years after the ceremony Herzl witnessed, and after the affair had metamorphosed from a routine espionage case into a French and international *cause célèbre*. By this time it was the litmus test of French politics, the symbol of the battle between the republican left and the unholy alliance of monarchists, the military, the Church, and anti-Semitic and anti-democratic rabble-rousers.

Did Herzl's memory betray him? Or was he tweaking the event better to promote his cause? By 1899 the Dreyfus affair resonated in an entirely different way than it had four years previously. In retrospect, it seemed to confirm Herzl's claim that the emancipation of the Jews had failed. Dreyfus's trial and disgrace was much more meaningful for the Jewish people from a perspective of four years than it had been at the time. The answer to these questions is complicated. Herzl had certainly heard anti-Jewish slogans in France and had reported hearing them, as in his coverage of the Panama scandal. Did faulty memory simply attach what he had heard then to the scene of Dreyfus's degradation, now that the latter had taken on such historical significance? We have no way of knowing. Some historians and editors who have addressed the subject have suggested that Herzl indeed reported the crowd as yelling 'Death to the Jews' but that the *Neue Freie Presse* revised the text before printing it. There are no grounds for this theory, nor any evidence for it – the newspaper's editors never censored Herzl's articles, and they often referred to Jewish issues and to anti-Semitism in France. Furthermore, had they indeed bowdlerized his article, Herzl would no doubt have protested. But it was Herzl's later account of Dreyfus's court-martial, not his contemporary one, that has become part of his myth. According to that version, it was the sight of the innocent Dreyfus being expelled from the French army and French society, and the cries of the crowd, that convinced him that the Jews needed their own country.

Herzl remained in Paris for a few months while after the ceremony. He referred to Dreyfus, briefly but with considerable sympathy, in several subsequent articles reporting the convicted man's sentence of exile. On January 7 he wrote: 'Dreyfus is already treated as a convict. Yesterday his moustache was shaven off.' On January 14 yet another French government, this one led by Charles Dupuy, fell. Its end was brought on by the revelation of yet another corruption scandal, this one involving the financing of a train line, in which Baron de Reinach was again implicated. Herzl reported on January 16 that the President of the Republic, Jean Casimir-Perier, had resigned. With the nearly simultaneous resignations of both a Prime Minister and a President hurling the already shaky Third Republic into one of its most severe crises, Dreyfus was largely forgotten. In the weeks that followed Herzl wrote seven long, detailed pieces about the ongoing presidential crisis, which ended only when Félix Faure was elected by a bare majority at a riotous National Assembly session where legislators traded blows. But the political crisis as a whole did not end, and Herzl continued to cover it. From time to time he submitted brief items about Dreyfus. For example, a day after the new President's election, he wrote: 'Yesterday Captain Dreyfus was brought in total secrecy to Gare d'Orléans in preparation for his exile to Devil's Island. He was dressed in a prison uniform and his head was shaved. He bore a parcel containing the uniform that had been slashed in his demotion ceremony.'

On April 6, Herzl informed his readers:

Captain Dreyfus arrived in Cayenne [French Guyana] on March 13. He was transferred to Devil's Island, where he is kept night and day under the surveillance of five soldiers. He can move only 150 meters from his cottage. Local conditions make it impossible for anyone to reach him either by sea or land. On arrival, Dreyfus once more declared his innocence. He intends to wait patiently until the truth prevails.

Throughout this period, Herzl's last months in Paris, he continued to report on the French political crises. Another government fell in February 1895, and other scandals hit the headlines during attempts to form a new government. De Reinach's name returned to the front pages when, in June, the rail scandal and the bribing of public officials again moved to center stage.

Jewish issues repeatedly arose in Herzl's coverage of these political tremors. Here and there he mentioned Dreyfus, but only as a footnote to the part that Jewish figures were playing in the scandals and how the scandals were affecting the economy. In two articles that appeared on May 25, Herzl reported at length on a debate in the National Assembly on a motion tabled by 'anti-Semitic delegate Denny' calling for a parliamentary debate on 'the Jewish takeover of the state bureaucracy.' Herzl's account of the political aspects of this issue are evidence of the importance he attached to informing his readers in Vienna about how Jews were being vilified in parliament. These events took place at a time when, as will be seen in the next chapter, he was already pondering the Jewish question in depth. He wrote that the Assembly Speaker demanded that Denny cite specific examples rather than make general accusations. And he quoted a socialist legislator who declared that

> Anti-Semitism is a cardinal sin against the principles of the French Revolution. We do not recognize any differences of race . . . nor do we share the views of the anti-Semites that the Jews are responsible for the ills of society, that only they are involved in financial scandals. This is just not true.

Herzl offered his readers the long list of speculators named by the Speaker, stressing that none of them were Jews. Referring to the Panama scandal, he declared, 'Christians are as avaricious as Jews in all of these swindles.' He then continued to quote from the same speech to the effect that in the past the targets of accusations regarding bank speculation had been Protestants. The socialist Speaker offered a brief history of the role Protestants and Jews had played in the development of the banking system, what he called 'movable capital.' He asserted that anti-Semitism had to be seen in light of feudalism's rearguard battle against capitalism. 'Anti-Semitism was brought to us from Germany,' he declared. In asserting that Jew-hatred was not home-grown but was, rather, an import from France's chief enemy, we may presume that he appealed to French patriotic sentiments. Herzl also provided an extended account of a speech made by the senior Jewish member of the National Assembly, Alfred Naquet, who had once been a follower of Boulanger. Naquet offered an erudite chronicle of Jewish life in France since the Revolution, highlighting the loyalty the Jews had displayed to their French homeland. According to Naquet, Judaism was a religion, no more: 'Talk for half an hour with a Jew from Hamburg, a Jew from London, a Jew from Paris – you will recognize three distinct nationalities,' he asserted. To the cheers of the socialists and catcalls from the right, Naquet declared that, while there were indeed many Jewish socialists, 'Marx, Lassalle, [and] some leaders of the German Reichstag, to name but a few,' France's Jews were patriots. And at this point, for the first time in Herzl's journalistic output, he placed the Dreyfus trial in its larger context – quoting Naquet's words, with all their pathos:

> We are defamed because of this miserable traitor Dreyfus, who as a Frenchman, Alsatian, and Jew, sinned thrice against the French homeland – while heroes who fell for France – d'Ercole, Major Kahn, Sergeant Bloch – are innumerable, and memorials have been set up for them, are not mentioned, as neither are our philosophers, poets, scholars, artists. How many Jews sit in the Academy!

Herzl must have already realized that such apologetics were missing the point. He told his readers that Naquet's florid speech was received with applause, but also that an anti-Semitic member of the Assembly had submitted a bill to repeal the law, passed during the Revolution, that had granted the Jews equal rights. Another member introduced a law to confiscate Jewish assets. Both were rejected, on a motion submitted by the cabinet, by a large majority – only two or three members voted in support of the anti-Jewish legislation. But one of these supporters called out during the debate: 'This is the republic of [Prime Minister] Ribot, the Jews, and the Freemasons.' Herzl made a point of telling his readers that the French parliament had nevertheless spent two entire days debating the question of whether the Jews indeed controlled the French state apparatus and whether to rescind their rights. While this political turmoil continued to shake France, Herzl left Paris that summer.

*　　*　　*

During his final autumn in Paris, Herzl wrote a play about the failure of Jewish emancipation, especially in the Austrian lands. It was called *The New Ghetto*, and it was his first work for the stage with an explicitly Jewish subject. He was unable to find a theater willing to stage it, and this failure helped spark the personal and political quest that would end with him writing *The Jewish State*. We know something about what Herzl was thinking and feeling during this time from his extensive correspondence with Arthur Schnitzler, the best-known Jewish Viennese author and playwright of his time. Herzl confided to his theatrical mentor that he had written the play as if in a trance, even though the subject had been growing in his mind for a long time. He first sat down to write it on October 21 (prior to Dreyfus's arrest) and completed it on November 8, just a few days after first reporting the army captain's arrest and before he had made any mention of the accused man being a Jew. From November through March he tried, without success, to interest a theater in producing it.

He was at a crossroads. His term as Paris correspondent for the *Neue Freie Presse* was coming to an end. He was being brought back to Vienna to serve as editor of the newspaper's *feuilleton*. He wanted to return to his career as a playwright, but his previous lack of success in that genre, and his growing fame as a journalist and essayist, induced him to try a new tactic. He would seek to produce *The New Ghetto* under a pseudonym, Albert Schnabel. He and Schnitzler wrote back and forth to plan a strategy that would keep his authorship of the play secret. They decided that Herzl would convey the play to a notary, who would show the play to the managements of several theaters in Berlin (Herzl decided not to offer it to theaters in Vienna). He obviously feared rejection and thus wanted to remain anonymous. He was also anxious to avoid any suggestion that he was using his standing as a journalist and essayist to pressure theater managers to accept his play. But the reasoning he offered Schnitzler was not always clear. It seems clear that the play's Jewish subject was no small factor in the ruse. Herzl told his friend that, if *The New Ghetto* were a success, he would write another four or five plays under the pseudonym before revealing his true identity to the public. If it were rejected, he would publish the text under the pseudonym along with an explanation that it had been rejected by the best German theaters – and why.

During his exchange of letters with Schnitzler, Herzl began to think of his new play not only in terms of a possible theatrical success but also as a programmatic piece. Schnitzler saw it that way as well, and was thus willing to indulge Herzl despite the work it meant for him. He told Herzl that he thought the play excellent, and at Herzl's request suggested some revisions and additions. In the more than 30 letters Herzl wrote to Schnitzler about *The New Ghetto*, he not only offered technical instructions about carrying out the deception but stressed that this was a play with a message. 'I do not know if it's a good play, but I feel it is a necessary one!' he wrote. 'The play has to reach the people . . . that's why it is written in blunt language – otherwise people will not listen to the end.' 'After all, I am writing for a nation of anti-Semites,' he stressed in another letter. When Schnitzler commented that too many of the Jewish characters were unsympathetic, Herzl responded that he did not want to prettify the situation. 'I do not want to defend the Jews or "save" them. All I want to do is to raise the issue as forcefully as possible,' he explained.

Throughout the Dreyfus trial, from December 1894 through January 1895, Herzl's inability to interest a theater in the play stood at the center of his correspondence with Schnitzler. While Herzl mentioned a number of political and literary events in Paris in these letters, he made not a single reference to Dreyfus. One theater manager after another turned down his play – even after Herzl permitted Schnitzler, in one case, to discreetly reveal to one of them the playwright's true identity. In April 1895, Herzl vacated the Paris apartment he had been living in and moved into a hotel. The rejection of his drama was a bitter, depressing disappointment.

In the end, *The New Ghetto* received its first production only in December 1897, under Herzl's real name, following the publication of *The Jewish State* and the First Zionist Congress. Herzl was by then a well-known public figure. When the play was published in book form, Herzl dedicated it 'with profound love' to Max Nordau, the well-known physician, author, and critic who became his partner in founding the Zionist movement. Nordau's ideas about the failure of emancipation were much like Herzl's and had taken shape under the same influences. While *The New Ghetto* presents Herzl's thinking before he arrived at his belief that the Jews needed their own country, his analysis of the Jewish predicament – as the play's name states – had been on his mind for some years and led him toward his subsequent political program. Despite being written in Paris, the play contained no reference to the issues faced by French Jews. Its analysis of the problematic status of the Jews was based exclusively on the situation in Vienna and the Habsburg Empire.

Some maintain that *The New Ghetto* is Herzl's best play. But like all his other works for the stage it is a didactic melodrama with more slogans than fully drawn characters. The plot is convoluted and lacks credibility. Its many long speeches are useful clues to Herzl's thinking but in the play they hold up the action. It offers a stereotypical description of nouveau riche Jews who marry to advance their businesses. Most of the characters are Jews, but one is an upstanding Christian friend of one of the Jewish protagonists, a cavalry officer from an aristocratic family that has come on hard times. He is prepared to enter into doubtful stock market speculations with Jews as middlemen. When his investments go sour, he of course blames 'the Jews.' Herzl also depicts Christian maids who are deferential to their Jewish mistresses while secretly loathing them. The play, in addition, takes several radical positions on social issues, among other things describing the conditions suffered by coal miners (the bad stock market bets have to do with coal). Another character is an esteemed rabbi who speaks of the community's responsibility for the poor in its midst, but explains that the Jewish community engages in stock market speculation 'to help the poor.' Yet he also advises his flock to keep a low profile and not to challenge the gentiles head-on when they suffer an injustice. In this figure, Herzl stereotypes the kind of Jew who invoked the Jewish faith to perpetuate the Jews' ambivalent position in gentile society. Herzl portrays Jewish women as spiteful and shallow – his female characters are interested only in clothes and diamonds, concerts and the theater. It was probably these portrayals that prompted Schnitzler to suggest to Herzl that he make his characters a little nicer. It is hardly surprising that this play about the failure of Jewish emancipation, with its negative stereotypes of bourgeois Jews, found few admirers. (The motifs would reappear, in a somewhat milder form, in the opening chapters of Herzl's utopian novel *Altneuland*.)

The play's argument is that while the Jews of Vienna and the rest of the West had emerged from the ghetto, they found themselves in a new one, gilded and seemingly open, but still a ghetto. The protagonist, attorney Dr. Jacob Samuel, displays all the accoutrements of the economically and socially successful urban Jews at whom Herzl aimed the barbs of his irony. Samuel's parents call him 'Kobi,' but to his snobbish wife, whose only interests are dresses, amusement, and her social status, he is 'Jacques.' The young Samuel is acutely sensitive to his generation's plight. He admires his Christian friend and learns social graces and manners from him, but he feels humiliated when he finds himself in the position of having to thank those who treat him as an equal. 'Something of the ghetto always remains in us,' he declares. He confesses to his Christian friend that the fact that he needs to learn the right facial expressions, the right body language, 'to bow without servility, to stand up straight without rebelling,' is not a product of the Jews' inborn flaws but a result of the way European Christian society has shaped the Jews:

> You have been free for some centuries, while we were not made by nature into what we are, but through history. By force you cast us onto a pile of money, and now you want us to get away from it in one day. First you condemned us to a servitude of a thousand years, and now we have to liberate ourselves overnight.

Samuel bears in his heart the humiliation he experienced when, a few years earlier, he got into a fight with this very same Christian cavalry officer. He had challenged the officer to a duel, but his Jewish friends forced him to cancel it. Christian society, he learns, has allowed the Jews to prosper economically, but still treats them with contempt. This has induced in the Jews an overwhelming desire to excel, to flaunt their wealth and thus to paper over their humiliation. This theme, which appears frequently in Herzl's writings, is the central moving force in the plot. The young Jewish attorney seeks to behave according to the norms of Christian society, with its aristocratic foundations, but in the end he is unable to do so.

At a social gathering in the Samuels' salon, a rabbi relates that the

Jews of the Habsburg Empire have done well and that they are helping their poor brethren of the East to emigrate to the West. Vienna's Jews suffer no persecution, the rabbi asserts. 'We are, after all, permitted to reside in our homeland [Austria], we enjoy the protection of the law,' he declares. 'Yes, we are still looked upon with hostility, as in past generations, in the days we lived in the ghetto. But the walls, in any case, have tumbled down.' Samuel replies to this with the play's central statement: 'Yes, the visible walls,' to which he adds, 'We have to get out!' The rabbi makes a show of agreeing, but again reverts to traditional Jewish subservience: 'In the time of the physical ghetto, we could not leave it without special permission . . . Now the walls have become invisible, as you say. But this notional ghetto is the Pale of Settlement imposed on us. Woe to him who dares to break out.'

This, in Herzl's view, is *The New Ghetto* – not one bounded by stone walls, but by a barricade built inside the Jewish soul. It is these walls that the young attorney speaks of when he remonstrates to the rabbi: 'Dear doctor, sir, these barriers we have to bring down in a different way, not like the old walls. The old barriers had to be breached from outside – the internal barriers have to be dismantled by us, by ourselves, from inside.'

The need to demolish this wall within would lead Herzl to the realization that, in the end the Jews would find no salvation in the gentile world, as liberal and enlightened as it might be. They needed an internal revolution. It was the insight that would eventually lead him to the Zionist idea. The theatergoing public and critics in Berlin, where the play had its premiere, did not like this message at all. After all, many of them were Jews of the very sort that Herzl was aiming his barbs at.

Herzl's sardonic portrayal of Jews as stock market speculators, juxtaposed with his description of the lives of indigent coal miners, who are killed when mines collapse because the owners have not invested in the necessary safety measures, sometimes borders on socialist critique. Echoes of such critique can be found in *Altneuland*, where Herzl portrays the Jewish society of the future as a kind of alternative to avaricious capitalism and revolutionary socialism. In *The New Ghetto*, Herzl displays an intimate knowledge of stock market shenanigans. This may seem surprising, but Herzl had, after all, delved deep into the activities of speculators in his coverage of the Panama scandal and the Jews involved in it. Herzl's aversion to stock markets – in his vision of a Jewish state, there is no such institution – was no doubt an outgrowth of his work in Paris. The speeches he wrote for Samuel, who visits a coal mine that has collapsed, were not pleasant for at least some of the people in his audience to hear:

> [The miners' children] break your heart. Here are small children whose faces are so serious that they look like old men, and it seems to me that they gaze in terror at the black hole that will one day devour them. Like their fathers, who have gone to heaven, they, too, will descend [into the mine]. There, in the bowels of the earth, young as they are, they will pull iron carts for 45 kreuzers a day ... And when they grow up, they will become cutters, crawling and crouching in the tunnels, cutting the coal overhead, in the dark, and any incautious move of their lanterns can bring out the toxic gases ... And tomorrow they will go down again. They have no choice – otherwise those above will die from hunger.

Samuel's friends and business partners do not understand what he is so upset about. After all, coal mines are lawful and legitimate enterprises. The rabbi reassures Samuel with a cliché: 'My young friend, nobody suffers more than he can bear. God has wrought this wisely. Those who walk barefoot have thick soles on their feet.' He also tells a medieval Jewish homily attributed to Rabbi Yehoshua of Speyer, who warns his people not to take too much interest in what is going on outside the ghetto walls. The same rule applies today, the rabbi maintains. Samuel's friends remain impassive when they hear his remonstration against a Jewish speculator who grows wealthy off convoluted, dubious transactions that, indirectly, lead to the mine disaster:

> Sir, you still don't understand how you cause us, the Jews, harm. Such massive movement of funds visits ruination on many people; and the victims blame the Jews ... Who can rise above the details and see the wider context of things? People see only people ...

That's why I am so unhappy if the people closest to me are deeply immersed in stock market affairs.

But his protests fall on deaf ears, even when Samuel resolves to respond to the cavalry officer, who blames the Jews ('a mob of Yids') for his financial losses. Samuel challenges him to a duel. As one might expect, the officer is the better shot. He shoots Samuel, inflicting a fatal wound. Before he dies, Samuel asks his loving mother to forgive him for the sorrow he has caused her, and expresses his hope that his father will understand him ('You are a man, after all.'). The play ends with Jacob Samuel's dying words. He is unable to speak clearly, but the meaning comes through: 'My brothers, Jews, they will grant us freedom only if you . . . [mumbles] I want – out! Out – out of the ghetto!'

Out – out of wealthy, liberal European society, which has granted equal rights to the Jews but is unable to truly liberate them. The play's central message is self-emancipation. The Jews must achieve emancipation themselves, not have it granted to them by others. Herzl had not yet read *Auto-Emancipation*, the pamphlet published by Leo Pinsker a dozen years previously, but the two men's analysis of the Jewish plight was identical. In 1894, when he wrote the play, Herzl had not yet found the answer to his dilemma, but the challenge was clearly stated. It was not the trial of Alfred Dreyfus, but Herzl's long analysis of the failure of emancipation and the rise of German and Austrian anti-Semitism, that led him to his radical conclusions.

CHAPTER FOUR

BETWEEN POLITICAL FICTION AND POLITICAL ACTION

HERZL TOOK A WINDING ROAD to political action, one that led, a year after the publication of *The Jewish State* in 1896, to the First Zionist Congress. But, at first, he had no idea what he was doing or where he was going. We find direct evidence of this in the dozens of pages and notes to himself that he jotted down while ensconced in his hotel in Paris at the beginning of June 1895. 'For some time past I have been occupied with a work of infinite grandeur,' he wrote, but then immediately qualified this: 'At the moment I do not know whether I shall carry it through. It looks like a powerful dream.'

What was this 'opus'? He did not know in his own mind whether he was producing a novel or a political program. Or perhaps it was a novel meant to promote political action? But, if so, what kind of political action? All these possibilities ran through Herzl's brain and he found himself torn between them. But his experience as a journalist and dramatist was of help – it prompted him to put his ideas, doubts, and every fragment of a thought into writing. He admitted that the fact that he did not know which kind of work he would end up choosing 'is the best proof of how necessary this written record is.' Out of all these confused and contradictory scribbles, some of them well-thought-out, profound historical and intellectual analysis, others speculative and even nonsensical ideas, the book that Herzl would finally produce slowly came together. The bumpy road he followed, so unclearly marked, is evidence of a real upheaval in his personal life.

It would turn him from the mediocre writer and playwright that he acknowledged himself to be into a leader of a political movement who conferred with Europe's most powerful men. This personal transformation would go hand in hand with a historical reassessment of the Jewish people that would transform the idea of a return to Zion from the reverie of a few clusters of Jews living on the fringes of European and Jewish society into a program that, eventually, diplomats and statesmen would not be able to ignore.

This stormy and creative period of June 1895, just before Herzl's return to Vienna, preceded his assumption of the editorship of his newspaper's *feuilleton*. During this same period he failed so far to find a theater willing to produce his play *The New Ghetto*, leading him to doubt whether he had a future in the theater. His diary entries evince inner turmoil and crisis. He wavered between writing a political novel or plunging into political action, but the fact that he was turning toward public affairs was undoubtedly a product of his years covering the French National Assembly. 'In Paris I found myself in the midst of politics – at least as an observer. I saw how the world is run. I was also amazed at the phenomenon of the mob – for a long time without comprehending it,' he wrote in his diary.

During all this Herzl also reviewed and selected the best of the pieces he had written on French politics for the *Neue Freie Presse*. The collection was issued in book form in October 1895 under the title *Das Palais Bourbon*, the name of the building that served as the seat of the National Assembly. Coming out as it did soon after his return to Vienna, under the imprint of a respectable German publisher in Leipzig, it showed that Herzl wanted to make himself into a prominent public persona not just in Austria but throughout the German cultural sphere.

His hesitations about his personal future are joined in his diary by entries wondering what the final form of his work of 'infinite grandeur' would be. If he put his bold dream in the form of a novel, he wrote, he would call it *The Promised Land*, the land of the Jews. The subject that was unsettling Herzl was the Jewish issue, '*die Judensache*.' He deliberately eschewed the common term 'the Jewish question.' As far as he was concerned, this was not a '*Jewish* Question,' but a question that

Europe and humanity as a whole needed to address and answer. It was thus clear to him from the start that, contrary to the thinking of the First Aliyah and the Hovevei Zion movement, it was not a problem the Jews could solve alone. It was an international, global issue that crossed borders and continents, one that only a concerted international effort could solve. Herzl's analysis of the Jewish issue led to the conclusion that it had to be dealt with on the diplomatic and international front, a view that would later be called 'political Zionism.' The plight of the Jews was no more than a symptom of a much more fundamental and severe problem – the European crisis of the end of the nineteenth century. No Jewish thinker before Herzl (with the possible exception of Moses Hess, whose book of 1862, *Rome and Jerusalem*, had received little attention) had placed the future of the Jewish people within this broad perspective of international politics.

When he began keeping a diary in June 1895, Herzl asked himself when he had begun to ponder the Jewish issue. He answered: 'Probably ever since it arose; certainly from the time that I read Dühring's book.' He recalled his sharp reaction on reading the book, which he recorded 'In one of my old notebooks, now stacked away somewhere in Vienna ... but I know that today I am repeating some of the things that I wrote down then.' The entries in his youthful journal, quoted in the previous chapter, confirm that Herzl had been shocked by Dühring's claim of the need to 'purge' German and European society of the Jews and their influence.

So the subject was not new to Herzl – it was an issue that he deliberated throughout his life. But, Herzl wrote, he had not had the means to bring his thinking before the public.

> As the years went on, the question bored into me and gnawed at me, tormented me and made me very miserable. In fact, I kept coming back to it whenever my own personal experience – joys and sorrows – permitted me to rise to broader considerations ... The Jewish question naturally lurked for me around every turn and corner.

Herzl confessed that at times, like other Jews of his generation, he would have preferred to run away from the issue. 'There might have been a time when I would have liked to get away from it – into the Christian fold, anywhere. But in any case, these were only vague desires born of youthful weakness . . . I never really thought of becoming baptized or changing my name.'

He related how, at the beginning of his journalistic career, he submitted a manuscript to the journal *Deutsche Wochenschrift*. Its (Jewish) editor, Heinrich Friedjung, suggested to him that he 'adopt a penname less Jewish than my own.' 'Herzl' too clearly identified him. But the young man refused. 'I flatly refused, saying that I wanted to continue to bear the name of my father,' he wrote. He also revealed in his diary that the idea of writing a 'Jewish novel' had first come to him in 1891, before he left for Paris, following the suicide of his best friend and fellow student Heinrich Kana. Kana had come from a poor Jewish family and never found his way in life. Herzl related that, in his novel, 'I wanted in particular to contrast the suffering, despised, and decent mass of poor Jews with the rich ones. The latter experience nothing of anti-Semitism which they are actually and mainly responsible for.' This sociological observation would later be represented by a principal character in *Altneuland*, David Litvak. Herzl originally intended to call him Samuel Kahn, which he thought more unambiguously Jewish, but the novel was set aside at this point.

Herzl also cited previous correspondence with people in Austria and Germany who sought to fight Jew-hatred by founding leagues against anti-Semitism. He praised the good intentions of these correspondents, but reached the conclusion that such ameliorative efforts were doomed to 'emptiness and futility.' He recalled in this context two seemingly insignificant events, one of which took place in a pub in Mainz and the other near Vienna. In both cases he heard explicit anti-Semitic epithets ('Hep-Hep,' the slogan of the German anti-Jewish riots of 1819, and 'Jewish pig'). The fact that Herzl remembered these events and even thought it necessary to write about them testifies to how profoundly they affected him, even if the specific incidents had no broader import – as Herzl himself noted. But they did not spark his interest in the Jewish issue, nor is there any indication that Herzl thought his personal career had in any way been held back because he was a Jew. On the contrary, Herzl's social and professional milieu – the press, the theater, and the literary world – was full of Jews. His work had been held in high esteem and he had been able to rise in his profession. His concern was not personal – rather, he was worried by the fundamental problem of the Jewish people's position in the modern world.

Among the dozens of these pages Herzl devoted to thinking through a solution to the Jewish issue, France hardly got a mention. That country comes up only in passing, and the Dreyfus affair is notably absent. And this while he was in Paris and reporting extensively on events there for his newspaper. Neither do his diaries contain any reference to a single traumatic and dramatic event that triggered all this contemplation of the Jewish issue. As shown in the earlier chapter, the common view that *The Jewish State* was a product of Herzl's shock at the Dreyfus affair has no basis in the facts. His writing shows that what was on his mind was the tenuous position of the Jews of Germany and Austria. In a draft of a letter he wrote at the time, addressed to the Rothschilds, he stated explicitly that 'all I want is to combat anti-Semitism where it originated: in Germany.'

Herzl wrote that the process began while he was a student. The appearance of Dühring's book and the emergence of racist parties in Austria, Germany, and Hungary prompted him to think about the future of the Jews in Europe. While he referred broadly to the works of the French anti-Semitic writer Édouard Drumont, the Dreyfus trial is mentioned only incidentally in the hundreds of pages of his diary. Herzl witnessed the ambiguous status of his people close to home, living in the society that was, at the time, considered the most friendly, amenable, and open to the Jews – that of Vienna, the capital of the tolerant Austrian-Hungarian Empire.

During the last decade of the nineteenth century, the very foundations of the Habsburg Empire were being called into question. The Jewish issue was but a small subset of the Empire's larger national problems. Herzl viewed the status of the Jews in this broader context, a point of view that made him all the more apprehensive about what would happen to the Jews as the political crises of Europe and Austria-Hungary played out. He was one of the first to see that this world, which on its surface seemed to be offering the Jews increasing freedom and acceptance, was fragile and likely to collapse.

Many of Austria-Hungary's statesmen and thinkers viewed the rise of national movements among the Empire's ethnic groups as a largely insignificant phenomenon. They realized that it needed to be addressed, but they did not think it presented any danger to the existence of the Empire itself. The expansion of suffrage would, they believed, satisfy some of the nationalists' demands. The Austrian socialists established special branches for different linguistic groups – Germans, Czechs, Croats, and so on – which they reasoned would provide for national self-expression within a larger framework of class solidarity that bridged national lines. The government granted some national groups the right to educate children in their own languages, seeing this as a way to allow each group to foster its specific ethnic identity within a larger integrated polity. Even the parliament in Vienna, the Reichsrat, included members not only from the core German-speaking areas but also parliamentarians representing the crown lands of Bohemia, Moravia, Silesia, Galicia, and Bukovina, each of whom was permitted to address the body in their native languages. Croatian and Italian could also be heard on the floor of parliament.

But these liberal reforms proved to be not nearly adequate for the crisis. Rather than mitigating, they aggravated it. Granting provincial schools the right to use local languages raised the problem of what to do in places of mixed populations, such as Prague, in which German speakers had long lived, or Vienna itself, to which tens of thousands of Czech speakers had migrated in search of jobs in the city's burgeoning industrial sector. Was it conceivable that children would study in Czech in the imperial capital, rather than in German, the language of the government and the hegemonic culture? The right to speak in native languages in parliament required consecutive translation into all the other sanctioned languages, slowing down debate and effectively paralyzing the work of the legislature. Even provincial representatives who knew German very well insisted on speaking their ethnic tongues – the Czechs in particular. In fact, many of the provincial members were not at all bothered by the paralysis – it presented them with a sterling opportunity to challenge the very need for the Habsburg monarchy and to pursue their separatist agendas.

But these demands caused a reaction among the Empire's German speakers, giving rise to pan-German and racist movements that proclaimed 'Aryan' distinctiveness. The emphasis on German racial identity led such movements – including student organizations, sports clubs and journalist associations – to reject and expel those who were not considered 'Aryans' or 'true' Germans. That meant not only Jews, but also Jews who had converted to Christianity, thus barring the way into society at large even to baptized Jews. Jewish students responded in a number of ways. In Vienna, they established their own fraternities, with Hebrew names that indicated an awakening of Jewish national feelings – Ivria (formed in 1882) and Kadima ('Forward' – 1892). Educated Jews, who had sought entry into Austria's German-speaking culture and society, now found themselves rejected and excluded.

Herzl observed all these developments closely, and repeatedly wrote about them in his diary. They laid out the contours of his political development and honed his sensitivity to the national issue as it shook the Jews' sense of being at home in the Habsburg Empire. In the period just before he left Paris and following his return to Vienna, Herzl was involved in the Vienna government's attempts to address the issue of languages of instruction. As a correspondent for the *Neue Freie Presse* with contacts in government circles, Herzl submitted to the Austrian Prime Minister, Count Kasimir von Badeni, a detailed program for the establishment, throughout the Empire, of schools for the speakers of different languages in accordance with the demand in different regions. There was also talk of Herzl being appointed editor of a new government-subsidized newspaper that would promote liberal multi-linguistic reforms. Herzl set down detailed and lengthy accounts of the progress of his talks with Badeni over the next several months. But in the end they led to nothing.

Today historians almost completely disregard the Habsburg regime's attempts to find liberal and pluralistic solutions to the national problem. It was not surprising that Herzl was respected by leading figures in the Vienna government. Many of them were members of the non-German nobility, including Badeni himself, who was a Polish aristocrat from Galicia. They thus had a natural interest in strengthening the multi-national character of the Habsburg Empire. Another important Polish figure was the historian Stanislaw Kozmian, a member of the Reichsrat, who was of great assistance to Herzl and who would later publish a sympathetic review of *The Jewish State* in a Polish-language newspaper published in Lemberg.

Herzl's diary evinces growing anxiety about Austria's ability to survive as a multi-ethnic state. He could see that the national issue was already adversely affecting the Jews, especially in Bohemia and Moravia, where the clash between Czech and German nationalists placed the Jews in a precarious position. In Prague, the Jewish economic and cultural elite had traditionally identified with the hegemonic German culture. As nationalist and racist sentiments among German speakers increased, many of the city's educated Jews, who had been expelled from German-speaking professional associations as they pursued 'Aryanization' policies, sought to join Czech organizations. But, in many cases, the Czechs rejected them, saying, 'Now that the Germans have thrown you out, you're coming to us?' A mob of Czechs rioted against Germans in Prague's Old Town Square, smashing the display windows of stores bearing German-language signs. Many of these stores were owned by Jews. The Jews – intellectuals and businessmen, students and journalists – thus found themselves caught in a vise with Germans on one side and Czechs on the other.

The worsening situation of the Jews in mixed Czech-German regions was, in Herzl's view, just one acute expression of the empire's crisis, but it had dramatic consequences, especially for the Jews. This subject continually came up in his writings. For example, in November 1897, two months after the First Zionist Congress, he wrote in *Die Welt*, the Zionist newspaper he had founded:

> The great language dispute in Bohemia has put Austria's Jews in a strange position. They loyally follow those [the Germans] who have been their worst enemies in the past, and who will soon be their enemies again. German-educated Jews, who grew up and reached adulthood while liberal ideas were at their height, wholeheartedly adhered to the German nation. They loved their German identity

deeply, and ardently served the German people, as well as the idea of civic liberty ... Then, suddenly, [the Germans] withdrew; suddenly they declared [the Jews] to be parasites sucking the life-blood of the German race. The scene changed abruptly, as sudden as awakening from a dream ... They were flabbergasted – everything they knew appeared to be a mistake, their entire life plans turned out to be based on fundamental errors. The sacrifices they had made were for naught, their patriotism squandered.

Similar conflicts occurred in Krakow and Lemberg, where the Jewish elite found itself torn between supporters of the Habsburgs and those who cast their lot with the rising Polish national movement. Herzl also followed the rise of virulent racist anti-Semitism in his native Hungary. As in Austria, Jew-hatred was a paradoxical product of Jewish success in business, culture, and the press. Jews had lived in Romania for centuries, Herzl noted in his diary, but a Jew who applied for citizenship in that kingdom was forced to run a hostile bureaucratic gauntlet only, in the end, to have his petition denied.

Vienna held municipal elections in May 1895 and the campaign reinforced Herzl's foreboding about how cross-national currents of the type so characteristic of modern society could have adverse effects on the Jews. As a result of political reforms instituted by the Austrian government, the capital's mayor was now elected by a broad voting public. The city's liberal establishment, supported by the national government and the Emperor, was challenged by a radical populist, Dr. Karl Luëger, who led a coalition of clericalists, German nationalists, and anti-Semites under the rubric of his Christian Social Party. He and his followers decried 'corrupt liberalism,' charged that the Jews controlled the Austrian economy and press, and warned that the Czechs were a threat to Vienna's German character. Luëger won an upset victory but, in order for him to be installed as mayor, the national government had to certify his election. The government responded by dissolving the city council and holding another election, which Luëger again won. The cycle was repeated several more times, but each time Luëger received a majority of the votes, proving especially popular among the 'third curia,' the voting group composed of middle- and low-income citizens. Eventually the government had no choice but to accept the will of the people, and the Emperor certified Luëger's election as mayor of Vienna.

The lengthy Vienna election season cast a dark shadow over Austrian politics throughout the summer of 1895, the very period in which Herzl was agonizing over the Jewish issue and trying to decide where his future lay. Luëger's accession to the mayor's office and his party's victory were, in Herzl's view, a severe and dangerous development – in his diary he termed it a new St Bartholomew's Night, a reference to the massacre of French Protestants in 1572. Herzl also saw the election as the end of Vienna's liberal era. The fall of the Badeni government a short while afterward made him all the more worried about the future of the Empire and its Jews. It was his analysis of the deteriorating Austrian political situation, not the Dreyfus trial, that sparked the dramatic turn in Herzl's engagement with the Jewish issue.

In Herzl's view, the Jews were in danger not just in Austria but throughout Europe. After all, Luëger, the populist racist, had been voted into office on a wave of popular enthusiasm – thanks to the democratic extension of the right to vote to a broad swath of the population. Vienna's Jew-hatred was not a vestige of medieval Church superstitions. Rather, it was anchored in the very fabric of modern society as more and more decisions were handed over to the people. At the beginning of the 1890s, Herzl had supported universal male suffrage and had tried to persuade his newspaper to support this cause. While he never changed his position on this issue, he now realized that democracy could have adverse consequences. His support for democratization therefore became tempered by a certain fundamentally romantic wistfulness for the role that the aristocracy could play in restraining dangerous popular tendencies during times of social and national tension. Universal suffrage was meant to reinforce democracy and tolerance, but could under such circumstances have the opposite result. The expansion of the right to vote for the Austrian parliament had strengthened the various nationalist movements, while in Vienna it had brought to power an anti-Czech, anti-Semitic nationalist. The liberals, Herzl wrote, 'believed that people can be granted equality through an edict in the official gazette.'

Luëger's rise in Vienna in 1895 has been compared to the rise of Hitler in Germany in 1933, despite the differences. Nevertheless, in both instances a nationalist and racist movement won power through democratic elections, proving that democratic elections were not always an effective defense against racism and extreme nationalism. Vienna at the beginning of the twentieth century became the breeding ground of the young Hitler's political and ideological world-view. He came to the Austrian capital from the provinces, and it was in Vienna that he absorbed pan-Germanism, the concept of the Aryan master race, anti-Semitism, and anti-Slavism. Herzl clearly understood something that many of his generation did not see.

In other words, he turned his attention to the Jewish issue because he sensed that his world was falling apart. If the country that had treated the Jews best during the nineteenth century was about to disintegrate and pose serious challenges to the well-being of its Jewish population, a radical solution had to be found. Herzl also from time to time wrote of his fears that a new European war would break out. Yet this foreboding left him clueless, searching, coming up with what seem sometimes to be totally delusionary ideas of how the Jews might escape and where they might find refuge. His diary from this period does not have the character of an ordered narrative. It is a collection of scraps of inchoate ideas, more an expression of his mental state than a blueprint for action. It is hardly surprising that his friends feared that he was taking leave of his senses. After all, normal people addressed these problems in a rational and responsible way. The idea that the Jews as a community had to find a haven outside Europe seemed total insanity. Worse than that, it was dangerous, as the dissemination of such ideas by a man of Herzl's standing and influence could actually further undermine the Jews' position in European society. This was the reaction of the editors of the *Neue Freie Presse*, who rejected Herzl's ideas out of hand, even if they were prepared to indulge their most famous writer.

Hundreds of notions ran through his head. As an experienced writer and a journalist trained to jot down material for future use, he recorded his thoughts on scraps of paper. He had read Goethe's *Bildungsroman, Poetry and Truth,* so he understood the inevitable disparity between a writer's idealism and the hard facts of life. His ideals were a jumble, expressing the tension between imagination and reality. The diary entries from this period abound in symbolic motifs for a novel, one that he would never write even if there are some echoes in his later *Altneuland*. And there was everything from almost childish imaginary games to sober plans of action. The plot of the novel that was running through his head was not exactly clear to him. But his repeated reminders to himself that 'I must read [George Eliot's] *Daniel Deronda*' suggest that he intended a protagonist who, in one way or another, rediscovered his Jewish identity. It was clear that Herzl aspired to include in this work not only a portrayal of the Jewish world he knew but of the entire Jewish Diaspora. The stereotypes of his time were evident in his description of two central Jewish characters in the planned novel: 'The hero is of the blond type, blue eyes, a determined look. His beloved is a willowy Spanish Jewess, dark hair, a noble race.'

But alongside this scheme for a work of fiction, Herzl considered composing a detailed report on the state of the Jews in all the lands they lived in, as he later recounted:

> I wanted to visit the localities where the vagaries of history had strewn Jewish communities: particularly Russia, Galicia, Hungary, Bohemia; later, the Orient, the new Zion colonies; finally, Western Europe again. All my faithful reports were to bring out the undeserved misfortune of the Jews and to show that they are human beings whom people revile without knowing them. For here in Paris I have acquired a reporter's eyes, which are needed for such.

But he also paid attention to what the French novelist Alphonse Daudet told him. Daudet confessed to being an anti-Semite, but when he heard that Herzl intended to write a book about the Jewish issue, he told him that the best way to attract attention would be a popular novel along the lines of *Uncle Tom's Cabin*. As Herzl wavered between a journalistic account and fiction, the boundaries sometimes blurred. It was clear to him that the goal of whatever he wrote or whatever action he took needed to be aimed at finding the Jews a safe haven outside Europe.

It would require a huge emigration project that would need broad-based international support, not to mention that of Jewish financiers. He made lists of practical steps, sometimes going down to fine details (for example, on the best way of obtaining the necessary credit to pay for the emigration program, and on how to transfer people's pensions to their new country). He even fantasized about the structure of this future Jewish society, and jotted down these completely unsubstantiated and disjointed ideas. Later, some of the less outlandish ideas would be incorporated into his political program in *The Jewish State*.

In one of these fantasies about how this future Jewish settlement would operate, he would persuade the *rebbe* of Sadigura, the leader of a Hasidic sect in Bukovina, to join his enterprise 'and be installed as something like the bishop of a province. In fact, win over the entire clergy.' On another piece of paper he wrote of crowning Vienna's Chief Rabbi Moritz Güdemann to the same exalted position, and of appointing one of the Rothschilds to an office like that of the Venetian Doge. He stipulated that 'The High Priests will wear impressive robes; our cuirassiers, yellow trousers and white tunics; the officers, silver breastplates.' Furthermore, 'the Senate will include all the prominent Jews who go with us,' while his own father would hold the post of 'first senator.' There would be a battalion called the Knights of Herzl. He set down a detailed protocol for the crowning of the first Doge, a procession in which the ambassadors of every country would walk along with the leaders of the Senate and Parliament, representatives of the chambers of commerce, and attorneys. They would be led by 'the High Priest of the capital city [and] the flag with a guard of honor composed of generals,' all wearing dazzling uniforms. He added that 'the high priests [would walk] under canopies, [while] the Doge will wear the garb of shame of a medieval Jew, the pointed Jew's hat and the yellow badge!'

Elsewhere in the diary, Herzl lets his fantasy run wild: he would challenge Luëger (and perhaps other Austrian and German anti-Semites) to a duel. Were he to be killed, 'my death could perhaps mend peoples' minds and hearts.' If he were to kill his rival and be brought to trial,

I will make a tremendous speech in the style of Lassalle [who was himself killed in a duel], shocking the jury, touching their heart, gaining the support of the court – and I would be pronounced not guilty and set free. The Jews may even propose me for parliament, but I would have to refuse the offer, since I would not be willing to enter the people's representative body standing, so to speak, on the cadaver of a dead person.

Herzl's fancy flew free in many other notes to himself. He composed a meticulous procedure according to which titles of nobility would be awarded only for service to society rather than bought. Out of respect for wealthy Jews who already held peerages, he promised that 'I shall validate those acquired elsewhere prior to the founding of the state . . . [but to ensure] that no grotesque titles will infiltrate our [country].' The country would award decorations along the lines of the Légion d'honneur, to be called 'Jewish Honor' and 'worn on a yellow ribbon and thus our ancient mark of calumny will turn into our new mark of distinction.' Furthermore, the Jews of Hungary would be 'the hussars of Judea; they could make splendid cavalry generals.' There will be a strict code of dueling. The ships that would sail for the Jewish haven would be loaded with coffins because 'We shall also take our dead along with us.' A museum like the Louvre would be founded. It would be worth considering a monopoly on the manufacture and sale of alcoholic beverages, and perhaps a dowry tax on wealthy young women. Over dozens of pages of his diary and in notes he attached to it his thoughts addressed the sublime and the trivial.

But anyone who viewed this as a plan of action, or alternatively as evidence of the hallucinations of an unbalanced mind, would be wrong. As Herzl himself wrote, 'These notes are not a burden for me – on the contrary, they are a great relief. I write and set my thoughts free, and they rise like bubbles in a flask.' Eventually a plan of action did in fact emerge from these hundreds of jottings, a plan devoid of literary and romantic fantasies. In the meantime, however, Herzl allowed his imagination free rein. Yet his notes contain many concrete symbolic elements that he would hold on to later, when he decided to pursue a political and diplomatic program. One of these was a flag:

'Perhaps a white flag with seven gold stars. And the white field will signify our new, clean life. Just as the stars are the working hours. Under the banner of labor we shall enter the Promised Land.'

But where was the Promised Land? Romantically, Herzl avowed: 'No one has ever thought to look for the Promised Land where it actually is, and it is so near – within ourselves.' It was nice as an aphorism but it hardly provided the very concrete answer that Herzl was desperate to find. Where, in fact, should the Jews go? Palestine? Argentina? At this point he reached no verdict, but simply listed the pros and cons of each. Since Europe, with its crises and conflicts, was the root of the problem, it would be best to get as far away from that continent as possible: 'Going to South America would have a lot in its favor on account of its distance from militarized and seedy Europe, . . .' he wrote hopefully. 'If we are in South America, the establishment of a state will not come to Europe's notice for a considerable period of time.'

On the other hand, international politics would make it difficult for the Jews to obtain their needed refuge in Palestine, a land close to Europe and full of European interests. But realpolitik should not have the final word. 'What speaks against Palestine is its proximity to Russia and Europe, its lack of room for expansion as well as its climate, which we are no longer accustomed to,' he wrote. 'In its favor is a mighty legend.'

In the end, 'the mighty legend' would win out. Even as he wavered between the two options he used language with potent historical associations. When the convoys would leave for the new land, each group of Jews would be led by its rabbis. 'They will be the first to understand us, the first to be excited by the cause and from the pulpit fire the public. Imagine how enthusiastically our old saying will now be intoned: Next year in the Promised Land.' Such words clearly could not apply to South America. Elsewhere he wrote, 'in principle, I am neither against Palestine nor for Argentina.' He left the question open, but a reader of his diary can see that, as time went by, Palestine became the strong favorite.

In the meantime, however, Herzl continued to list South America's advantages. It would be easier to obtain territorial concessions there in exchange for loans from Jewish financiers, he asserted, 'because of the financial needs of the South American republics.' Furthermore, on that continent it would be easier to move a part of the local population to other locations without creating a crisis, simply by ensuring that there would be work available in their new locations. Nevertheless, he was aware of the problematic nature of this statement and quickly added that 'we [will] bring immediate prosperity to the absorbing country' and that 'we shall of course treat members of other faiths with tolerance and mutual respect . . . In this, too, we shall be an example for the entire Old World.' As he tossed out these ideas, it occurred to Herzl that a solution to the Jewish question might well be a key to a broader, global settlement:

> Today the thought occurs to me that I may be solving much more than the Jewish question. Namely, *tout bonnement* [very neatly], the social question! . . . One difficulty in the social question is precisely that everywhere men are bogged down in ancient abuses, lengthy stagnation, and inherited or acquired wrongs. Whereas I propose a virginal soil. But if it turns out to be true, what a gift of God to the Jews!

In another place he argues that the Jews' exemplary society would achieve the goals of socialism. And if any were to accuse him of preaching state socialism, he would agree, 'as long as the state does the right and just thing, i.e. not pursue the advantages of any group or sect, but strive for gradual amelioration for all.' The Jews are producing 'a surfeit of intellectuals,' he wrote, and these talented people, who could not find a place in European society, would be absorbed into and enrich the new Jewish commonwealth. There they would work in partnership with the common people and Jewish capital like that of the Rothschilds, which was currently impeding the world economy and contributing to the rise of anti-Semitism.

Notably, Herzl made no attempt to offer a sharp and incontrovertible definition of Jewish identity. He did, however, make an effort to learn about Jewish communities around the world. In his diary from February 1897, he recorded in amazement information he heard from a

Jerusalem hospital director whom he met in Vienna about the heterogeneity of the city's Jewish population:

> He told me wonderful things about Palestine, which is said to be a magnificent country, and about our Jews from Asia. Kurdish, Persian, Indian Jews come to his office. Strange: there are Jewish negroes who come from India. They are the descendants of slaves who were in the service of the expelled Jews and adopted the faith of their masters. In Palestine you can meet warlike mountain and steppe Jews, fighting warriors.

Herzl realized that the great variety of Jewish identities disproved racialist claims. He would use it not only in responding to anti-Semites but also to respond to one of his supporters, the Anglo-Jewish author Israel Zangwill, who, in a conversation with Herzl in November 1895, referred to the Jews as a race. Herzl rejected this concept categorically. In his diary, he referred sharply, and somewhat venomously, to Zangwill's seemingly 'negroid' physiognomy: 'I cannot accept it that we are a race: it is enough to look at myself and him . . . All I am saying is this: We are an historical entity, a nation composed of different anthropological elements. This also suffices for the Jewish state. No nation has uniformity of race.'

Significantly, at a time when racist theories were popular in Europe, even among some liberal thinkers, Herzl utterly rejected racial theory as a basis for national identity. Just as he argued against racial uniformity, so he dismissed the need for linguistic unity in the future Jewish state, citing Switzerland as an example. 'Language will present no obstacle. Switzerland, too, is a federal state of various nationalities,' he wrote.

What, then, made a Jew a Jew? Herzl was too smart and politically seasoned to get caught in a restrictive definition. Yet he offered a formula – a surprising one for a non-religious man like himself – that evinced his profound awareness of the complexity of the issue and the need to find a common denominator that would be acceptable to different groups of Jews. 'We recognize ourselves as a nation through our faith [*Wir erkennen uns als Nation am Glauben*],' he asserted.

Elsewhere he wrote: 'Our belonging to each other historically is based on our ancestral faith, for we have long since adopted the languages of many nations.'

This was descriptive rather than prescriptive, reflecting the nature of the way most of the Western and Central European Jews of Herzl's time, place, and station understood their religion – as the outer framework of their Jewish national identity. A Jewish person who gave up his religious affiliation has given up his claim to be Jewish in any sense – even in the view of a non-religious man like Herzl.* The link between Jewish national identity and religious affiliation should be viewed, with all due caution, as the context for a brief passage in which Herzl considered – and immediately rejected – the possibility that the Jews, at least those in Austria, might collectively convert to Christianity.

The idea appears in the context of a comprehensive discussion of anti-Semitism that Herzl included in his diary. He recalled, in a June 1895 diary entry, that two years previously he had speculated that it might be possible to solve the alienation of the Jews from European society with the help of the Pope and the Catholic Church. He hypothesized that a group of Jewish leaders, including Herzl himself (who had no standing as a leader of the Jewish community), would appeal to all the Jews of Austria and propose that they convert to Christianity, 'freely and honorably.' The conversion would take place in a public ceremony, not covertly, as many of the Jews who sought to flee their Jewish identities by converting had. 'The conversion was to take place

---

* This is not the place to go into detail about the long-running 'Who is a Jew' debate in Israel. But Herzl clearly took the position that would later form the basis of the Israeli Supreme Court ruling in the famous case of Brother Daniel, a Jewish Holocaust survivor who converted to Catholicism and joined a monastic order. Upon taking up residence in Israel, Brother Daniel invoked the Law of the Return, which grants automatic Israeli citizenship to every Jew who settles in the country. His application was turned down, but he was offered citizenship on the basis of his residency in Israel rather than on the Law of Return. But the court rejected his petition on the grounds that, while religious belief and practice are not the substance of Jewish identity, a Jewish individual's decision to adopt a different religion was not just an act of taking another religion, but of placing oneself outside the bounds of Jewish nationhood. This ruling was later written into the Law of Return. While this formulation is not without its problems, it is well grounded in Jewish experience. It may be unique to the Jewish people, but the right to define one's own nationhood is, after all, a sine qua non of modern national self-determination.

in broad daylight,' he wrote, recalling his idea, 'Sundays at noon, in St. Stephen's Cathedral, with festive processions and amidst the pealing of bells.' But his notion had a weird codicil involving the leaders – and Herzl himself, of course. They, he stipulated, 'would remain Jews, escorting the people only to the threshold of the church and themselves staying outside, the whole performance being elevated by this touch of great candor.' In placing himself among those who would remain Jews, Herzl confirmed another statement of his – that he had never considered converting to Christianity himself. He imagined that 'We, the steadfast men, would have constituted the last generation. We would still have adhered to the faith of our fathers. But we would have made Christians of our young sons before they reached the age of independent decision, after which conversion looks like an act of cowardice or careerism . . . I had thought out the entire plan down to all its minute details.' He even imagined bringing up the idea with the Archbishop of Vienna, or even with the Pope. The latter, he thought, would try to persuade him to be baptized himself, but Herzl would refuse and insist on remaining Jewish. The playwright Herzl even drafted this heroic dialogue between the Pope and this stiff-necked Jew.

But Herzl quickly realized that it was a ludicrous scheme, perhaps a good premise for a play but not a serious prescription for his people. He shared it only with the two liberal Jews who owned the *Neue Freie Presse*, both of whom laughed at their senior correspondent. Herzl shelved the idea and never brought it up again. Most likely, no one would ever have known about it had he not mentioned it in his diary. But there is no escaping the fact that his reference to it meant that it must have preoccupied Herzl for some time as he desperately sought a way to address the plight of the Jews. It is no coincidence that in this same section of his diary he wrote: 'There are matters in these notes which may appear absurd, exaggerated, crazy. But had I exercised self-criticism, as I do in my literary works, my ideas would be emasculated.' Eventually, Herzl formulated a proposal for meeting these challenges, but in the meantime he was seeking to escape the pressures engulfing him in his Paris hotel by jotting down such notes. In the evenings he fled his room, sometimes to meet friends, sometimes to attend the opera.

Herzl's favorite opera was Wagner's *Tannhäuser*. Upon returning from a performance of this work on June 5, 1895, he wrote in his diary that 'We, too, will have such magnificent theater halls,' and that theater and opera would be a means of forging a national consciousness. Later, in *Altneuland*, Herzl would have his characters attend, at Haifa's opera house, a performance of a work called *Shabbetai Tsevi*.

Herzl's taste for Wagner, *Tannhäuser* in particular, may seem surprising in light of the later association of Wagner with the racist ideology of the Nazis. Perhaps even more surprising is the fact that Herzl had the overture to *Tannhäuser* played at the opening of the Second Zionist Congress in 1898. But the Nazis adopted as their own most of the great figures of German culture, including enlightened and liberal ones like Schiller, Goethe, and Beethoven. True, Wagner, unlike these others, also wrote an anti-Semitic pamphlet, *Judaism in Music*, but the fact is that his music was central to the intellectual world of the late nineteenth century, especially in the German-speaking sphere, Jews included.

Herzl's admiration for Wagner has to be seen in context. Wagner began his career as a young artistic and political radical, an associate of both the poet Heinrich Heine and of Friedrich Engels. With their musical and dramatic innovation and their proclamation of a new cultural and social age, his operas appealed to a broad range of people. They were swept away by his musical genius and by the liberating messages it conveyed. It was Wagner who turned opera from mere entertainment, an art form that often deteriorated into cheap sentimentality and even kitsch, into a comprehensive cultural experience. Audiences of the late Romantic nineteenth century were in particular enthralled by his heroes, men who sought redemption and liberation from social mores and constrictions. While their quests had a religious cast, they did not fall under the rubric of a specific faith – one reason why Wagner gained so many admirers among Central Europe's middle-class and educated Jews. He proved that sublime and emotionally charged music bearing profound moral content did not have to come in the form of Christian masses, oratorios, cantatas, and requiems.

Tannhäuser tells a classic story of personal redemption. The legend on which it is based comes from Christian folklore, but the opera's protagonist is a symbol of humanity as a whole, a man who seeks moral purity and transcendence beyond the bounds of religious and church affiliation. The Catholic Church, in the person of Pope Urban II, is depicted as stern and heartless. Few remember today what was well known in Herzl's time – that Wagner's adaptation of the legend, which turned the traditional pious saint of Christian folklore into a rebellious defender of carnal love, was inspired in large measure by Heinrich Heine's poem of the same name, a vicious lampoon of the Church and the Pope. Heine tells of his hero's wanderings from city to city after the Pope's rude rejection of his plea for absolution (he had sinned, in the eyes of the Church at least, for having spent a year as lover of the goddess Venus). The Jewish-born poet and master of linguistic dissonance gave the Christian knight an ironic line: 'I arrived in Frankfurt on *Shabbos*,' the insertion of this Yiddish/Hebrew word being intended to shock his German readers.

Wagner was also indebted to Heine for the plot of his previous opera, *Der fliegende Holländer* (*The Flying Dutchman*), based on the legend of a Dutch seaman doomed to wander the seas for ever for a crime he did not commit. Just as Goethe took the story of Faust, the scholar who sold his soul to the Devil, and turned it into an apotheosis of man's grappling with the sublime, which could, surprisingly, appear in the guise of Mephisto, so Wagner turned the story of the cursed ship's captain into a parable of a restless soul seeking the anchor of redemption. That anchor is a woman who will agree to share his life of endless wandering as a man without a homeland.

Wagner was not the first to give the legend a moral dimension. Heine had turned the popular ghost story into a quest for and achievement of salvation. Wagner wrote in his memoirs that he had been profoundly moved when he read Heine's story, seeing the tale as a paradigm of deliverance through the love of a woman, a unique interweaving of the legend of the Wandering Jew with the story of Ulysses. It was this fabric that, Wagner wrote, he had sought to bring to life in his opera. There the cursed sailor who terrorizes ships at sea turns into a seeker of liberation, of a safe haven, and of a homeland, a man who rather than scaring us arouses our empathy. It should hardly be surprising that these themes appealed to Jews both as story and as music.

Herzl carried on his internal dialogue, with its meticulous programs and sometimes preposterous ideas. But from this jumble of thoughts he extracted his principal goal – a detailed plan for the establishment of a Jewish state. It was a grand project that raised myriad practical questions. How could the process get started? How would the necessary support for the project take shape? The deeper Herzl delved into these issues, and as the way before him grew clearer, the more he realized how revolutionary his ideas were – not just for the Jews, but for international politics and European society as well.

Herzl's first notes to himself about how to get started still hovered in the world of fantasy. They were completely disengaged from his position as a journalist and a private individual who had no political support or standing. 'First of all I will negotiate with the czar the liberation of Russia's Jews, . . .' he instructed himself. 'Then I will have talks with the German Kaiser, then with Austria, and then with France about the Jews of Algeria.' He understood, however, that it was all a daydream at this point. Until he had the means to gain access to the corridors of power, he had to focus on more realistic goals. Herzl thus wrote two letters, one to Baron Maurice de Hirsch and the other to Rabbi Dr. Moritz Güdemann. Hirsch represented the wealthy Jewish bankers whose financial success had brought them honor, prestige, and titles of nobility, but who were also the targets of acerbic social criticism that made no little contribution to the rise of anti-Semitism. Rabbi Güdemann, as Chief Rabbi of Vienna, represented the religious establishment that Herzl respected despite his own non-observance, realizing that rabbinic support could be essential to his plans. But both these figures firmly rejected Herzl's overture, a fact that in the end dictated his line of action.

Herzl's diary contains a lengthy account of his meeting with Baron Hirsch in June 1895 and their subsequent correspondence. Like the Rothschilds, the Hirsch family was a prominent member of Europe's Jewish moneyed aristocracy. The baron's father had made his fortune as banker to the Bavarian royal house, from which he had received his title. His mother was a Wertheimer, a family that had served as 'court Jews' and bankers to southern German princes since the eighteenth century. Baron Hirsch married into the Bischoffsheim banking family, firmly establishing his reputation as a man of finance in Brussels. He doubled the capital he had inherited from his father by managing the huge credit enterprise that enabled the construction of the Orient Express, the rail line connecting Constantinople to Europe's major cities. His mansions in Paris and London and his estate in Hungary were the stuff of legend; his title of nobility and the honors granted to him by the Sultan had made him one of the world's most famous Jews. His friends included the Prince of Wales (later King Edward VII), the son of Queen Victoria, and the Habsburg heir, the son of Emperor Franz Joseph, Archduke Rudolf. Baron Hirsch was famous for his generosity and his philanthropic support of Jewish charities. He was one of the principal backers of Alliance Israélite Universelle, the French-Jewish organization that was mainly involved in developing French-language schools for Jewish communities in North Africa and the Levant. In addition, Hirsch supported Jewish immigrants to the US, and initiated the establishment of Jewish farming colonies in Argentina and Brazil, by founding the Jewish Colonization Association to support these colonies.

That made Hirsch the most obvious person for Herzl to appeal to for support. He did so carefully and with all due reverence, fearing that Hirsch would see him as just one more *schnorrer*, another Jew seeking a handout. In his letter he introduced himself as a correspondent for the *Neue Freie Presse*, but stressed that 'I do not want an interview with you, nor to talk about a disguised or undisguised financial matter . . . I simply wish to have a discussion with you about Jewish political matters.' Hirsch at first turned down the request politely (in a letter sent from London, the baron asked Herzl to put his ideas into writing). Herzl sent another letter saying that it would be difficult for him to summarize in a brief letter his extensive plan centered on 'Jewish politics,' and certainly did not want a memorandum of his to be placed on the baron's desk alongside the letters he no doubt received 'from beggars, parasites, fraudsters, and charity professionals.' Herzl's insistence, and perhaps the tone of audacity his letters displayed, seem to have aroused Hirsch's curiosity. In a subsequent reply, he acceded to Herzl's request, informing him that he, the baron, would a few days hence pay a 48-hour visit to Paris. He would be pleased to see Dr. Herzl on June 2 at 10:30 in the morning at his home on the Champs-Élysées.

Herzl was excited. 'I judged the man correctly and hit him at the *locus minoris resistentiae* [place of least resistance],' he wrote. He prepared painstakingly for the meeting, drafting a 22-page memorandum revealing his plan. He confessed to his diary that he would have to overcome the discomfiture he usually felt 'when dealing with famous or well-known people.' He bought new gloves and wore them a day earlier, 'so that they might still look new, but not fresh from the shop.'

While he had become acquainted with prominent figures in French society and politics during his years in Paris, he had not frequented the baron's circles. His acquaintances and contacts had been journalists, writers, members of parliament, and a few more or less famous Jews, but not financiers like Baron Hirsch. Herzl was aware that Hirsch was one of the world's richest men, and his diary offers his impressions, those of a modest member of the bourgeoisie ('I dressed carefully and with discretion,' he wrote):

> I drove up to the Rue de l'Élysée. A palace. The grand courtyard, the noble side-stairway – to say nothing of the main staircase – made a strong impression on me. Wealth affects me only in the guise of beauty. And there everything was of genuine beauty. Old pictures, marble, muted gobelins. *Donnerwetter!* Amazing! People of my standing never think of these corollaries of wealth when they disparage it. Everything had truly great style and, a bit dazed, I let myself be handed from one attendant to another . . . The baron, I thought to myself, must have hired someone to be in charge of good taste.

Upon arriving, Herzl was, of course, made to wait a bit until Hirsch graciously received him. Herzl first sought to ascertain whether he could have a whole hour of the baron's time, because otherwise 'I'd rather not start at all.' Hirsch asked him to begin and instructed his aides not to disturb them.

Herzl drew out his notes and began a lecture. It was an utter failure, and Herzl's account in his diary emphasizes the gap between them that both men felt. On the one side stood Herzl, petitioning Baron

Hirsch, for all intents and purposes, to head an enterprise that would lead, in the end, to the establishment of a Jewish state. On the other side was Baron Hirsch, one of the world's wealthiest Jews, at home in the courts of lords and kings and a munificent supporter of Jewish charitable works, but naturally averse to any action that might seem like an attempt to translate his economic might into Jewish political power. Herzl was asking Hirsch to become king of the Jews, but that was the last thing Hirsch, an experienced man of the world with a lot of common sense, wanted.

Herzl didn't even have a chance to complete his learned and well-thought-out presentation, because Hirsch kept interrupting with comments that made it clear that he did not like what he was hearing. 'I do see that you are an intelligent man, . . .' he told his guest. 'But you have such fantastic ideas!' When Herzl proposed applying to the German Emperor and raising a billion marks as a 'Jewish national loan fund,' Hirsch, who knew the Kaiser well and had some experience with finances, said Herzl's proposal was delusional. The conversation ended amiably and graciously, with a promise from Hirsch that it would continue. But when Herzl returned to his hotel he wrote in his diary: 'I only got as far as page six – I had 22 pages!' He wrote Hirsch a detailed letter, asking for a second meeting – a request that received no response.

Herzl drew the obvious conclusion – it was not just his long and exhaustive speech that had displeased Hirsch. The baron was generous, attentive to the plight of the Jews, prepared to support every philanthropic initiative, including emigration – but he would not lend his hand to political activity. Yet Herzl did not despair entirely. He sent Hirsch another detailed letter, which received no real reply, in which he attempted to persuade him that he was neither a delusionary nor a dreamer. This letter displayed the kind of chutzpah which would characterize many of Herzl's initiatives, and which would stand him in good stead in times of trouble. He acknowledged that he was not a man of action, but that 'this pen is a Great Power,' and tried to characterize both his correspondent and himself: 'You are the great Jew of money [der grosse Geldjude], I am the Jew of the spirit.' He understood why the baron was treating him sardonically, but 'one day you will recall this Whitsunday morning.' He beseeched Hirsch not to dismiss his ideas because of his relative youth. 'In France, at my age of 35,' he pointed out, 'men are ministers of state, and Napoleon was Emperor.' This may well merely have reinforced Hirsch's opinion that Herzl was not a man he should take seriously.

In Herzl's letter was a fascinating intimation of his thinking about how his political vision might become reality. He invoked the unification of Germany:

> Believe me, the politics of a whole people – especially of a people dispersed all over the world – can be carried out only through extraordinary means, which appear as if they were floating in the air. Do you know what the German Reich was created out of? Out of dreams, songs, and black-red-gold ribbons [the colors of the German democratic national movement]. Bismarck had only to briefly shake the tree planted by the visionaries.

He added that 'the exodus to the Promised Land' involved not just a mass transportation operation and should not merely be reduced to an itemization of expenses. The enterprise would require 'tremendous propaganda, the popularization of the idea, through newspapers, books, pamphlets, talks by traveling lecturers, pictures, songs.' He knew that the aristocratic banker was liable to scorn such things, and he realized that Hirsch might well ask him whether he had a flag to wave at the head of the Jewish convoy. He replied with a sentence that would later become one of the slogans of the Zionist movement: 'A flag, what is that? A stick with a rag on it [*ein Fetzen Tuch*]? No, sir, a flag is more than that. With a flag one can lead men wherever one wants to, even to the Promised Land.'

If Herzl's interview with Hirsch was a failure, from it he gained insights that would serve him well in the future. Another, more realistic, man would have given up. Another man, less determined, might have despaired. But Herzl responded differently, and in keeping with his personality – for him disappointment was an incentive to crystallize his ideas. He considered turning to another source of Jewish wealth, the Rothschilds. He would convene the entire family at one of its estates for a lecture about his program. He did not wait to ponder whether such a convocation was likely – he filled pages and pages of his diary with plans for this 'family council.' At the same time he prepared a memorandum for the German Emperor.

In the meantime, he sought a way into the heart of Vienna's Rabbi Güdemann. Herzl's wooing of this religious figure preoccupied him during the summer and autumn of 1895. The two men exchanged frequent letters. Herzl's impression was that the rabbi was sympathetic to his ideas. After repeated delays, and thanks to the intercession of mutual friends, the two men met face to face. The meeting was a bitter disappointment for Herzl, and it also gave rise to feelings of enmity between the two men.

Herzl's correspondence with Güdemann showed how fraught with internal tensions this approach proved to be. Herzl sent his first letter to Rabbi Güdemann from Paris on June 11, 1895. It contained all of his own concerns and apprehensions. Since he and the rabbi, as Viennese Jews, already had some acquaintance with each other, Herzl permitted himself to write in a slightly intimate tone, while at the same time apologizing for the temerity of his approach. He notified the rabbi: 'I have decided to take the lead in an action on behalf of the Jews and am asking you whether you would like to help me.' He requested that Güdemann make available to him any material he had on the extent of anti-Semitism and its public manifestations, and on the dimensions of Jewish emigration from Austria, 'e.g., from Galicia and Lower Austria [meaning Vienna and its environs].' He did not reveal his political program to the rabbi in this first approach. In subsequent letters he was more explicit.

Rabbi Güdemann proved evasive at first, avoiding a meeting with Herzl by making a variety of technical excuses. But his initial reaction was otherwise favorable. He viewed Herzl as an ally in the fight against anti-Semitism – but only, apparently, before he realized what project Herzl proposed to pursue. He was even a bit surprised by Herzl's sudden concern about 'our cause' and presumed that he was turning to religion – perhaps, the rabbi thought, he wanted to become observant. But Herzl quickly corrected the rabbi's misimpression. 'Despite all my reverence for the faith of our fathers I am not fanatically observant and shall never be,' he wrote, reiterating, 'That I am not planning anything contrary to religion, but just the opposite, is shown by the fact that I want to work with the rabbis, with *all* rabbis.'

It was evident why Herzl turned to Rabbi Güdemann. Enlisting the leader of the Jewish religious establishment in Vienna would open many doors and many Jews would follow him. It would also enable him to place a familiar community leader at the head of his project – for all his self-confidence, he was well aware that he had no public standing, neither among the Jews nor in gentile society. He candidly told Güdemann that he hoped, through the rabbi, to gain access to the Vienna branch of the Rothschilds, and even to the German Emperor. When Rabbi Güdemann asked him how his interest in the Jewish question came about, Herzl replied in much the same terms that he had used in his diary, referring to his encounter with Dühring's book, adding: 'Now that everything is so clear in our mind I marvel at how close to it I frequently was and how often I passed by the solution.' He acknowledged to Güdemann that the rabbi was likely to think him a madman (he used the Judeo-German word *meschugge*), but he assured him that he was entirely serious and that he planned to devote his life to the Jewish cause.

Rabbi Güdemann's initial interest, which seems to have been genuine, grew steadily cooler as he discovered that Herzl's solution to the Jewish problem was a political one. At first he tried to dissuade Herzl, who was unsure about how to appeal to the public, and suggested that he make do with writing a novel. Gradually, and especially after the two men met in Munich in mid-August, his reservations about Herzl grew. Herzl came to understand that behind the rabbi's polite words lay firm opposition to the very nature of the idea of a Jewish state. Indeed, Rabbi Güdemann may not at first have grasped the radical nature of Herzl's program. Perhaps he initially viewed it as a humanitarian solution to the plight of the Jews. It could also be that his enthusiasm cooled after discussing the program with community leaders and receiving a cold shower from them.

Whatever the case, Herzl did not manage, in the end, to enlist Rabbi Güdemann in his cause. Furthermore, when Herzl launched his public campaign and published *The Jewish State*, the rabbi sided with his colleagues in the religious establishment, who publicly denounced Herzl and the Zionist idea on the grounds that it constituted a clear and present danger to the position of Jews in European countries and was, furthermore, a violation of Jewish religious principles. In April 1897 Rabbi Güdemann published (through the same Jewish press that issued Herzl's *The Jewish State*) a polemic against Zionism. Herzl responded in his diary scathingly, wounded, it seems, like an unrequited lover:

> Dr. Güdemann has published a malicious counter-pamphlet entitled *Nationaljudentum* [*Jewish Nationalism*]. Evidently at the behest of the local '*upper Jews*' ... I shall answer him – and, following the Machiavellian precept, it will be devastating ... The publisher Breitenstein tells me that as soon as Güdemann's tract appeared, Rothschild sent for 30 copies.

Herzl replied with a cutting review in a Vienna newspaper.

But Rabbi Güdemann was hardly the only Jewish leader to distance himself from Herzl's ideas. The Rothschilds treated him with indifference, not even deigning to reply to his request to present his plan to a family council.

Herzl racked up one disappointment after another. On June 19 he wrote to Bismarck, who, since his insulting and humiliating dismissal by the young Wilhelm II in 1890, had been living as a solitary, lonely old man at his estate in Friedrichsruh. Herzl's letter was emotional and full of flattery for the architect of German unity, whom he referred to as the man 'who has stitched a torn Germany together with his iron needle in such a wonderful way that it no longer looks as patchwork.' He implored Bismarck for an audience where he could present his Jewish political program. He even went so far as to write: 'May I remind Your Excellency that you once spoke about matters non-exclusively Jewish with another Jew [Lassalle] who, like me, did not have a mandate.' Here Herzl was referring obliquely to the surprisingly good relations that the conservative Chancellor Bismarck had had with the founder of German social democracy. Herzl received no reply to this letter, either.

Paradoxically, however, all these failed efforts did produce something – they helped Herzl formulate his ideas. In preparation for his meeting with Hirsch, Herzl had fashioned his jumble of ideas into a well-thought-out document. While he was not given time to read all of the program's 22 pages to the baron, he now had a first draft of his plan. His long correspondence with Rabbi Güdemann then forced him to hone some of his positions, especially with regard to religion. And his hope of presenting his plan to a Rothschild family council compelled him to draft, rewrite, and polish a political memorandum so that, in speaking to the family, he would not fumble, as he had with Hirsch, in answering questions his interlocutors might put to him.

The memorandum was never submitted to the Rothschilds, but essentially it became the pamphlet *The Jewish State*. On June 11, Herzl wrote in his diary: 'If I cannot mobilize either the Rothschilds or the dwarf millionaires, I will publish the plan as a book: *The Solution of the Jewish Question*.' That is precisely what he did. Herzl turned his mishmash of ideas, some of which were admittedly ridiculous, into a political program. His indecision about whether to write a novel or commence public action led to a call to the public in the form of a political pamphlet. He may have run into a wall of rejection when he asked for the help of Jewish financiers and religious leaders, but Hirsch's cool civility, the Rothschilds' disregard, Rabbi Güdemann's objections, and his inability to gain access to the corridors of political power braced Herzl and compelled him to refine his ideas and tactics.

Herzl's talent as a writer, journalist, and playwright helped him along in his political activity. His public appearances were informed by the theater. As a writer, he knew that symbols, theater, and opera were critical to creating national consciousness, a point he stressed in many of his writings and speeches. 'Only the phantastical arouses people,' he wrote. Even when he was in the midst of his political maneuverings and initiatives, he continued to view his own life as if it were a novel. So when, in April 1902, it became clear that all his efforts to obtain the Sultan's consent to a Charter for Palestine came to naught, he wrote in his diary: 'Thus concludes this volume of my political novel.' On another occasion he confessed ironically: 'Actually, I am still a playwright. I pick up poor beggars off the street, dress them up in fancy clothes, and they enact before the world an exquisite drama concocted by me.'

The program Herzl fashioned, in the space of a few months, from his random notes, with all their contradictions and absurdities, was a radical, sweeping one that frightened, and even revolted, many Jews. To many it sounded utopian and pointless. But it brought together many Jewish streams, all seeking their way, from Eastern Europe's Hovevei Zion to Vienna's Jewish student fraternities and Jewish activists in London into a single movement. In doing so, it also first placed the Zionist idea on the international political map. The notions and ideas that Herzl's fevered brain began producing in June 1895, as he sat in his Paris hotel room, could well have ended in nothing more than a nervous breakdown. Instead, they reached the light of day after their goal had been clearly delineated and appeared in public as a clear agenda, grounded in historical and political analysis.

CHAPTER FIVE

FROM THE JEWISH QUESTION TO *THE JEWISH STATE*: THE REVIVAL OF JEWISH PUBLIC SPACE

IN THE END, Herzl's hesitations about how to put the 'Jewish issue' before the public helped him achieve maximum impact when he did so. In the summer and autumn of 1895, first in Paris and then after his return to Vienna, Herzl met with dozens of people to discuss his ideas. He sought out the advice of Jews and non-Jews, made connections, and solicited backing and assistance. In the process of this intensive labor, he first made the acquaintance of Jewish activists from different European countries, learned about Jewish organizations, and made his first acquaintance with the Hovevei Zion movement, which has been active since the 1880s in encouraging Jewish immigration to Palestine.

The result was that when Herzl resolved to publish *The Jewish State*, a revised version of the memorandum he had drafted to submit to the Rothschilds, its appearance was already eagerly anticipated by many. As a result, it immediately found a readership. It would not be an exaggeration to say that no other Jewish work of the modern age was so quickly disseminated and as widely read as Herzl's book. At the time of its publication, Herzl held no public position, but his extensive activity – meetings, letters, travels, establishing bonds with others – had made his name known across broad swaths of Europe's Jewish population.

The Jewish State: Proposal of a Modern Solution for the Jewish Question was issued by a Jewish publisher in Vienna and Leipzig in February 1896. A month earlier, on January 17, following a visit by

Herzl to London, the Anglo-Jewish newspaper the *Jewish Chronicle* published a summary of Herzl's ideas under the title 'A Solution to the Jewish Question'. A week later, on January 24, the Hebrew-language newspaper *Hatzefirah*, based in Warsaw, published an item about the *Jewish Chronicle* article, bringing Herzl's proposal before Hebrew readers across the Russian Empire. The February 23 issue of the monthly journal *Zion*, associated with the German branch of the Hovevei Zion movement, included a favorable response to Herzl's book. On February 23, Herzl asked Sylvie d'Avigdor, the daughter of a British Hovevei Zion sympathizer, to do an English translation. What we would today call Herzl's promotion of his book was a great success – as a journalist, he was well aware of the importance of public relations in the promotion of political causes.

It thus happened that upon publication, *The Jewish State* was reviewed and commented on in dozens of Jewish newspapers in Central and Eastern Europe. Europe's lively Jewish press, one of the products of the modern media revolution, consisted of newspapers published in a variety of languages, ensuring that news of the book and its ideas reached a wide audience. Within just a few months the book itself had been translated into many languages. In 1896 alone an English translation appeared in London, a Hebrew one in Warsaw, a Yiddish version in Galicia, a Romanian one in Botoşani, a Bulgarian one in Sofia, a Russian one in St. Petersburg, and a French one in Paris. The Hebrew translation was rendered by Michael Berkowitz, who later served as Herzl's Hebrew secretary. A copy of d'Avigdor's English translation was sent that May to the former Liberal Prime Minister William Gladstone, who voiced his support for the Zionist idea. The *Neue Freie Presse* printed an item on Gladstone's positive response. While the newspaper's owners did not particularly like the idea its most famous correspondent was promoting, it could hardly ignore the splash the book made, especially when it was touted by such a leading figure as Gladstone.

Herzl sent out lots of copies. A copy of the English translation was dispatched to Herbert Spenser, the British philosopher. A Russian version, with a long covering letter, went to Grand Duke Vladimir, the younger son of Czar Alexander II – the members of Hovevei Zion would never dare to approach him in such a way.

Herzl's advocacy of a political solution to the Jewish question had repercussions across Europe. In June, when Herzl set out on his first trip to Constantinople, his train made a stop in Sofia. Hundreds of Jews awaited him at the train station and called out 'Leshanah haba'ah beYerushalayim!' 'Next year in Jerusalem!' A proclamation supporting Herzl was published by several of the Jewish student fraternities in the Austro-Hungarian Empire – Kadima, Ivria, Gamala, Libanonia, all in Vienna, and Hasmonea in Czernowitz. The Hebrew names that these young people chose for their organizations reflected a reawakening of Jewish identity among the hundreds of Jewish students from all corners of the Empire who streamed into Austria-Hungary's universities. While the Jewish fraternities did not have explicit national political agendas, the charged atmosphere in Vienna led them to develop a Jewish cultural identity that was not necessarily connected to religious observance, while retaining a potent link to Jewish history and to Palestine. They were well primed to receive Herzl's ideas. It was among these students, many of whom were Ostjuden, Eastern Europeans, that Herzl found his first supporters.

The Jewish fraternities' declaration, which appeared in May, just three months after The Jewish State was published, was unequivocal:

Despite the fact that the proposal to solve the Jewish Question through territorial concentration and the establishment of a political commonwealth [Gemeinwesen] has already been raised many times, the revival of Jewish statehood has never been expressed in such a clear and forthright way as it has been in the recently-published tract by Dr. Theodor Herzl.

The declaration asserted that despite the religious and social aspects of the Jewish question, Herzl's view was that

It is a national question and can be solved only by turning it into a matter of international politics. We are one people now rediscovering itself through its sufferings, and our power lies in our unity. We possess all the human and material forces necessary for the formation of a state – even a model state. All that has to be done is to grant us sovereignty in some part of the world.

Either Argentina or Palestine could serve for the re-establishment of the Jewish commonwealth, but Dr. Herzl supports Palestine unequivocally. Only this country can kindle in the Jewish people that kind of enthusiasm necessary for such an enormous project.

According to the authors of the declaration, 'this sublime idea' needed, first and foremost, the support of 'free-thinking and educated people.' More than other peoples, they maintained, the Jews recognized the seminal role played by intellectuals. They thus appealed to Jewish scholars to put their *Herz* – their heart – into Herzl's program, to teach their people that 'Judaism seeks to be free.' They should help Herzl found an organization that could make the vision of *The Jewish State* a reality.

It hardly mattered that a good part of Herzl's book was written in dry legal prose. It aroused the imaginations of masses of Jews in Eastern and Central Europe. Yet the Viennese Jewish bourgeoisie and religious establishment viewed his ideas with suspicion, even hostility. To Orthodox rabbis it reeked of heresy – they warned that Herzl was another Shabbetai Tsevi, the mystic who in the mid-seventeenth century had announced that he was the Messiah who would lead the Jewish people back to the Holy Land, and who eventually converted to Islam. Reform rabbis saw Herzl as a threat to their ideology, which was based on purging Judaism of national sentiment. Many well-off Jews in Central and Western Europe feared that Jewish nationalism could undermine their claims to equal rights under the law in Europe, a status they had achieved with considerable success.

But Herzl's book filled a vacuum for the educated Jews of Eastern Europe, those who had, as part of the *Haskalah*, the Jewish enlightenment of the nineteenth century, cast off the yoke of the rabbis and Jewish religious practice yet maintained strong and proud Jewish identities. The concept of the Jews as a nation, on a par with the other awakening nations of Europe, fired these Jews with enthusiasm. Hovevei Zion was the initial product of that fervor. *The Jewish State* changed the discourse from trying to achieve individual civil rights to gaining recognition as a nation.

'We are a people – *one* people!' This declaration reverberated in each language into which *The Jewish State* was translated. It was a defiant challenge to the emancipation, which by placing the individual Jew and his rights at its center had eclipsed collective Jewish identity. Herzl now invoked Jewish historical memory, which had always combined a national-ethnic consciousness with a religious one, in the context of contemporary Europe's modern national movements. As Europeans increasingly viewed themselves as members of national communities, he said, the integration of the Jews could no longer be seen in merely personal or religious terms. Jewish emancipation had gotten under way just as European nationalism was on the rise, and as a result solely personal and religious emancipation was doomed to fail.

In the first sentence of his book, Herzl asserted: 'The idea I put forth in this book is a very old one – it is the restoration of the Jewish state.' While some of his readers might not have gone as far as accepting the goal he proposed, he did speak to their concerns:

> We have honestly endeavored everywhere to integrate ourselves into the social life of our surrounding communities and to preserve only the faith of our fathers. Yet we are not permitted to do so. In vain are we loyal patriots, our loyalty in some places running to extremes; in vain do we make the same sacrifices of life and property as our fellow-citizens; in vain do we strive to increase the fame of our native land in science and art, or her wealth by trade and commerce. In countries where we have lived for centuries we are denounced as strangers, and often by those whose ancestors were not yet resident in that land, where Jews already had experienced suffering.

Herzl was well aware that Jew-hatred grew in part out of envy and resentment. But he also understood that anti-Semitism was an extremely complex phenomenon, with both religious and social aspects. Yet, fundamentally, he maintained, 'the Jewish question is not a social or a religious one, notwithstanding that it sometimes takes these and other forms. It is a national question . . .' Its solution thus required political action in the context of international diplomacy – it was not a problem that could be resolved within individual states, but only as part of an international arrangement.

Placing the Jewish issue in a national context challenged the common wisdom of many disparate parts of the nineteenth-century European and Jewish publics. The supporters of emancipation made every effort to make it a purely religious matter, reducing the whole Jewish question to a matter of freedom of religion for the members of a minority faith. Large segments of the Orthodox Jewish community, especially in the West, had also adopted this position, viewing themselves as 'Germans (or Frenchmen) of the Mosaic faith.' It was this view that led some of these people to begin to call themselves 'Israelites' rather than 'Jews.' The term 'Judaism' (*Judentum* in German) was also a new coinage, created as a parallel to the term 'Christianity,' one that implied that a Jew was simply a person who practiced the Jewish religion.

Herzl was certainly not the first to have this insight that the Jews should think of themselves as a nation. The Jewish-German historian Heinrich Graetz's monumental chronicle of the Jews depicted them as a group with a distinct national identity in their interactions with other nations. His work was widely translated and was the vehicle by which many Jews of the time became acquainted with the richness of their people's history. But Herzl differed from Graetz in that from his analysis of the Jewish situation he derived a plan of action. Emancipation, he argued, had not solved the problem of Jewish identity. Despite all the Jews' efforts 'to be like all the nations' they were rejected. The only possible solution was a national-territorial one, a new and distinct political entity. Herzl's diagnosis was that it was a matter not of the individual rights of the Jews but of the rights of the Jewish collective. They had to reclaim their standing as a nation among nations, and to re-establish a Jewish polity.

Herzl knew very well that many of his readers would rebuff his call for a renewal of Jewish independence on the grounds that his analysis was flawed. Even those who accepted his thesis would argue that his program of action was utterly unworkable. In anticipation of this objection, he stressed, right at the beginning of *The Jewish State*, that he did not view his proposal as a utopia. It was completely realistic, he claimed. Had his goal been a utopia, he maintained, he would have cast it in the form of fiction. Clearly he was thinking of his own doubts, the previous June, about whether to write a novel or a manifesto. In fact, a novel, *Altneuland*, would come in due course, but only in 1902, after his political efforts were well under way.

Herzl proposed a clear and interesting distinction between his program and those of utopias. The typical dream polity portrayed in the latter literary works was 'a complicated mechanism with a plethora of interlocking gears, but there is nothing to prove that they can be set in motion.' In contrast, 'the present scheme . . . includes an actual propelling force. In consideration of my own inadequacies, I shall content myself with indicating the cogs and wheels of the machine to be constructed . . .' A large part of *The Jewish State* is thus devoted to detailed accounts, in technical language, of the legal and financial institutions the project required and the means of putting his plan into action. Some of this part of the work may seem overly formalistic, but for Herzl it was vital. People might disagree with his proposals, but they could not, he was certain, dismiss them as fantasies. No utopian work, he said, not the first of the genre, Thomas More's *Utopia*, nor any of its progeny, included a concrete and detailed roadmap for making its vision reality.

But beyond his slogans, and before turning to his program for the establishment of the Jewish state, he offered a survey of the reasons for the failure of all other attempts to resolve the Jewish question in the modern age, as well as an account of anti-Semitism. First, he contended, 'The Jewish question exists wherever Jews live in significant numbers.' While anti-Semitism was a relic of the Middle Ages, in modern times 'even civilized nations do not seem to be able to shake it off, try as they will.' He saw no reason to offer a defense of the Jews against the charges leveled at them, because the roots of Jew-hatred ran much deeper.

Considering his native Hungary, Herzl maintained that assimilation via intermarriage had proved unsuccessful. It had proved efficacious to some extent among the aristocracy. There, he said, 'The

Jewish families ... re-gild the old nobility with their money ... But what form would this phenomenon assume in the middle classes, where (the Jews being a bourgeois people), the Jewish question is mainly concentrated?' The advocates of assimilation, he said, ignored the fact that the indigent Jewish proletariat could not be integrated into general society. Any attempt to solve that class's problems by mass emigration was doomed to failure, because the massive entry of Jews into countries where they had not previously been a presence would create social pressures that would necessarily produce anti-Semitism. 'What could be achieved by transporting a few thousand Jews to another country? Either they will come to grief at once, or they will prosper, and then their prosperity will create anti-Semitism,' he wrote.

Another proposed solution was the 'productivization' of the Jews – which meant removing them from the middle class and turning them into peasants. Herzl made good use of his historical knowledge, arguing that such an approach was based on a fundamental misunderstanding of the agricultural life.

> The peasant is a historical category, as is proved by his costume, which in some countries he has worn for centuries, and by his tools, which are identical with those used by his earliest forefathers. His plow is unchanged; he carries seed in his apron, mows with the historical scythe and threshes with the time-honored flail ... It is absurd, indeed impossible, to make [the Jews into] modern peasants on the old model.

Furthermore, agriculture was undergoing modernization, a phenomenon especially notable in the United States, where farming was being industrialized. The consequence was that the traditional farmer was disappearing. It would thus be ridiculous to attempt to turn Jews into old-time farmers. Furthermore, doing so would simply produce Jew-hatred among the peasants, who would, from their point of view, view Jewish cultivators as competitors.

Herzl took care to distinguish between modern anti-Semitism and that of previous generations:

[T]he main current of the aggressive movement has now changed. In the main countries where anti-Semitism prevails, it does so as a result of the emancipation of the Jews ... While in the ghetto we have, curiously enough, developed into a bourgeois people, and we stepped out of [the ghetto] only to enter into fierce competition with the middle classes. Hence, our emancipation set us suddenly within the middle-class circle ...

These processes led, on the one hand, to a rise in Jewish economic power, and on the other to the rejection of the Jews by society around them – a rejection that impelled Jews toward revolutionary movements. 'When we sink, we become a revolutionary proletariat, the subordinate officers of all revolutionary parties,' he wrote. Caught, socially, between the hammer and the anvil, the Jews were perceived both as an exploitive bourgeoisie and as radicals who threatened the very foundations of society. There was only one way out of this predicament – to extract the Jews from European society. 'Let sovereignty be granted us over a portion of the globe large enough to satisfy the rightful requirements of a nation; the rest we shall manage for ourselves,' he declared.

In an age in which new nation-states were coming onto the scene, he argued, 'the creation of a new state is neither ridiculous nor impossible.' The previous century, he pointed out, had seen the rise of new countries with much weaker social foundations than the Jewish people had. If peasant nations could establish states, the Jews, who boasted a strong middle class and a large educated elite, could certainly do so.

As he did in his diaries, in *The Jewish State* Herzl grappled with the question 'Argentina oder Palästina?' While he did not come down firmly on one side or the other, there can be no doubt where his heart lay. True, Argentina was one of the richest lands in the world, huge in territory but small in population, and it would benefit from setting aside a portion of its land for the Jews. But Herzl was also aware that 'The present infiltration of Jews has certainly produced some discontent, and it would be necessary to enlighten the Argentine Republic on the intrinsic difference between [this influx of individuals] and the new [organized] immigration of Jews.' He clearly had his reservations about this course.

Over the course of *The Jewish State* the arguments in favor of Palestine grow stronger. Writing of the Jewish nation's historical connection to its ancestral land, Herzl reflected prevailing views about Europe's civilizing mission. He may have pursued this line also because he thought that it would appeal to non-Jewish readers. In a period when the independence movements of the Greeks, Serbs, Romanians, and Bulgarians had been partly supported by the European powers and public on the grounds that these new nations would broaden the bounds of European culture, such an argument would sit well with the prevailing *Zeitgeist*.

He also knew that he had to assuage European apprehensions about the future of Christian holy places should Palestine come under Jewish rule:

> Palestine is our never-to-be-forgotten homeland. The very name of Palestine would attract our people with a force of marvelous potency. If His Majesty the Sultan were to give us Palestine, we could in return undertake to reform the whole financial system of Turkey. We should then form a portion of the rampart of Europe against Asia, an outpost of civilization as opposed to barbarism. As a neutral state, we should remain in contact with all of Europe, which would have to guarantee our existence. The Holy Sites of Christianity would be safeguarded by assigning to them an extraterritorial status as is well known in the law of nations. We would set a guard of honor around these sanctuaries, answering for the fulfillment of this duty with our existence. This guard of honor would be the great symbol of the solution of the Jewish question after eighteen centuries of Jewish suffering.

Herzl saw poetic justice of an important kind in the idea that, by serving as trustworthy custodians of Christianity's Holy Sites, the Jews could demonstrate to the Christian world that they would not do to the Christians as the Christians had done unto them. What stands out here is Herzl's grasp of the fact that the enormous revolutionary enterprise of establishing Jewish territorial sovereignty could not move forward merely on instrumentalist arguments. The Jews, and the non-Jews whose support they required, needed symbols and stories to motivate them to undertake this enormous project. Argentina or some other distant land might logically serve as a Jewish refuge, but such places could never motivate the spirit. And if the spirit were not moved, the Jews would not pack up and leave Europe, nor would the Europeans facilitate them doing so.

Herzl focused in *The Jewish State* on the practical matter of getting the project started. To this he devoted the second and central part of his work. His principal claim was that what he advocated was not immigration of the usual sort but an organized operation aimed at creating a Jewish territory with standing in international law. Herzl put his finger on the problem – that the Jews, a nation like all other nations, still lacked a recognized public authority that could assume responsibility for this mass migration. There were Jewish communities, Jewish charitable institutions, Jewish organizations, but there was no institution that could act in the name of the Jews as a global national entity. In other words, it was necessary to establish a recognized Jewish public organization that could act in the name of the Jewish people.

Herzl implied something that now seems obvious, but which no one had given any thought to until he pointed it out. All the myriad debates about the Jewish question, with all its complex implications, had not produced for the Jews – neither as a religion, nor a nation, nor as some combination of the two – a real body that could represent them. The destruction of the Temple and the Jewish polity by the Romans in 70 CE also meant that the Jews as a people had lost their *parhessia*, their public standing, and as a consequence no longer had a recognized leadership which could speak on their behalf. The nations that won political independence in the nineteenth century had emerged from national movements and had their foundations in historical memory, newly established or renewed public institutions, and academies for the preservation or renewal of their national languages. Sometimes, as in the Balkans, with its Orthodox Christian population, historical, ethnically-based churches became the foundation of national

movements. The churches were religious institutions, but they preserved in their rituals traditional languages and collective memories
of ancient kingdoms and heroes, and these could be translated into a
new national consciousness. So the Greek Orthodox Church served
as a foundation for Greek nationalism, and similar phenomena were
evident elsewhere in Eastern Europe. The Jews lacked anything of the
sort – and, as we have seen, Herzl was quickly disabused of the hope
that Jewish financiers or leading rabbis would play this role.

Herzl thus concluded that the precondition for establishing a
Jewish state was the creation of a legitimate and recognized Jewish
public sphere in the form of national institutions. He offered the first
vague and tortuous outlines of such an institution in *The Jewish State*.
While writing the book he still did not have a clear idea how the necessary infrastructure could be created, but he was convinced that
without it his ideas would never take on substance. The idea of convening a congress would come up only during the course of the public
discourse that *The Jewish State* set off. Just as he had wrestled with the
question during the summer of 1895 in his hotel in Paris, Herzl now
inquired and debated and considered different paths forward only to
find that some of them were dead ends. Nothing was clear from the
start – it all took form in the course of discussion and action.

At the center of *The Jewish State*'s proposal to create a Jewish
public realm – that is, an accepted and efficient representative of the
Jewish people – was the establishment of two institutions, a Society
of Jews and a Jewish Company. Notably, the names of these two entities appear in English in his German text. He had learned during
his visits to England that, under the British legal system, companies
granted a public charter under private law could have quasi-state functions. Herzl wanted to register Zionist companies in England and then
prevail on the Ottoman authorities to grant these institutions concessions in Palestine, analogous to, for example, the way the British
East India Company had obtained concessions from local rulers in
India. Herzl had a law degree, which he mentioned on the title page
of *The Jewish State*. While readers of Herzl's constitutional-legal prose
often have difficulty comprehending all the intricacies of the arrangements he proposed, proper legal grounding was imperative because

he wanted to make political changes, not merely establish another humanitarian or philanthropic organization like the Alliance Israélite Universelle, which had never stepped beyond its educational and social agenda.

Readers were not always clear about the distinction between the two entities Herzl proposed to create. He himself stated that the purviews of the two bodies 'cannot be kept strictly apart in this outline. These two great bodies will have to work together constantly.' However, basically the Society of Jews would be responsible for organizing the Jews for emigration from the countries of the Diaspora, while the Jewish Company would assume responsibility for settlement of the Jews in their new territory. In a coinage that would later enter the Zionist lexicon, the Jewish Company would be something like a 'state-in-the-making.'

The Society of Jews' first task, Herzl wrote, would be to see to the orderly liquidation of the assets of the emigrating Jews. This would not be a rushed exodus. Instead, the migration of the Jews 'will be gradual, continuous, and will cover many decades . . . The poorest will go first to cultivate the soil. In accordance with a preconceived plan, they will construct roads, bridges, railways, and telegraph installations, regulate rivers, and build their own dwellings.' When this infrastructure was in place, the members of the middle and wealthy classes would come, their departure from Europe and resettlement organized by the Jewish Company and its branches in various countries. At first, individual Jews would be encouraged to sell their assets at market prices, but, as the rate of emigration increased, 'the development of this movement might cause a considerable decline in the prices of real estate, and may eventually make it impossible to find a market for it.' This is where the Jewish Company would step in. 'It will take over the management of abandoned [Jewish] real estate until such time as it can dispose of it to the greatest advantage. It will collect rents, let out land on lease, and install business managers – these, on account of the required supervision, being, if possible, tenants also.'

When new homes were built in the territory that would be provided to the Jewish Company, it would ease the process for immigrants by granting them these homes in exchange for their homes in their

countries of origin. This would also prevent the exit of the Jews from throwing European countries into financial crisis. This idea of public guardianship of the property of Jewish migrants would protect Jewish assets and would also provide the Jewish Company with a powerful financial instrument.

In parallel, the Jewish Company would purchase land in the new Jewish territory. Herzl stressed that the political agreement that would transfer effective government of this territory to the Jewish Company would not transfer ownership of land to Jewish immigrants. Herzl realized that the internationally recognized grant of a territory for Jewish settlement did not mean that the privately owned land in that territory would be given to the Jews. Land there would have to be bought at market rates from its private owners, including state-owned land. The tasks he assigned to the Jewish Company were:

- Improvement and cultivation of land.
- Construction of housing for workers: 'They will not resemble those dismal workmen's barracks of European cities . . . rather, detached houses in little gardens will be united into attractive groups in each locality.'
- Allotment of land for private construction.
- Organization of work battalions for the construction of initial economic and social infrastructure.
- Establishment of a social welfare system.
- Establishment of employment bureaus and the guarantee of income through work (a subject Herzl had addressed in detail during the debates over welfare policy in Austria).
- Introduction of industrial incentives, first in order to provide the needs of the new settlers, and thereafter for export; alongside a publicly owned industrial sector, loans and tax credits would be provided to individual entrepreneurs, with the aim of creating a mixed economy.
- Creation of financial tools to fund these activities, through the establishment of a national bank and the sale of shares and bonds.

On the matter of organizing emigration from Europe, Herzl envisioned a mixture of private initiatives and organized voyages, based on country of origin. 'Our people should emigrate in groups of families and friends,' he wrote. 'But no man will be forced to join the particular group of his former place of residence,' even if that were desirable. He added: 'Preferably there will be only one class on board trains and boats.' He still hoped to make the rabbis part of the emigration process:

> Every group will have its rabbi, traveling with his own congregation. Local groups will afterward organize themselves voluntarily around their rabbi, and each locality will have its own spiritual leader. Our rabbis will devote their energies to the service of our cause, and will inspire their congregations by preaching it from the pulpit. They will not need to address special meetings for the purpose; an appeal such as this may be uttered in synagogue ... For we feel our historic affinity only through the faith of our fathers.

The Society of Jews would establish branches wherever Jews lived and seek to operate through local communities and institutions.

Herzl offered further details, while at the same time qualifying them by writing that he could offer only 'a few suggestions, as this part of my scheme will most probably be condemned as hallucinatory.' But he asserted that efforts should be made to prevent, as far as possible, sudden uprooting of Jews from their homes and customary lives. 'Just as we wish to create new political and economic relations, so we shall preserve as sacred all of the past that is dear to our people's heart,' he wrote. Involved as he was on the intellectual scene, aware of global developments, he added with a certain measure of irony:

> Anyone who has seen anything of the world knows that just these little daily customs can easily be transplanted elsewhere. The technical contrivances of our day, which this scheme intends to employ in the service of humanity, have heretofore been principally used for

our little habits. There are English hotels in Egypt and on the mountain crests of Switzerland, Viennese cafés in South Africa, French
theaters in Russia, German operas in America, and the best Bavarian beer in Paris. When we journey out of Egypt again we shall not
leave the fleshpots behind. Every man will find his customs again
in local groups, but they will be better, more beautiful, and more
agreeable than before.

Herzl then turned to the way the new territory would be run, while
the ultimate issue of sovereignty was left in abeyance for some time.
Yet, it was thus critical that the Jews in their new land create a public
authority – borrowing from Roman law, he said that the Society of
Jews would act as a *gestor*, a legal representative acting on behalf of
the Jews in the territory. As a precedent, he noted that in his time new
nations were winning their independence as 'Colonies secede from the
mother country; vassals fall away from their overlord; newly opened
territories are immediately formed into free states.' But the foundation
of a state, he argued, was not territory, but the nation: 'People are the
personal, land the impersonal groundwork of a state, and the personal
foundation is the more important of the two.' It was his intention to
build that foundation.

With the commencement of the settlement enterprise, the Society of Jews would establish a council of legal experts, which would
be tasked with writing a constitution for the new society. Herzl's
political experience is evident in the sections of *The Jewish State*
that address the constitution, which draw on his observation of the
French National Assembly and of the unintended and problematic
consequences of the expansion of suffrage in Austria and Vienna in
particular.

'A good constitution should be of moderately elastic nature,' he
wrote. Citing Montesquieu to support him, he argued that mixed sys-
tems like 'a democratic monarchy and an aristocratic republic are the
finest forms of a state.' Herzl clearly preferred the former, in which,
as he saw it, the monarch serves as a check on the excesses of democracy. His examples were Britain and Austria-Hungary. But no Jewish
monarchy was possible because of the long hiatus in Jewish statehood

and the lack of a 'historically famous family' to assume the throne. He thus suggested that the Jewish polity should constitute itself as an aristocratic republic.

All the citizens of the Jewish state would be equal before the law: 'No member of the Jewish state will be oppressed.' Any inhabitant would have an equal opportunity to rise to the top. Yet Herzl objected to unrestrained democracy, just as Montesquieu and the American Founding Fathers did. It is somewhat embarrassing to read him lauding the aristocratic constitution of Venice, which he romanticized to a fault, but he made a point of stressing that the Jewish state would not repeat Venice's errors (although he did not say what they were) because 'we are a modern nation.' He referred repeatedly to the corruption, demagoguery, and governmental paralysis that populism produced in Paris and Vienna. He was clearly thinking of France's dysfunctional Third Republic and Luëger's electoral victory in Vienna, along with the Bonapartist penchant for circumventing elected democratic bodies by the use of plebiscites:

> A democracy without monarchial restraint . . . tends to lead to vacuous discussions in parliaments, and produces that objectionable class of men – professional politicians. At present, nations are not fit for unlimited democracy, and will become less and less fit for it in the future. For a pure democracy presupposes a predominance of simple customs, and our customs daily become more complex with the growth of commerce and increase of culture. 'Le resort d'une démocratie est la vertu,' said the wise Montesquieu. And where is this virtue, that is to say, this political virtue, to be found? I do not believe in our political virtue; firstly, because we are no better than the rest of modern humanity . . . I also hold a settling of questions by referendum to be an unsatisfactory procedure, because there are no simple political questions which can be answered merely by Yes and No. The masses are also more prone even than parliaments to be led astray by false opinions and to be swayed by loud-mouthed demagogues. It is impossible to formulate a wise internal or external policy in a popular assembly.

ITT ÁLLT AZ A HÁZ
MELYBEN

HERZL TIVADAR
1860 - 1904
A ZSIDÓ ÁLLAM MEGÁLMODÓJA
SZÜLETETT
✡
כאן עמד בית הולדתו של
תיאודור הרצל
✡

HERE WAS THE HOUSE
WHERE

THEODORE HERZL
WAS BORN

Plaque on the site of the house in Budapest where Herzl was born.

Herzl as a young man.

ЕВРЕЙСКА ДЪРЖАВА.

ОПИТЪ

ЗА МОДЕРНО РАЗРѢШЕНИЕ НА ЕВРЕЙСКИЙ ВѢПРОСЪ

ОТЪ

ТЕОДОРЪ ХЕРЦЛЪ

ДОКТОРЪ НА ПРАВОТО.

ПРѢВЕДЕ ОТЪ НѢМСКИ: ДРУЖЕСТВОТО „ЦИОНЪ" ВЪ СОФИЯ.

СОФИЯ
ПЕЧАТНИЦА „ЛИБЕРАЛНИЙ КЛУБЪ"
1896.

ד"ר תיאודור הירצל

מדינת היהודים

(Der Iudenstaat)

דרך חדשה בפתרון שאלת היהודים.

מתרגם ברשיון מיוחד מאת המחבר ע"י

מיכל בערקאוויטש.

הוצאת "תושיה".

ווארשא. תרנ"ו.

בדפוס האלטער ואייזענשטאדט, נאלעוקי 7.

МЕДИНАТЪ ГАІЕГУДИМЪ
т. е. *Еврейскій штатъ*
Соч. Д-ра **Т. Герцля**
Пер. М. Берковича
Изданіе „ТУШІЯ"
ВАРШАВА.
Тип. М. И. Гальтера и М. Айзенштадта, Налевки 7.
1896

ЕВРЕЙСКОЕ ГОСУДАРСТВО

ОПЫТЪ

СОВРЕМЕННАГО РѢШЕНІЯ ЕВРЕЙСКАГО ВОПРОСА

ТЕОДОРА ГЕРЦЛЯ.

ДОКТОРА ПРАВЪ.

(Переводъ съ нѣмецкаго).

С.-ПЕТЕРБУРГЪ.
Типографія М. Стасюлевича, Вас. Остр., 5 лин., 28.
1896

L'État Juif

ESSAI D'UNE SOLUTION DE LA QUESTION JUIVE

Par Théodore HERZL.

Docteur en Droit.

(Extrait de la Nouvelle Revue Internationale)

PARIS
LIBRAIRIE DE *LA NOUVELLE REVUE INTERNATIONALE*
23, BOULEVARD POISSONNIÈRE, 23

A JEWISH STATE

AN ATTEMPT AT A MODERN, SOLUTION
OF THE JEWISH QUESTION

BY

THEODOR HERZL, LL.D.

TRANSLATED INTO ENGLISH BY
SYLVIE D'AVIGDOR

LONDON
DAVID NUTT, 270-271, STRAND
1896
ONE SHILLING

DER

JUDENSTAAT.

VERSUCH

EINER

MODERNEN LÖSUNG DER JUDENFRAGE

VON

THEODOR HERZL
DOCTOR DER RECHTE.

LEIPZIG und WIEN 1896.
M. BREITENSTEIN'S VERLAGS-BUCHHANDLUNG
WIEN, IX., WÄHRINGERSTRASSE 5.

דער

יודענשטאאט

פֿערזוך

אינער

מאדערנען לאזונג דער יודענפֿראגע

פֿאן

טהעאדאר הערצל
ראקטאר דער רעכטע.

קאלאמעא ה'תרנ"ז
פֿערלאג: רעדאקציאן דעם "העם" (דאס פֿאלק).
קאלאמעא גאליציען.

STATUL
EVREILOR.

ÎNCERCAREA

UNEI

DESLEGĂRI MODERNE A CHESTIUNEI EVREESCI

DE

THEODOR HERZL
DOCTOR IN DREPT

Traducere din germană de .˙.

— BOTOŞANI —
EDITURA LIBRĂRIEI GOLDSLEGER & Comp.
1896.

Title pages of the first editions of *The Jewish State* in its many translations.

Herzl and the Zionist
delegation en route to
Palestine, 1898.

Herzl and the Zionist
delegation in Jerusalem,
about to meet Kaiser
Wilhelm II.

Kaiser Wilhelm II riding with the German Foreign Minister Bernhard von Bülow in Jerusalem.

Herzl at the rostrum of the Second Zionist Congress in Basel.

Left Joseph Chamberlain, British Colonial Secretary; *centre* Vyacheslav von Plehve, Russian Interior Minister; *below left* Pope Pius X; *below right* Italian King Victor Emmanuel III.

Above Herzl's funeral in Vienna;
left Herzl Street, Tel Aviv, c.1914;
below The Haganah ship *Theodor Herzl*
with illegal immigrants, mostly
Holocaust survivors, in Haifa harbour,
1947. It was guarded by British soldiers
before its passengers were deported
to internment camps in Cyprus.

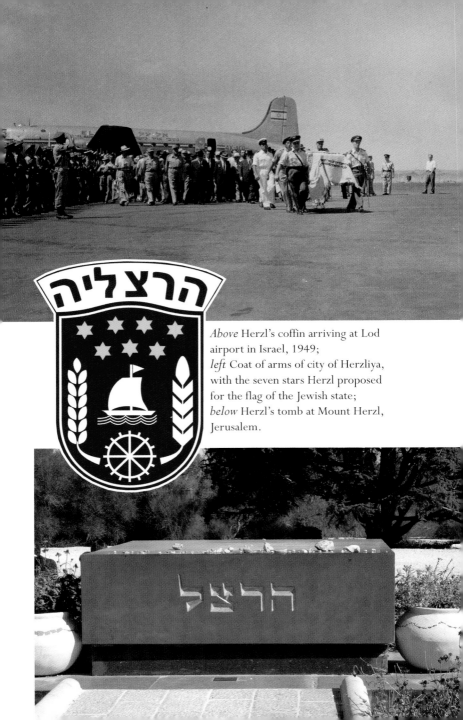

Above Herzl's coffin arriving at Lod airport in Israel, 1949;
left Coat of arms of city of Herzliya, with the seven stars Herzl proposed for the flag of the Jewish state;
below Herzl's tomb at Mount Herzl, Jerusalem.

Herzl's dislike of professional politicians stayed with him for the rest of his life and would be on display in *Altneuland*. Yet, despite his aversion to a certain type of Jewish functionary that he had to deal with, he would in the end advocate the organization of the Zionist movement and its institutions in the form of a parliamentary democracy. These institutions would later serve as the foundation for the State of Israel and its governing bodies, for better and for worse.

In the final part of *The Jewish State*, Herzl offers a brief survey of some other aspects of the future state. Since this section contains some of the book's best-known passages, they are worth examining in some detail:

Language: Herzl did not think it problematic that the Jews who would settle in the new land would not share a common language. Hebrew no longer served that role, he noted: 'We cannot converse with one another in Hebrew. Who among us has a sufficient acquaintance with Hebrew to ask for a railway ticket in that language?' His skepticism about whether Hebrew could serve as the language of the Jewish state was a result of his lack of acquaintance with the revival of Hebrew as a language of literature and thought that began during the *Haskalah*. Hebrew, he thought, could serve only as a language of prayer. But he would later moderate this view to some extent. In *The Jewish State* he maintained that each group of Jews would continue to speak the language it brought with it, and offered Switzerland as an example of a multi-lingual society. In the end, 'the language which proves itself to be of the greatest utility for general intercourse will be adopted without compulsion as our national tongue.' Herzl did not think much of Yiddish, either, saying that 'we shall give up using those miserable stunted jargons, those ghetto languages . . .' He would later soften his position on this language as well, as he gained a better acquaintance with the Jews of Eastern Europe through his political activity. Max Nordau, who would be Herzl's partner in the Zionist movement, would persuade him at a very early stage to have *The Jewish State* translated into Hebrew and Yiddish, 'for the Russians,' as he said. On the other hand, Herzl's discussion of this issue displays just how deeply he felt rejected by that same European culture of which he felt so much part. 'Every man can preserve the language in which his thoughts are at home, . . .' Herzl said. 'We shall remain in the new country what we now are here, and we shall never cease to cherish with sadness the memory of the native lands out of which we have been driven.'*

The status of religion and rabbis: Herzl valued religion as an important and vital component of Jewish identity and, as related above, sought to obtain rabbinic support for his political program. However, he asserted without hesitation that the Jewish state would not be a theocracy. His complex attitude toward religion, not easily categorized, would later become a signal trait of the Zionist movement as a whole. Militant believers and militant non-believers would both have trouble citing Herzl in their support (not that this stopped them – they merely quoted Herzl selectively and, at times, distorted his words):

> Faith unites us; science gives us freedom. We shall therefore prevent any theocratic tendencies from coming to the fore on the part of our clerics. We shall keep them within the confines of their synagogues in the same way that we shall keep our professional army within the confines of its barracks. Army and clergy shall receive honors as high as their valuable functions deserve. But they must not interfere in the matters of state which confer distinction on them, otherwise they will cause internal and external difficulties.

There would be no institutional separation between religion and state because the Jewish religion would enjoy a leading role. Despite this, Herzl maintained that members of all other national and religious communities would enjoy full civic equality:

> Every man will be as free and undisturbed in his faith or his disbelief as he is in his nationality. And if it should occur that men of

* This pain, mixed with anger, simmers under one of the early drafts of *The Jewish State* to be found in Herzl's diary. 'Each will continue to speak his language. I am a German Jew from Hungary and I cannot be anything other than a German. Today no one recognizes me as a German. That will come, after we are already there, so each person needs to preserve the nationality he gained . . . We see from Switzerland that a federated state of different nations can endure.' This personal reference is absent from the published version, which also offers a more considered position on linguistic identity.

other creeds and different nationalities come to live among us, we should accord them honorable protection and equality before the law. We learned toleration in Europe. This is not said sarcastically.

Army: In retrospect, the two sentences that Herzl devoted to military matters look naïve, if not ludicrous. Herzl clearly did not foresee Arab opposition to large-scale Jewish settlement in Palestine, both because the Ottoman Empire ruled the land and because no active Arab national movement yet existed there. Since Herzl believed that a Jewish commonwealth in Palestine would be established by international agreement and guaranteed by the great powers, his position was not as absurd as it may seem today: 'The Jewish state is conceived as a neutral one. It will therefore require only a professional army, equipped, of course, with every requisite of modern warfare, to preserve order internally and externally.'

In the final section of *The Jewish State*, Herzl took up this subject from a different angle – in reference to the political and psychological theories that were gaining popularity in his generation. According to these doctrines, human beings needed enemies to provoke them into action, both as individuals and collectives. Some might think, Herzl maintained, that 'the Jews, once settled in their own state, would probably have no more enemies.' This could lead to a situation in which, because they would be 'well-off and serene, and since prosperity enfeebles and causes decline, they might soon disappear altogether.' Herzl's response was that the Jews would always have enemies. He had no illusion that the creation of a Jewish state would end anti-Semitism, although it would reduce it by eliminating the constant friction between Jews and non-Jews. But, he wrote:

> I think the Jews will always have sufficient enemies, just as every other nation has. But once settled in their own land, it will no longer be possible for them to scatter all over the world. The Diaspora cannot take place again, unless the civilization of the whole earth were to collapse; and such a consummation could be feared by none but foolish men. Our present civilization possesses weapons powerful enough for its self-defense.

His characteristic cultural pessimism led Herzl to deduce that modern Jew-hatred could not be ended in Europe, but he nevertheless believed that modern culture was immune to catastrophes and atrocities. Yet he knew that the Jews need never worry that they would lack an 'enemy' to spur them into social solidarity – the war against anti-Semitism would give them plenty to fight against, even after the attainment of Jewish sovereignty.

Flag: Repeating what he had written in his diary, Herzl asserted:

> We have no flag, but we need one. If we wish to lead many people, we must raise a symbol above their heads. I would suggest a white flag with seven golden stars. The white field symbolizes our pure new life; the stars are the seven golden hours of our work day. For we shall march into the Promised Land under the sign of labor.

Herzl noted that all these ideas were simply the initial sketches of transitional legislation. Until the completion of a comprehensive modern legal code, which should quickly be promulgated, all immigrants would be judged in accordance with the laws of their countries of origin. The new code needed to be exemplary, 'imbued with all the just social claims of the present day.' In parallel, the Jewish state would sign extradition agreements with all other countries, and immigrants would be required to fulfill all their obligations to their countries of origin before their departure. The Jewish state would not turn into an asylum for Jewish criminals – that is not what Jewish solidarity means.

There is much more in the booklet. It is less than a hundred pages long but comprehensive in the number of issues it addresses. It is obvious that Herzl's preliminary work and the many drafts he produced in Paris helped him put together such a broad document. It combines historical analysis that challenges much conventional wisdom, a call to action, precise planning of large-scale immigration and settlement, and the basic outlines of the new state, all packaged together with gripping slogans that could captivate different parts of the public. Undoubtedly these catchphrases were intended for those who would have trouble digesting the book's dry policy and legal arguments. Some examples: 'The Maccabeans will rise again!'; 'The Jewish state is crucial for the world; it will therefore be created!'; 'Those Jews who wish it will have their state!' But these were just a small part of a much more serious work. It was a book without precedent in Jewish history, a modest few pages that spurred many people to action.

Yet it would be wrong to exaggerate the impact of *The Jewish State*. Most of Europe's Jews did not hear about Herzl's book. Many of those who heard of it or read it opposed the political program it laid out. Still, many thousands were deeply impressed and galvanized. The translations that quickly appeared spread Herzl's message far and wide, as did the many articles about *The Jewish State* that appeared in the Jewish press.

It should be kept in mind that Herzl himself had no idea what the next step would be. A close reader of *The Jewish State* will find not even an intimation of how to get from the current state of affairs to the detailed outcomes that Herzl laid out. This seemed to belie Herzl's claim that his book was not a utopia but a plan of action. Yet Herzl thought on his feet – he learned by trial and error. It was only during his composition of *The Jewish State* that he first learned, for example, about Leo Pinsker's 1882 proto-Zionist pamphlet *Auto-Emancipation*. This was characteristic of the way he worked, and the way his personality and his views developed. Herzl heard of Pinsker in September 1895, from one of the dozens of people he consulted with at the time. A leader of the Alliance Israélite Universelle told him that 'in Russia I would find many adherents. In Odessa, for example, there had lived a man named Pinsger [sic] who had fought for the same cause, namely, the regaining of a Jewish homeland. Pinsger is already dead. His writings are said to be worthwhile. Shall read them as soon as I have time.'

Only half a year later, on February 10, four days before the publication of *The Jewish State*, did Herzl finally get around to reading Pinsker's manifesto. He wrote in his diary:

Read today the book *Auto-Emancipation* . . . An astonishing correspondence in the critical part, a great similarity in the constructive one. A pity that I did not read this work before my own book was printed. On the other hand, it is a good thing that I didn't know of it – perhaps I would have abandoned my own undertaking.

Presumably, this display of modesty was an attempt to paper over his unfamiliarity with earlier writers on his subject and Pinsker in particular. It hardly seems likely that Herzl would have been deterred from writing *The Jewish State* had he known of Pinsker's work.

His acquaintanceship with Hovevei Zion followed a similar trajectory. One of the sketches of his plan that he jotted down in June 1895 includes a section under the heading 'Negotiations with Zion.' Most probably he meant Hovevei Zion or one of the various organizations founded to support that organization's settlement movement. He made his first explicit reference to Hovevei Zion in a diary entry reporting his journey to England in November 1895, when he met with a number of people whose support he sought. Of one of these, Colonel Albert Edward Goldsmid, he wrote: 'He showed me the flag of the Howe we Zion.' The next day he met the local secretary of Hovevei Zion in Cardiff and recorded the movement's name as 'Chowe we Zion.' He obviously had no idea what the name meant and assumed that the final syllable of 'Hovevei' (which means 'lovers of' or 'devotees of') was the Hebrew prefix 've,' which means 'and.'

Yet there is something telling about his ignorance. It testifies to the process of self-education that in the end turned Herzl into a political leader. He certainly wanted to be a leader – his diaries are full of self-aggrandizing, sometimes even megalomaniacal comments. But, lacking political experience and organizational and institutional tools, he grew into a leader through his own activity, through the huge energies he put into it, through persistence and determination. He carefully recorded his disappointments and his learning curve in his diary, and these entries track the process of his growth.

Some of the immediate reactions to the publication of *The Jewish State* demonstrate how rapidly developments followed one after the other:

- On February 20, 1896, a week after publication, Herzl spoke, for the first time, before the oldest of the Jewish student fraternities in Vienna, Kadima, where he was enthusiastically received.

- On February 23 he accepted Sylvie d'Avigdor's suggestion that she translate his book into English.

- On February 26 a favorable review of *The Jewish State* appeared in Berlin's Orthodox Jewish newspaper (but three days later one of Vienna's best-known Jewish philosophers, Theodor Gomperz, published a review rejecting Herzl's ideas categorically).

- On March 3, a leader of Sofia's Jewish community who had studied in Vienna and had been among the founders of Kadima wrote to Herzl to congratulate him on his 'political essay.' He told Herzl that he was waiting in suspense for Herzl to convene a conference of 'all the Zionists from all lands in order to organize the apparatus of liberation.'

- On March 7 the editor of the Jewish newspaper in Kolomea, Galicia, notified Herzl that he would put his newspaper at Herzl's disposal. He asked for permission to publish *The Jewish State* 'in Hebrew letters.'

- On March 9, Herzl's correspondent in Sofia notified him that he would be lecturing on *The Jewish State* at a large public assembly to be held before the Passover holiday.

- On March 11, Herzl was visited by the Reverend William Henry Hechler, chaplain of the British Embassy in Vienna. The two became friends and Hechler was instrumental in gaining Herzl access to a number of German noblemen and, ultimately, to the German Emperor.

- On March 14, the Hovevei Zion chapter in Vienna called on Herzl to take action to bring his plan to fruition.

- On March 16, the Zion organization in Sofia resolved to support Herzl.

- On March 28, Herzl took part in a Passover Seder with the Viennese Jewish fraternity Unitas, which called on its members to support his program.

- On March 29, an assembly of Jewish students and young people in Lemberg, Galicia's capital, declared its adherence to the principles laid out in *The Jewish State* and called on Herzl to head an organization to carry out his program.

- On April 5, members of Hovevei Zion in Paris reported to Herzl that their organization had resolved, at a general meeting, to support Herzl.
- On April 9, a Jewish student activist in Paris proposed to translate *The Jewish State* into French.
- On April 22–24, Herzl visited Karlsruhe, the capital of the Grand Duchy of Baden, where he met, thanks to Hechler's mediation, with its hereditary ruler, Grand Duke Friedrich I. The latter was the first European ruler to meet Herzl and he would be instrumental in paving Herzl's way into the court of his nephew, Kaiser Wilhelm.
- In early May, Herzl commenced correspondence with a leader of Eastern European Orthodox Jewry, the Hasid Aharon Marcus of Podgórze, near Krakow.
- On May 15, Herzl held his first meeting with the Papal Nuncio in Vienna.
- On May 20, the head of the Jewish National Society in Cologne made contact with Herzl.
- At the end of May, Herzl made first contact with the Hovevei Zion movement in Russia. Menachem Ussishkin, who chaired the movement's Moscow Branch, visited Herzl in Vienna.
- From June 15 to 30, Herzl made his first visit to Constantinople. He traveled in the company of Philipp Michael Nevlinksy, a journalist and Polish aristocrat who had earlier worked for the Foreign Ministry of Austria-Hungary and knew Sultan Abdul Hamid II. Nothing practical resulted from the visit, but Herzl was received by the Secretary of the Ottoman Foreign Ministry, the Sultan's Secretary, and in the end was received by the Grand Vizier as well.

*   *   *

This feverish level of activity would continue – all while Herzl continued to work full time as an editor at the *Neue Freie Presse*. Before long he was not just a run-of-the-mill journalist who had written a book called *The Jewish State* but had become a public personage, developing diplomatic contacts – without any organization behind him and without any mandate to do so. But his close circle of acquaintances and supporters, and his wide and growing network of correspondents, began to take on the nature of a political movement. He continued to travel – to London, Paris, Karlsbad (where he met Ferdinand, Prince of Bulgaria) and continued, from Vienna, to broaden his network of connections with both Jews and non-Jews. These included the Turkish Ambassador and members of the Jewish community of Jerusalem, such as the educator David Yellin, the writer and administrator Yehiel Michael Pines, and the historian and educator Zeev Yavetz.

Thus came into being, gradually and without prior planning, the human and organizational fabric that would enable Herzl to convene, on March 7, 1897 in the Hovevei Zion offices in Vienna, a 'preliminary committee' to lay the groundwork for a convention of Zionists from all over Europe. The participants included not only Herzl and his associates from Vienna but also representatives from Berlin, Breslau, Katowice, Tarnów in Galicia, and elsewhere. They elected an organizing committee to make preparations for an all-Zionist congress. At the beginning of May of that year the first rallies in support of Herzl's movement were held in New York, and on May 12 Herzl reached the conclusion that his movement needed a newspaper of its own, leading to the establishment of the weekly *Die Welt*.

After wrestling with no few doubts, and in the face of warnings from some of his supporters not to hold a public convention, Herzl decided to go ahead. Invitations were sent out from Vienna to Jewish individuals and organizations, who were asked to attend an event to be held on 'the first, second, and third of Elul [the Hebrew month that falls at the end of the summer]' in Basel, Switzerland. Herzl signed himself as 'chairman of the preparatory committee for the Zionist Congress.' The invitation, sent out in German and Hebrew, contained the following language:

> There our brethren from all over the world will tell us about their circumstances and developments, there it will become clear what the Zionist movement demands from its supporters, there our activity – which has been splintered and divided – will be united. There

we shall witness an Ingathering of the Exiles, which will unite all forces for one great and tremendous effort.

The Congress aims at an immediate and possible end. Any other reports about it are empty air. All activities of the Congress will be totally public. Its debates and decisions will not contravene the laws of any country or our civic duties. We would like especially to guarantee that all acts of the meeting will be acceptable to Hovevei Zion in Russia and to that country's supreme government.

Friends and enemies alike await the Congress, and we have therefore to prove to all that our wishes are clear and our capacity great. If the Congress does not fulfil its goals, our movement will suffer a setback that will last for a long time. All depends on massive participation of our brethren from Russia, where most of our people reside. We hope that you will recognize your duty and come to our convention. At the meeting, it will be possible to speak in Hebrew. In Basel there is a kosher hotel.

The prescient reader will note Herzl's acknowledgement of the complex political circumstances in which he operated. In his invitation, he sought to assuage the fears of Russian sympathizers that the Congress might be viewed by the authorities in their country as subversive and revolutionary activity. He also took into account the different views of the organizers themselves. This was the establishment of a Jewish public space, to be anchored in institutional structures. He was quite conscious of this, when, in a letter dated March 26, 1897, he referred to the Congress, which had yet to meet, as a 'National Assembly.' That may have been an exaggeration for public relations and ideological purposes – the Congress obviously could not speak on behalf of the entire Jewish people, or even as the voice of most of it. But there had not been an institution like it since the destruction of the Jewish polity eighteen centuries earlier.

CHAPTER SIX

THE CONSTITUENT ASSEMBLY: THE BASEL CONGRESS

IN SUMMING UP the First Zionist Congress, which convened in Basel in August 1897, Herzl recorded what came to be an iconic passage. After the establishment of the State of Israel in 1948, it took on the aura of a prophecy: 'Were I to sum up the Basel Congress in a word – which I shall be very careful not to do publicly – it would be this: At Basel I founded the Jewish state. If I said this out loud today, I would be answered by universal laughter. Perhaps in five years, and certainly in fifty, everyone will admit it.'

Herzl rightly realized that, at the time, any such declaration would sound ridiculous. After all, he was speaking of a fairly modest event, involving fewer than 200 delegates, only 69 of whom represented organizations that could in some way be called Zionist. The rest were people he had invited personally who spoke for no one but themselves. But Herzl followed his prediction with an analysis that justified his claims regarding the transformative nature of the gathering held in the concert hall of Basel's civic center, the Casino. Few readers have paid much attention to the passage in his diary that followed his famous declaration, but it displays far more profound historical and political insight than the memorable and grandiose statement that preceded it:

The foundation of a state lies in the will of the people for a state . . . Territory is only the material basis; the state, even when it possesses territory, is always something abstract . . . It was at Basel that

I created this abstract entity which, as such, is invisible to the vast majority of people. And with minimal means, I gradually worked the people into the mood for a state and made them feel that they were its National Assembly.

The reference to a National Assembly clearly alludes to the legacy of the French Revolution: it deliberately echoes the words of Abbé Sieyès, one of the leaders of the French National Assembly of 1789, who posed the rhetorical question 'What is the Third Estate?' in reference to the class that was the prime mover of the Revolution. His ringing response had been: 'It is nothing – but its goal is to be everything.' Herzl consciously paraphrased the Abbé when he wrote: 'Today the Presidium of the Zionist Congress is nothing; we still have to establish everything.'

This creation of a Jewish public space for the first time in thousands of years was indeed the Congress's signal achievement. It is no coincidence that it was Herzl who assumed this task. The idea itself was not new – proto-Zionist and Zionist schemes had been brought up by some members of the Eastern European Jewish intelligentsia before he came along, and Jewish settlements had already been founded in Palestine. But Herzl was the first person to understand that the Zionist goal could not be achieved without the establishment of a recognized institutional authority that could claim to speak publicly on behalf of the Jewish people. What was needed were not only Jewish charitable organizations providing assistance to individual immigrants, nor half-clandestine consultations, nor authors whose readership consisted primarily of those who already supported the positions they voiced. In the modern world, new states were founded only when they won the ideological, political, and diplomatic support of the world powers and the public. It was thus necessary to act overtly, openly, and demonstratively, and to back up statements of purpose with the establishment of institutions and organizations that could act in the public arena. The claim of these bodies to speak for the entire Jewish people might remain open to challenge, but without such institutions the national movement would be unable to achieve its goals.

In this sense it was Herzl's biography, so different from that of the founders of Hovevei Zion, that enabled him to make this breakthrough. Herzl's acquaintance as reporter and editor with the world of politics had also made him a stickler for detail, such as his insistence that the delegates wear formal dress to the Congress's opening session. The point was to imbue the event with a quasi-parliamentary milieu. As Herzl said, 'And now it became clear why I had to spend four years going to the Palais Bourbon [the seat of the French National Assembly] . . . At critical moments I learned to coin *mots présidentiels* [presidential phrases].' No Zionist writer or activist before Herzl had understood this, nor did they have the experience that would have led them to such an insight. As often happens in history, a public need met up with an individual suited to meet that need. Herzl was, in Hegel's terms, a 'world-historical individual.'

Which does not mean that it was easy. The months between the decision to convene the Congress and his prophetic words at its conclusion were fraught with obstacles and difficulties. For a long time it was not even clear whether the Congress would take place at all. During these months Herzl, a man lacking in political experience and without knowledge of the intricacies of Jewish affairs, learned an important lesson; there may have been no Jewish polity, but there was a surfeit of internal Jewish politics. He found himself encountering obstacles placed in his way not only by the opponents of the Zionist idea but also by his most enthusiastic supporters. His allies intrigued, jockeyed for honors, and wielded their huge egos. Herzl's diary entries from this period are full of grumbles, sometimes bitter and angry remonstrances, against all this maneuvering. The blunt language in his diary testifies to what extent he had to hold himself back from saying in public, and during the Congress sessions, what he really thought of some of the people around him. Herzl the journalist and playwright gradually, and not without a lot of heartbreak, metamorphosed from a visionary into a politician.

The first major issue was the site for the Congress. Herzl preferred Switzerland from the start, Zurich specifically, so as to underline the Congress's neutrality with regard to European power politics. But the Russian representatives on the Preparatory Committee balked at holding the conference in Switzerland because that country served as a refuge for Russian radical revolutionaries. They feared that such a venue would make the Zionist gathering look like that of a subversive movement. Herzl reluctantly agreed to Munich, a center of German culture in a convenient location, well served by trains from Eastern Europe, where most of the delegates would be coming from. But the Jewish community in Munich objected. It feared that the Congress, promoting an idea that there was a Jewish people that sought its own homeland, would cast doubt on the claim of those German Jews who saw themselves as 'Germans of the Mosaic faith.' The objection of the Munich Jewish community compelled the planners to relocate the Congress (just two months before it was to convene) back to Switzerland. But out of consideration to the Russian delegates, the city would not be Zurich, but, rather, Basel.*

Herzl thus reverted to his original idea, but took political advantage of the switch. He publicized the exchange of letters between the Preparatory Committee and the Munich community in *Die Welt*. Before doing so, however, he inquired of a non-Jewish Bavarian acquaintance, Prince von Wrede, whether the Bavarian government would object to having the Zionist Congress in its capital. When it turned out that the Bavarian government would not oppose this, Herzl lashed out against the 'pitiful patriotic protests of the Munich community leaders.' He knew that the publication of the objections of Munich's Jewish leadership would be great publicity for the Congress. Secure in the knowledge that the Bavarian government had no objections, Herzl wrote in *Die Welt* that he could proceed with the Congress in Munich without the community's consent, but that, so as not to embarrass it and create further division among the Jews, he had decided to move it. *Die Welt* also published a letter, signed by Herzl, from the Preparatory Committee to the leaders of the Munich Jewish community:

---

* The Munich Pact of 1938, in which Britain and France agreed to partition Czechoslovakia and hand part of its territory over to Hitler, has become the archetypical act of appeasement. It stained the very term 'Munich' in international politics and Jewish consciousness. Had it indeed been the venue of the First Zionist Congress, Herzl would have asserted 'In Munich I founded the Jewish state' and his famous statement would have had an entirely different ring to it today. Zionism owes thanks to the rabbis and community leaders of the Munich Jewish community for preventing what would have been a somewhat embarrassing historical irony.

We intended to convene the Congress in Munich because of the city's hospitable nature and its being a transportation hub. We did not expect a protest from the Jewish side, and non-Jews will not understand the nature of this objection.

It seems to us that those Israelites who do not see themselves as national Jews but as belonging to another nation should have left us to our national sentiments. We do not speak on their behalf, only for ourselves. We respect their nationalism – let them also respect ours, as is the usage among the nations.

Given that the Bavarian government had no problem with a Zionist Congress in Munich, Herzl charged that the Munich Jewish leadership was trying to outdo its own government in patriotism. That they did so may have been no surprise to Herzl, but it illustrated the major challenge he faced among the people he sought to lead. He knew very well that he had to maneuver among many interests in order to ensure that the Congress would not fail before it began. While he did not always succeed in defusing the mines in his path, he recorded them all in his diary. He did so in his signature way, with an understanding of the challenges confronting him and the movement he would give birth to in Basel. About a week before the opening of the Congress he wrote:

I will have to tread on eggs that nobody sees:
1. Egg of the *Neue Freie Presse*, which I must not compromise nor furnish them with a pretext for easing me out.
2. Egg of the Orthodox.
3. Egg of the Modernists.
4. Egg of Austrian patriotism.
5. Egg of Turkey, of the Sultan.
6. Egg of the Russian government, against which nothing unpleasant must be said, although the deplorable situation of the Russian Jews *will* have to be mentioned.
7. Egg of the Christian denominations, on account of the Holy Places.

To these he added:

Egg Edmond Rothschild
Egg Hovevei Zion in Russia
Egg of the colonists, whose help from Rothschild must not be
    compromised . . .
Egg of envy, egg of jealousy.

Herzl may not have exaggerated at all when, at the end of this list of constraints, he wrote that it would be 'a Herculean task' to safely navigate between the rocks of international politics and the hard places of the Jews themselves.

The *Neue Freie Presse* egg was a personal challenge for Herzl, his career, and his future. Despite their firm opposition to Herzl's private activism, the paper's publisher and editor-in-chief were indulgent, perhaps because they did not really take seriously what they saw as the obsession of their most famous writer. But when *Die Welt* was founded and Herzl assumed its helm, his employers viewed his editorship of another paper – with no little justification – as a conflict of interest. Furthermore, the anti-Semitic press trumpeted the connection, declaring that it proved that the *Neue Freie Presse* itself was a Zionist newspaper. The Vienna paper's management threatened to dismiss Herzl, and during the summer of 1897 it was not at all clear to Herzl, who had taken a leave of absence from the newspaper for the Congress, whether he would have a job to return to. In the end the owners decided to live with the contradiction in Herzl's status, on the one hand an editor of their newspaper and on the other not only the President of the Zionist Congress but also the editor of the Zionist newspaper. But Herzl's diary entries from the period show that he had no idea for several weeks what the outcome would be. He took a gamble, but at the same time it became ever more clear to him that he was being swept into activity that he would not be able to set aside even if it cost him his very respectable and prestigious position. Eventually, the two sides reached a tacit compromise. Herzl would not sign his full name to his articles and pieces in *Die Welt*. Instead, he would use the penname 'Benjamin Seff,' his Hebrew name (Binyamin Zeev), or remain anonymous. On the other hand, it was no secret that Herzl was the editor of the Zionist weekly.

The decision to found *Die Welt* was taken a few months before the Congress. It was a bold move but proved worthwhile for Herzl. It gave him and his circle a publication in which to present their program and to forge a heterogeneous group of activists from different countries into members of a coherent movement. Since the institutional framework of the movement had not yet been established, the founders had to obtain private funding for the newspaper. In the end, Herzl's father agreed to finance it. Its expenses were estimated at 11,000 gulden a year – quite a considerable sum. The name of the publication was carefully chosen. Herzl wrote: 'At night the name for the paper occurred to me: *Die Welt* [*The World*], with a *Mogen David* [Star of David], inside which a globe should be drawn with Palestine at its center.' It was a fitting symbol for Herzl's conviction that the Zionist cause belonged to the entire world, not just to the Jews.

Despite the small number of initial subscribers, the newspaper managed to make a place for itself, serving as the official organ of the Zionist movement until 1914. Because it was published in German, the cultural language of most Jewish intellectuals in Eastern Europe, it served not just as a Zionist mouthpiece but also became a source of information about Jewish communities throughout the world. On the eve of the Congress, the paper enabled Herzl to voice his opinions in print in a way he could not have done at the newspaper where he worked, the *Neue Freie Presse*. Material from *Die Welt* was cited and quoted in non-Jewish newspapers in many countries, thus further disseminating information about Zionism. As in other instances, Herzl's experience was important – he understood how vital the mass media was for the formation and consolidation of a political movement that did not have behind it strong social forces or generous funders.

The lead story of *Die Welt*'s first issue, which appeared on June 4, 1897, featured the outlines of Herzl's political manifesto. It was this manifesto that would serve as the basis for the resolutions passed by the First Zionist Congress – what would later be called the Basel Program. Herzl opened the article with the provocative and ironic statement: 'Our weekly is a Jewish rag [*ein Judenblatt*].' He used the derogatory term that anti-Semites and even the general public used to brand the large newspapers in Germany and Austria that were owned and edited by Jews, the *Neue Freie Presse* among them. Herzl added: 'We take this word, which some see as a sign of shame, and turn it into a badge of honor.'

This Jewish rag, as Herzl called it, was not to be a newspaper of wealthy Jews but, rather, 'of the poor, the downtrodden, the young – but also of all those who, while not destitute themselves, have found their way back to their people.' Its political goal was a universally agreed solution to the Jewish problem, in the form of 'a great and beautiful idea ... [T]o establish a homeland, guaranteed by international law [*eine völkerrechtliche gesicherte Heimstätte*] for those Jews who are unable, or unwilling, to be assimilated in their current place of residence.'

Herzl knew very well that the use of concepts taken explicitly from the political lexicon ('homeland,' 'international law') would engender apprehension about his movement's revolutionary nature and its political consequences, with the implications they had for the Ottoman Empire. Defending himself against such accusations, Herzl wrote that 'we count among us reactionaries as well as revolutionaries: we seek to achieve our goals through moderate and reasonable progress.'

In a separate article in that same first issue, Herzl went on preemptive defense against those who claimed that Zionism's political goals would hurt the Ottoman Empire. His strategy was to flatter, sometimes in an exaggerated way, the Sultan. Herzl wrote that he was aware that 'various complications in the Orient call for correcting the situation,' yet he quickly added: 'Nobody calls now for a partition of Turkey, as this would mean a world war.' The government in Constantinople needed financial support to stabilize its rule, he maintained, and in this the Jews could be of assistance. In correspondence that preceded the appearance of *Die Welt*, Herzl had tried to pass a communication through a contact in Constantinople to an important journalist there, Ahmed Midhat Effendi, a close associate of the Sultan. In his message, Herzl said that *Die Welt* would try to foster European sympathy for Turkish interests ('In this journal, we mean to give Turkey, so to speak,

an advance payment of our gratitude'). Herzl indeed kept this promise, writing in *Die Welt*:

> Sultan Abdul Hamid, the reigning monarch of Turkey, is a gracious
> ruler, sympathetic to every kind of human suffering. Those who
> know him realize that this Caliph, who is hated by many, is aware of
> the hardships of many of his subjects, and who out of his patriarchal
> disposition would like to be a merciful father to them all.

This flattery fit in with another move Herzl made in that summer of
1897, arising from the coincidence of the convening of the Congress
and the outbreak of a Turkish-Greek war. The war broke out on April
17, while preparations for the Congress were under way, having been
set off by a Greek revolt on Crete, which was still under Turkish rule.
The war was over in a couple of weeks with the defeat of the Greeks.
Herzl viewed this coincidence as a historic opportunity. His intellectual and cultural sympathies clearly lay with the Greeks, who were
seeking to move onto the next stage of their long war of liberation;
but the political and diplomatic circumstances offered an opportunity
for a Zionist pro-Turkish humanitarian gesture. The *Neue Freie Presse*
strongly opposed the continuation of Turkish rule of Crete. While it
was not easy for Herzl, he indicated in his contacts with various Turkish personages that the Zionist position was different from that of the
Neue Freie Presse, and that this could be seen clearly in *Die Welt*.

On April 4, even before the war, which began with anti-Turkish
riots in Crete, Herzl wrote in his diary: 'Fresh unrest on Crete. This
news gives me a peculiar presentiment: that it may be the beginning of
the liquidation of Turkey.' When war broke out and a Turkish victory
seemed imminent, Herzl was not indifferent to the possible implications of the conflict and was attentive to the international context of
the Zionist enterprise. It was an awareness that few of his supporters
shared, as he confided to his diary:

> The Greco-Turkish war, which in the last few days has changed
> from a cold to a hot war, will in its further course probably affect
> our cause as well. How? If a peace congress for the settlement of

Greco-Turkish differences will be the outcome, we shall present our request to the congress of the powers. If Turkey is victorious, which is probable, and if she receives reparations in cash from Greece, which is even now financially unsettled – something improbable, to be sure – the Turks will have less need of Jewish aid.

The idea that the Zionist movement – which had yet to be founded! – might be represented at a peace conference to be held at the end of the war was yet another manifestation of Herzl's view that Zionist goals could be achieved only in a broad diplomatic framework. Some twenty years later, the thing that Herzl believed was about to happen before his eyes – the dissolution of the Ottoman Empire – did indeed occur at the peace conferences following the end of World War I.

In any case, during the agitated months leading up to the Zionist Congress, as Herzl battled the opponents of the Zionist idea and coped with the internal squabbles among his inner circle of activists, he tried to organize a humanitarian fund to aid Turkish war wounded. It was his opinion that such a gesture would signal to Constantinople that it had nothing to fear from the Zionist movement that was about to be established, and that such a move would even intimate to the Turkish authorities that the Zionists could be helpful financially. Herzl pursued this idea in a number of ways:

- On April 23 Herzl first proposed collecting donations for the Turkish war wounded. One of the leaders of the student fraternity Kadima sought to organize a group of Jewish medical students to serve as volunteers on the battlefield. Herzl wrote to the Turkish Ambassador in Vienna, Mahmoud Nadim Pasha, recommending that he accept the student initiative.

- On April 27, Herzl convened, at his home, a meeting to found the committee to raise funds for Turkey. He also invited representatives of the Sephardi Jewish community in Vienna, who were subjects of the Sultan, and it was decided that they would manage the project.

- On April 28, Herzl sent a detailed letter to Ambassador Nadim Pasha: 'I beg to congratulate Your Excellency on the splendid victories of Turkish arms.' He informed the Ambassador of the founding of the charitable committee in Vienna and of parallel committees in other cities. He was careful, however, to add that, for general political reasons – not Jewish ones – many Jews in Western countries would find it difficult to support Turkey. But he promised that, when peace prevailed, 'the sympathies of the Jews will be on a far grander scale.' In the meantime, he wished to express his support for Turkey and to hope that his position would be conveyed to the highest authorities in Constantinople.

- On May 12, Herzl recorded in his diary that a cease-fire seemed imminent, and 'This sends our collection for the wounded soldiers down the drain.'
- On May 24, Herzl notified one of his correspondents in Constantinople that the Vienna Rothschilds had contributed 500 gulden to the fund.
- On May 27 he received from the Chief Rabbi of France, Zadok Kahan, a check for 1,000 francs, which he passed on to Ambassador Nadim Pasha.
- On May 30 it turned out that the managers of the fund in Vienna, members of the city's Sephardi community, had managed to collect only 800 gulden in contributions, and that the medical students who had offered their services as volunteers did not have funds for their trip. Herzl decided to pass on to them the donated funds to enable them to travel to Turkey.

In the end, the effort was not a great success, but Herzl had gotten his message across to the Turks in several ways. He continued to court his Turkish contacts as preparations for the Congress progressed. In letters to officials in Constantinople he reiterated that 'the immigrant Jews in Palestine would become the subjects of His Majesty the Sultan.' He added, however, that this was 'on condition of their right to self-defense being absolutely guaranteed.' Land purchases, he stipulated, 'would be made entirely without constraint: Nobody will be dispossessed. Ownership is a private right that cannot be violated. The Sultan's private domains could be paid for in cash according to their value, if he desires to sell.'

Herzl also tried, via *Die Welt*, to mollify Turkish fears that the future Zionist movement would be an 'international association.' Such fears, he wrote, grew out of prejudices about the role of Jews, according to which the aim of Zionism was the 'establishment of a global organization which will enslave the whole world under Jewish influence.' Herzl rejected this charge with 'revulsion' and responded to the fear that the movement would be an illegal association. Given the increasing attacks by anarchists on European statesmen, most countries on the continent had passed laws against 'international associations,' and Vienna had initially even prohibited the first Zionist meeting planned to be held in the city. In *Die Welt*, Herzl went to great lengths to explain that the Congress did not intend to establish such an organization in the sense that Zionists would be involved in the internal affairs of 'our lands of birth.' Rather, 'the Congress is international only to the degree that the Jewish question is international.' Here Herzl was parsing sentences, making semantic distinctions that in part were not reasonable. But they underlined what strident and sweeping accusations were being made about the very holding of the Zionist Congress and the establishment of an international Jewish organization in its wake.

In addition, Herzl made a point of stressing in *Die Welt* that Jews were not the only supporters of his ideas. In an article headlined 'Toward the Zionist Congress in Basel,' which appeared in the issue of August 26, 1897, just before the Congress began, he wrote:

> The Zionist movement has already drawn the attention of serious statesmen everywhere. Every day brings us reports about the attention of important daily newspapers and journals. The best way to describe this would be to say that the Jewish Question has become the Question of Zion.

The exaggeration, for journalistic and public relations purposes, is clear. But the fact is that Herzl had, in the months leading up to the Congress, managed to gain unprecedented support from a variety of political quarters. British and American newspapers reported, in February 1898, a *Die Welt* interview with Prince Dimitrie Sturdza, a former Prime Minister of Romania, who said:

I consider Dr. Herzl's idea to be excellent; in fact I may say the one and valuable way of solving the Jewish question. (It must be borne in mind that Romania has an enormous Jewish population.) The Jews are the one people who, living in foreign countries, do not assimilate with the inhabitants as others do.

It was clear that these sentiments did not grow out of love for the Jews. The Prince had other motives. But, as Herzl would discover as he went on, support for Zionism could come not only from philo-Semites and humanists, but also from people who had more questionable motives. This was an irony that would accompany the Zionist movement all along its way.

At the same time, during the summer of 1897, Herzl engaged in contacts with one of the leaders of the Egyptian national movement, Mustafa Kamil, who was then in Vienna lobbying for the interests of the Egyptian people. Herzl told Kamil that he supported the Egyptian national movement. He did so both on principle and in consideration of Zionist interests and in the context of his realist approach. But he also showed that he was aware of how history could sometimes produce political ironies:

The Egyptian emissary, Mustafa Kamil, who has been here before, came to visit me again. He is on a tour to garner support for the affairs of the Egyptian people, who seek to get rid of the English yoke. This Oriental gentleman makes an excellent impression; he is educated, elegant, expresses himself eloquently. No doubt he will play a role in the politics of the Orient, and maybe we shall meet him there.

The descendant of our oppressors in *Mizraim* [Egypt] now groans about the sufferings of slavery, and his route takes him to me, the Jew, and it is to me that he looks for journalistic support.

I believe, although I did not say this to him, that it would be good for our affairs if the English would leave Egypt; they will then need an alternative road to India . . . then Palestine would be their salvation – a railroad from Jaffa to the Persian Gulf . . .

As happened to Herzl more than once, practical and realistic considerations suddenly drew him into fantasies. But he grew progressively more perceptive about the complexities of Middle Eastern geopolitics.

In the end, Herzl overcame the crises and put out the fires. The Zionist Congress opened in Basel on August 29. For the contacts and correspondence he conducted before the Congress he won compliments – if sometimes backhanded ones – that no doubt raised his spirits. One example came from one of the editors at the *Neue Freie Presse*, a man especially close to him even if he disagreed with Herzl regarding Zionism. 'You are driving the whole world crazy,' he told Herzl. 'A real Pied Piper of Hamelin.'

Herzl arrived in Basel on August 25, where he oversaw the final preparations from an office that the Basel municipality placed at the disposal of the Congress. He decided to change the venue of the Congress from a theater – which he felt was inappropriate – to the concert hall in the municipal civic center, the Casino. All the arrangements were improvised, disorganized, under tremendous time pressure. There was no lack of further ironies. Herzl did not approve of the move of the Congress to Basel until he had ascertained that there was a kosher restaurant in the city, so that rabbis and observant Jews would not be deterred from attending (as noted, Herzl made a point of noting the availability of the restaurant in the invitation to the Congress). He spent a great deal of time at the Braunschweig restaurant, although his opinion was that 'the food is pretty awful.' But *noblesse oblige*, and so does politics.

On the Saturday morning before the Congress's opening, Herzl attended Sabbath services at the Basel synagogue, 'out of respect for religion,' and made sure that his attendance was noted in the Jewish press. The head of the Basel Jewish community called him up to recite the benediction for the reading from the Torah, an honor Herzl had not prepared himself for and was certainly not familiar with. A friend who had accompanied him served as prompter, feeding him the words of the prayer. Herzl wrote in his diary that when 'I climbed the steps to the altar, I was more excited than on all the Congress days. The few words of the Hebrew blessing [*der hebräischen Broche*] caused me more excitement than my welcoming and closing address and the whole direction of the [Congress] proceedings.'

Herzl's famous pronouncement, 'At Basel I founded the Jewish state,' was but the high point of his comprehension of the momentous nature of the Congress. Here and there in his diary he asserted that, despite all the petty rivalries and intrigues, 'the Congress was sublime.' He described the Congress hall at the moment when he entered through a rear door, while Max Nordau sat in the presiding officer's seat. 'The long green table on the dais, with the elevated seat of the Presidency,' he wrote, 'the platform draped in green, the table for stenographers and the press, all made such a strong impression on me that I quickly walked out again, so as not to lose my composure.' It might sound melodramatic, but Herzl's sense of awe was perfectly understandable. He was, after all, a man who had spent many years in the halls of the French National Assembly and the corridors of the Reichsrat in Vienna. What he saw in the concert hall was the embryo of a parliament. It was not a fantasy, but an actual body, an institution that was the foundation of legitimacy of the Jewish people as it reconstituted itself as a modern nation. Herzl repeatedly stated the historic significance of the event in his diary. He even sent his children, wife, and parents, who are seldom mentioned in his diary, Congress postcards from the presidium table. He admitted: 'This is perhaps the first act of childishness I have committed in two years, since the movement began.'

Herzl's keynote speech at the opening of the Congress was less impressive than one might have expected. More powerful and profound was the long programmatic speech offered by Herzl's most celebrated recruit into the Zionist movement, Max Nordau. Nordau was at that time perhaps the most famous essayist in the German language, whose celebrity extended to France and England. With his strong sense of social history, Nordau did a fine job of highlighting the ambiguities and internal contradictions of Jewish emancipation. He argued that the grant of equal rights to the Jews did not express any deep belief on the part of the non-Jewish population that the Jews ought to be accepted as equal citizens. On the contrary, he declared, it was to a large extent a shallow gesture, a performance of a perceived duty that carried no conviction. That being the case, Nordau predicted that emancipation would prove to be fragile and brittle in any time of crisis. Herzl himself acknowledged how powerful his colleague's speech had been when he congratulated him, as Nordau stepped down from the podium, with a quote from Horace, saying that his speech had created 'a monument more enduring than bronze' ('*Monumentum aere perennius*').

The relative flatness of Herzl's speech could have had several causes. He was an incisive journalist and writer but not an accomplished public speaker. All the eggshells he had had to tread over so carefully in the weeks leading up to the Congress no doubt inhibited him from displaying the fervor so characteristic of his writing. It may well also be that the non-stop writing he had engaged in over the previous few years had to an extent dulled his ability to express himself freshly and originally, causing him to repeat to the assembly before him formulations that they had already agreed to and had been persuaded of – the very things that had brought them to Basel in the first place.

Nevertheless, his speech contained several phrases that have entered collective memory, statements that duly impressed the audience that first heard them. The most keen of them was no doubt: 'We have returned home. Zionism is the return to Judaism even before our return to the Land of Israel.' This insight went hand in hand with Herzl's fundamental understanding that the underlying task of the Zionist project was the construction of a nation. The search for and purchase of a territory for that nation to inhabit could occur only after the Jews had developed a national consciousness, reiterating that the determining factor was the political will to be a nation. With some exaggeration, he claimed that one of the Congress's achievements was that it brought together groups of religious and non-religious Jews. That, in and of itself, proved that the Jews were a nation and not a faith community:

Zionism has already succeeded in achieving something wonderful, which has until now been viewed as impossible: the strong linkage between the most modern and the most conservative elements in Judaism. That this occurred without either of these two elements being required to make concessions which would have hurt its

honor or entailed deep spiritual sacrifices is another proof – if such
a proof were needed – that the Jews are a people. Such unity is possible only against a national background.

In the programmatic part of his speech, he proposed that several
initiatives should be pursued in parallel. Jewish culture needed to be
fostered as an expression of national awareness. (Herzl had already, at
meetings of *Die Welt*'s editorial board, asked one of his colleagues to
write a series of articles on figures such as Moses Hess, George Eliot,
and Benjamin Disraeli.) Jewish agriculture had to be fostered. Jewish
self-help institutions needed to be founded, to reduce dependence on
donations from wealthy philanthropists. And all these needed to be
subordinated to an untiring effort to obtain international legal recognition of the future status of Jews in Palestine. This recognition
could not be obtained through the lobbying of individuals, who could
at most obtain crumbs of benevolent support for a few settlers. Only
a politically organized people with representative institutions could
conduct political negotiations that would achieve 'guarantees anchored in public law.' He added that an organized mass exodus of Jews
to Palestine, as opposed to the settlement of individuals that had been
pursued up to that date, would be possible only after the achievement
of a political agreement. To reassure both Jews who were apprehensive
about Zionism and European political leaders, Herzl again asserted
what he had stated in the past: 'One cannot speak of a full and complete exodus of the Jews. Those who would prefer and wish to stay and
assimilate in their present places of residence will do so.'

He stressed again that Zionism was not a revolutionary movement.
It did not seek to intervene in the internal politics of the countries in
which Jews resided, and it was 'legal and civilized and full of love for
humanity.' It was in no way a messianic movement either (Herzl used
the Greek term 'chiliastic,' meaning an effort to bring on the end of
days). He also disputed those Orthodox Jews who claimed that Zionism was a form of false messianism, a forbidden effort to hasten the
messianic redemption by human agency.

To accomplish this, Herzl realized, the Congress's main task was
to establish permanent institutions: 'And finally, the Congress,' he told

the delegates, 'will seek to ensure its continuity; we shall not disperse without leaving our mark and without action.' And, in fact, this turned out to be the Congress's major legacy – it was not merely an impressive and celebratory, yet a one-time event, but the crucible of the public institutions of a political entity, the beginning of the state-to-be. The Basel Program, as Herzl proposed it and as accepted by the Congress after debate, called for a series of actions that blended the established activity of Hovevei Zion with innovative elements:

- Encouragement of the immigration of Jewish farmers and craftsmen to Palestine.
- The establishment in different countries of appropriate local and international institutions, all 'according to the laws of each particular country.'
- Encouragement of Jewish education to foster Jewish national consciousness.
- Preparatory activities to obtain the consent of European governments to the goals of Zionism.

That, as Herzl had defined it previously in his writings, was 'establishing a homeland for the Jewish people, guaranteed by public law.'

Beyond this program, one of the principal achievements of the Congress would be the decision to set up permanent institutions of the Zionist movement. Some of Herzl's colleagues may not have fully understood him when he insisted on the creation of an apparatus that resembled that of an independent state – a quasi-parliament, in the form of a Zionist Congress that would meet annually; and an executive arm, the Zionist Executive, which Herzl was elected to chair. At Herzl's suggestion, embryonic financial institutions were founded: a Zionist bank, a difficult project that would, in the end, require more effort from Herzl than any other (and which would lead him to come up with a number of creative ideas, only some of which would be carried to fruition). What all this amounted to was the creation of a Jewish *demos*, an organized and institutionalized electorate, membership of which would require the payment of annual dues. These dues were deliberately called the 'shekel,' echoing the voluntary tax Jews in ancient times paid to the Temple in Jerusalem. It was a term that evoked the solidarity that had once reigned between the Jews of the Diaspora and those living in the Land of Israel, connecting all of them to Jerusalem. A year later, at the Second Zionist Congress, it was decided that women who paid the shekel would also be entitled to vote and to be elected to office – this at a time when not a single European country had yet granted women the right to vote. Unquestionably, it was the establishment of this institutional infrastructure, not just the adoption of the goals stated in the Basel Program, that provided the solid basis for Herzl's statement 'At Basel I founded the Jewish state.'

With this spirit ('We are the start of an enormous enterprise') and hyperbole deriving from his thrill at the historic significance of the event, Herzl summed up the Congress with an article that appeared in *Die Welt* immediately following its adjournment, on September 10, 1897. The Congress, he wrote, was not an assembly of speechmakers and fantasists who returned to their homes after a 'comic assembly.' It offered evidence of the existence of an organized, institutionalized nation. The point may have been obscured by his rhetoric, but the meaning was clear:

> The poor Jewish nation . . . is unable and unwilling to die, and its rise suddenly, in all the glory of its sufferings and hope, gleams in its eyes. We are a poor people, but we are a people, *one* people: this is the testimony of the representatives of hundreds of thousands who were assembled in Basel.

One could quarrel with the 'hundreds of thousands,' but not with the fact that the convening of the Congress and the creation of the institutions of the Zionist movement were steps in the process of consolidating a nation. Herzl recognized that many of his supporters, those associated with Hovevei Zion, still saw Zionism as no more than the encouragement of settlement in Palestine. For that reason, Herzl reiterated, 'We need the sympathy and support of public opinion and the relevant governments.'

This was also the focus of Herzl's opening speech at the Second

Congress, also held in Basel, on August 29, 1898. 'We feel and recognize ourselves as a people,' he declared. In pain mixed with anger, he complained about religious opposition to the idea of the Congress. His disappointment at failing to persuade Chief Rabbi Güdemann of Vienna to join the movement, and at the anti-Zionist pronouncements of other rabbis was clear:

> We encounter the hostility of certain so-called 'official' Jewish circles. This became evident in the surprising protests of some rabbis. It is indeed one of the more odd things that these gentlemen pray for Zion while at the same time going to war against Zion.

It is on this occasion that Herzl also raised for the first time the idea of a Zionist 'takeover' of Jewish communities. Like some other ideas of his, this one was ahead of its time. He came to understand that if Zionists sought to speak with the nations of the world and their sovereigns in the name of the Jewish people, they needed an internal mandate that the convening of a Congress alone could not give them. It was thus a political necessity that the Zionists gain influence in and control of Jewish communities. Herzl knew, on the basis of the information at his disposal, that Zionists had reasonably good chances of gaining power in Jewish communities in a number of areas, Galicia in particular. He proposed that Zionist candidates compete in elections to the Austrian Reichsrat in urban constituencies in Galicia where many Jews lived – areas in which Jewish candidates had previously been elected or had good chances of being elected in the future.

In stressing the need to gain political power as a means of realizing the Zionist movement's goals, Herzl made an emotional statement of a kind he had never made before. He spoke of the deep link between the Jews and the Land of Israel:

> No piece of land has been coveted by so many, and out of that passion it remained desolate and destroyed. But we believe that this desolate corner of the Orient has not only a past, but just as ourselves, has also a future. On this land, where so little grows now, ideas for all of mankind have grown; and it is because of this that no

one can deny that there is an indelible link between us and this land – if there ever existed any legal claim to any territory on this earth.

Herzl maintained that the game being played by the great powers in the Middle East could be beneficial to the Jews. After all, the Jews lacked power and were not a threat to the position of any of the actors in the region. This explains Herzl's attempts to obtain the support of every possible player in the international system. It was one of the subjects that preoccupied him – despite a notable lack of success – during the year between the First and Second Congresses. Of course, he had to cope with complex organizational tasks, not to mention the never-ending challenges of internal politics, with its petty intrigues and accusations that he was wielding autocratic power. But on top of all that, he spent the first two years after the First Congress broadening the international political contacts he had fostered previously. All this was aimed at gaining the public international support that the Zionist enterprise vitally needed.

Herzl's diaries and letters from this period testify to his feverish work in bringing his ideas to fruition. One idea that he did not succeed in launching was floating an international Zionist loan issue backed by Jewish financiers. On the other hand, he managed to create other Zionist financial institutions by the eventual establishment of a Zionist bank and its holding company, the Jewish Colonial Trust (*Otzar Hityashvut HaYehudim*). Another institution, established in 1901, was the Jewish National Fund (*Keren Kayemet le-Israel*), charged with buying up land that would remain under the ownership of the Jewish national institutions and would not be turned over to private hands. These two institutions were only a part of the Zionist network. Membership in the Zionist Organization grew slowly but steadily, and its annual Congresses increasingly drew the attention of the international press. As Herzl had proposed, the movement's financial institutions were registered in London (even though the Zionist Executive's seat was Vienna) in order to take advantage of England's more liberal corporate law. Eventually this step proved even more prescient than Herzl could have envisioned – imagine what might have happened after World War I and in the wake of the Balfour Declaration had these bodies been registered in the defeated and disintegrating Austro-Hungarian Empire, rather than in the country that was granted a League of Nations Mandate for Palestine.

To increase awareness of the symbolic significance of these new institutions, Herzl even played with the idea of constructing a building to serve as the permanent site of the Zionist Congresses in Basel. He sketched such a building in his diary, in an Oriental Baroque style – much like the Dohány Street Synagogue in Budapest and other lavish European synagogues of the time. Nothing came of the idea, but the drawings were characteristic of his way of thinking:

> The Jewish House [*das Judenhaus*] in Basel will be one of the out-standing sights in Switzerland. But it will primarily be a symbol for all the Jews. With nations you have to speak in a childish language: a house, a flag – these are the symbols of communication. The Jewish House in Basel is the first opportunity to create a new Jewish style . . . The hall will receive overhead light, like a hall of parliament.

Herzl's diplomatic activity did not bring about the results he sought. He and his colleagues devoted considerable time to developing contacts in the court at Constantinople. They used a number of people as intermediaries – among them Jewish businessmen and operatives who traded with the Levant, both Jews and non-Jews, and men who promised the moon. One such intermediary was the Orientalist and Turkologist Arminius Vámbéry, a Hungarian Jew, born Hermann Bamberger, who had converted to Islam and was close to Ottoman ruling circles. Yet despite his repeated visits to Constantinople and his brief and insignificant audience with the Sultan, no breakthroughs were achieved. Herzl did not always understand how to wade through the layers of ambiguity that enveloped the policies of the Sultan's court.

Herzl was not always successful in reaching European rulers. Initially, the closest he came was the Grand Duke of Baden, the uncle of Emperor Wilhelm II of Germany, a connection he made through the Reverend William Hechler, chaplain of the British Embassy in Vienna. In the Grand Duke, Herzl found an enthusiastic proponent of Zionism, full of hope, who promised to bring Herzl's ideas before

the Kaiser. In the years to come, Herzl would find much encouragement from this quarter. It was through the Grand Duke that Herzl
first learned of Wilhelm's intention of making a trip to Palestine. That
information helped Herzl establish his first ties with the German Ambassador in Vienna, Prince Philip von Eulenburg, who, Hechler told
Herzl, had been instructed by the Emperor to submit to him material
on Zionism in advance of his journey to Palestine. In September 1898
Herzl once again, through the Ambassador, submitted a request for an
audience with the Kaiser. Wilhelm was scheduled to arrive in Vienna
to attend the funeral of Empress Elisabeth ('Sissy') of Austria, Franz
Joseph's wife, who had been assassinated by an anarchist in Geneva.
The request was politely turned down, but as noted before the Am-
bassador arranged for Herzl an appointment with German Foreign
Minister von Bülow, who had accompanied his monarch.

It was Herzl's first chance to speak directly with a top-tier European statesman. This impromptu meeting clearly indicated to Herzl
that von Bülow had no love for the Jews. He was apprehensive of the
large number of Jews who were attracted by revolutionary socialism
and had no fondness for wealthy Jews, either. He also said to Herzl that
he was concerned about Zionism's radical and revolutionary nature.
But Herzl responded to this challenge in a peculiarly creative way. He
explained to the Foreign Minister that the Jews were at heart individualists, citing Moses as proof: 'I mentioned something that I had
recently read – pre-Mosaic Egypt was a socialist state. Through the
Decalogue, Moses created an individualistic form of society, and the
Jews remained ever since individualists.' Although it seemed to Herzl
that he had succeeded in allaying some of von Bülow's fears, the Foreign Minister adopted a disparaging tone that Herzl may not have been
aware of. Von Bülow remarked that Herzl's social ideas reminded him
'of Plato's polis' – and that was no compliment coming from a German
Foreign Minister known for his scorn of philosophy. While the meeting was urbane and enabled Herzl to display himself as a man of the
world, it was clear that von Bülow remained skeptical about Zionism
and that there would be no meeting with the Kaiser in Vienna.

Nevertheless, as we have seen before, it was this meeting with von
Bülow and the ongoing contacts with Ambassador von Eulenburg

that ultimately led to Herzl's journey to Palestine to meet the German Emperor. As has already been seen, that meeting did not produce the results Herzl had hoped for, but it gave him an opportunity to see, for the first time, the object of his dreams, the Land of Israel. This, his sole visit to Palestine, would make its mark on his novel *Altneuland*. It seems unlikely that this work, with its carefully crafted and concrete descriptions of that country, could have been written had Herzl not seen the land with his own eyes.

CHAPTER SEVEN

ALTNEULAND – A PLAN, NOT A FANTASY

HERZL PUBLISHED his utopian novel *Altneuland* (*Old-New Land*) in 1902. The book was quickly translated into Hebrew and Yiddish, with editions in both languages published in Warsaw that same year. Not long afterward further translations appeared, including one in Ladino, the Judeo-Spanish lingua franca of the Sephardic Jewish Diaspora, published in Salonica in 1914 under the title *Vieja-Nueva Tiera*. The translator into Hebrew was Nachum Sokolov, a leading Zionist journalist, who chose as its Hebrew title *Tel Aviv*, literally 'Mound of Spring,' a conjunction of old and new used in the Bible by the prophet Ezekiel. In 1910, when the Ahuzat Bayit company chose this name for the new Jewish garden suburb it built on the outskirts of Jaffa – a neighborhood that would eventually become the first Hebrew city – it would be a concrete monument to Herzl's book, suggesting that Herzl's novel was not a utopian dream of a distant future but, rather, a plan of action.

Altneuland is indeed different from the utopian genre Herzl ostensibly chose for his novel. That tradition began in 1516, when Thomas More published his *Utopia*. More described an ideal society where humans lived in keeping with the highest moral principles. *Utopia* became a model for dozens of other depictions of ideal societies, books that were offered as templates for perfect states. One of the most famous of these, *La Città del Sole* (*City of the Sun*), was written by the Italian Dominican philosopher and theologian Tommaso Campanella in the seventeenth century. The genre was adopted by many authors during the Enlightenment, and socialist and communist theorists produced futuristic novels describing the societies they favored. The best known of these was written by the radical French thinker Étienne Cabet, whose *Journeys Through Icaria* appeared in 1840. Karl Marx did not think much of these socialists, dismissing them in *The Communist Manifesto* as 'merely utopians.' Marx sought to draw a clear line between his *Manifesto* and the visions of these writers, who appeared to him as indulging in little more than pious wishful thinking. Herzl was well aware that utopian works were often disparaged in this way, so, while adopting the utopian format, he took pains to make sure that readers would see that his imagined land was no fantasy, but concrete and real.

At the end of the nineteenth century, two utopian novels were particularly popular. The first was by the American socialist writer Edward Bellamy, who in 1888 published *Looking Backwards: 2000 to 1887*. Bellamy's novel was widely read in Europe, where it was translated into many languages. Just two years later, the *Neue Freie Presse*'s economics editor, Theodor Hertzka, like Herzl a Budapest-born Viennese Jew, published *Freiland* (*Land of the Free*), his vision of a socialist utopia. The name and contents of this book undoubtedly inspired Herzl's own, but the odd coincidence of their similar names and backgrounds only further highlights how different they were.

The utopian genre also played a role in the intellectual and social ferment of European Jewish society at the end of the nineteenth century, the same ferment that gave birth to the Zionist movement. In 1885 Edmond Eisler, an educated Jewish businessman from Upper Hungary (today's Slovakia), anonymously published a utopian novel with the title *Zukunftsbild* (*An Image of the Future*), describing the re-establishment of the Judean kingdom. Written in 1882, it was obviously inspired by the Russian pogroms that followed the assassination of Czar Alexander II as well as the emergence of an anti-Semitic movement in Hungary, led by Count Győző Istóczi. A member of parliament, he called for the forced emigration of the Jews from Hungary, preferably to Palestine. Eisler's novel opens with a dramatic depiction of mass pogroms, and the author directed his call for the renewal of Jewish statehood to Benjamin Disraeli.

Another book that preceded Herzl's was written by Elhanan Leib Levinsky, a Russian Jewish *maskil* with ties to the Hovevei Zion movement in Odessa. His utopia appeared in Hebrew in 1892 in the journal *Pardes* under the title 'A Journey to the Land of Israel in the Year 2040.' It describes a Jewish society in Palestine, with an emphasis on the cultural aspects of this new polity. Another work, written against the background of the impact of the Dreyfus trial, appeared in 1898, this one authored by a French Jewish journalist, Jacques Bahar, who represented the Jews of Algeria at the First Zionist Congress. His novel, *L'antigoisme à Sion (Anti-Goyism in Zion)*, offered an account of how a Jewish state would manage the trial of a non-Jewish officer accused of espionage.

None of these proto-Zionist works created much of a stir; in all probability, Herzl was not aware of them. Today they are of interest only to scholars who plow through archives. But Herzl was well acquainted with the socialist works and even referred to them from time to time in his writings (especially to the books by Cabet, Bellamy, and Hertzka), but repeatedly insisted that his own work differed from theirs entirely. *Altneuland*, he maintained, was not a utopian work depicting an ideal, perfect society intended as a contrast with reality, but, rather, a plan of action in the form of a utopian novel. In addition to being a vision of the future, it contained practical proposals for bringing it about. This was typified by the call to action of the book's epigraph, 'If you will it, it is no dream,' which would become the unofficial motto of the Zionist movement.

That Herzl intended his book as a plan of action, not just a depiction of an ideal future, is also evident in his decision to depict his future society with flaws – ones that can be overcome to be sure, but flaws nonetheless. In classic utopian novels, all is good, beautiful, and ideal. There are no warts. Herzl's book was clearly different.

As we have seen, Herzl had the idea of writing a novel as early as 1895, when he wavered over how best to bring his innovative ideas about solving the Jewish question before the public. His diary from that time contains preliminary sketches for such a novel, but they were abandoned when he resolved to pursue public political activity. Yet he apparently did not forget the observation made by his friend Alphonse Daudet that nothing had been more effective in changing public attitudes about slavery in the United States than the novel *Uncle Tom's Cabin*. As it happened, *Altneuland* appeared in 1902, at a time when many of Herzl's supporters were losing their enthusiasm for Zionism. Despite the relatively impressive publicity the Zionist movement had received since the First Zionist Congress five years previously, Herzl's diplomatic efforts had been fruitless. Furthermore, he had been unable to raise a significant amount of financial support for the movement. European statesmen had not enthused over the Zionist scheme; the approaches to Constantinople had led nowhere; and wealthy Jews had proven tightfisted. The publication of *Altneuland*, essentially Herzl's plans in the guise of a popular novel, was meant to give a further impetus to his ideas and to serve as a means of breaking out of the small circle that had thus far taken part in Zionist activity. Herzl's novel was no bestseller, but it was popular enough, as its rapid translation into other languages showed. And it indeed disseminated the Zionist idea among a much larger public.

Like other utopian novels, *Altneuland* suffers from a sentimentalism that sometimes borders on kitsch. Its frame story is artificial and forced, and the book is replete with lengthy didactic and erudite discourses that interrupt the flow of the plot. Yet a reader willing to move past this arrives at a comprehensive and rousing political program of a type seldom attempted either in Zionist literature or in that of other political movements. Few national movements have produced a document of such quality and on such an impressive intellectual level. As to its title, Herzl wrote that it was inspired by that of the Altneuschul, Prague's 'Old-New Synagogue,' which he first visited in 1885 and which he saw as a symbol of Jewish cultural continuity in Europe.

The story begins in Vienna at the turn of the century – the time when the book itself was written. It centers on a young Jewish attorney, Dr. Friedrich Löwenberg, who is described as 'an educated, desperate young man.' Like many other young Jews of his generation, he belongs to the freethinking university educated proletariat and has few professional prospects. Many such young men had found 'that those who left their ancestors' world of commerce became involved, as educated men, in all kinds of questionable dealings. They involved treating unspeakable maladies or setting up suspect legal enterprises. Lacking other outlets, some became journalists, dealing in public opinion.' Löwenberg is spurned by his beloved, the daughter of a wealthy Jewish textile merchant. She prefers the match her parents have made for her with a crude and uneducated but well-off man, and in the passage describing their engagement Herzl incisively portrays the vulgar nouveau riche Viennese Jewish bourgeoisie. It is these circles that also make fun of both the Zionist movement and the Jewish settlement project in Palestine ('I'll be the Jewish ambassador in Vienna!' one guest declares, and most of those around him echo 'Me too! Me too!'). Some of this is much like the satire of his own social milieu that Herzl had employed in his play *The New Ghetto*.

But this depiction, almost a caricature with even a faint whiff of anti-Semitism, reflected Herzl's astute diagnosis of Jewish society. Also present at the engagement party is a rabbi from Moravia, the only guest who does not mock the Zionists. He is profoundly apprehensive about the status of the Jews in the regions of mixed Czech and German population. These are the Jewish communities that Herzl himself had predicted would become the victims of national conflicts in the Austro-Hungarian Empire. The rabbi worries that 'In the provincial towns . . . our people are in actual peril. When the Germans are in a bad mood, they break Jewish windows. When the Czechs are out of sorts, they break into Jewish homes. The poor wretches are beginning to think of emigration. But they don't know where to go.'

No one listens to him. One of the guests promises that in the case of riots the authorities and police can be counted on, as always. Yet another guest makes, in jest, what a contemporary reader can only understand as a chillingly prophetic statement – one that even Herzl would not really take seriously: 'I feel it coming . . . We'll all have to wear the yellow badge.'

This is the background for Löwenberg's personal problems. Despondent about his professional future and his unrequited love, he decides to respond to an unusual newspaper advertisement that seeks 'an educated, desperate young man willing to make a last experiment with his life.' His response takes him to Adalbert Kingscourt, an eccentric American millionaire who plays the role of a Greek chorus, commenting on the action from the point of view of an outsider to Jewish society and its ills. Originally a Prussian cavalry officer going by the name of von Königshofer, he wearied of the idle life of a career officer, emigrated to the United States, and made a fortune for himself. Following a series of personal tragedies, Kingscourt has resolved to abandon the civilized world. He has purchased a Pacific island, where he intends to spend the rest of his life. But he first sets out for Europe to provision himself with all he needs, from modern technology to books. He also seeks a companion who will agree to spend the rest of his life on the island. Löwenberg, his future looking bleak, enthusiastically agrees to the proposal, and his determination pleases the former officer. Löwenberg feels duty-bound to tell Kingscourt that he is Jewish and to ask if this bothers him. Kingscourt chuckles: 'That is an absurd question. In my eyes you are a human being.'

Prior to their journey, Kingscourt makes available to Löwenberg a considerable sum of money to cover his debts and obligations. A convoluted passage relates how Löwenberg discovers a poor Jewish family, the Litvaks, who have come to Vienna from Galicia and are on the verge of starvation. The father is a poor peddler who wanders among the cafés where Löwenberg spends his time. There is a small boy named David, who impresses Löwenberg with his intelligence and humanity. In a melodramatic scene he gives all the money he has received from Kingscourt, the huge sum of 5,000 guilders, to this poor family, saving the father, the mortally ill mother, David, and his baby sister Miriam from hunger and death.

Following Löwenberg's operatic gesture, the two men set sail for Polynesia in Kingscourt's luxurious private yacht. Kingscourt asks Löwenberg if he would like, on the way, to see his fatherland one last time before parting from the world. Löwenberg, confused, thinks that Kingscourt is talking about returning to Austria. But the latter corrects him: 'God forbid! ... Your fatherland lies ahead of us – Palestine.' Löwenberg disputes this: 'I have no connection to Palestine ... I think that only anti-Semites can call Palestine our fatherland.' After a further exchange, Löwenberg accepts the proposal and the two of them sail to Palestine and disembark at Jaffa.

This visit to the Palestine of 1902 by his two protagonists enabled Herzl to portray the state of the country as he saw it at the time of his writing, both its neglect and the potential he thought it had. This account draws to a large extent on Herzl's impressions during his own visit to Palestine four years previously. Many details indicate that he had reviewed his diary in order to provide his readers with a vivid and authentic description of the country. The two protagonists form 'a very unpleasant impression' of Jaffa: 'The town was in an extreme state of decay.' They ride to Jerusalem 'in a ramshackle railway.' Herzl could hardly forget his own train ride to Jerusalem in 1898, while he was racked with fever. But Kingscourt, with his American can-do spirit, says: 'But much can be done here with afforestation, if half a million young giant cedars were planted . . .'

Jerusalem astounds and shocks them, just as it did Herzl. On the one hand, 'It was night when they reached Jerusalem – a marvelous, white, moonlit night.' But the next day, the sight of the city is less salubrious. The two travelers are accosted by 'shouting, odors, a flurry of dirty colors.' They find themselves in 'the noisome little lane that leads to the Wailing Wall, and were revolted by the appearance of the praying beggars there.' Löwenberg tells his companion, 'There's nothing left of the Jewish kingdom but this fragment of the Temple wall.'

Another visitor to the Wall overhears Löwenberg. He is a Jewish ophthalmologist from Russia, who takes Löwenberg to task in perfect German. 'His German accent,' Herzl tells us, 'was foreign but cultured.' The doctor rebukes Löwenberg: 'You are, sir, a stranger to your own people. If you ever come to us in Russia, you will realize that a Jewish nation still exists. We have a living tradition, a love of the past and faith in the future. The best and most cultured men among us have remained true to Judaism as a nation. We desire to belong to no other.' The echo of Herzl's own discovery of Eastern European Jewry, the *Ostjuden*, is unmistakable. The Jewish eye doctor, visiting Palestine with his daughter, also a physician, persuades the two companions to accompany them on a visit to the Mount of Olives. The view sends shivers down the spines of all four travelers. It was just as

Herzl had described it four years previously. Herzl has the doctor from Russia pronounce the same words and use the same images that Herzl had used in his diary: 'It reminds me of Rome ... A splendid city, a metropolis, could be built upon these hills once more. What a view from here! Grander than that from the Janiculum.'

Kingscourt, who makes uncomplimentary comments about the Jews from time to time, is impressed by the doctor and his daughter when they express their hope that Jews could resettle in Palestine: 'So practical and yet so foolish,' he says. 'I always imagined the Jews quite differently.' This, of course, foreshadows what happens afterward. It is from the doctor that the two traveling companions first hear about the new Jewish settlements in Palestine. On his recommendation, they visit Rehovot. When they reach the *moshava* they see tilled fields, vineyards, and orange groves. The settlers give them a special welcome, 'singing Hebrew songs,' the description of which is taken, almost word for word, from Herzl's description of the *fantasia* ceremony offered to him during his visit to Rehovot in 1898. The guests are amazed, especially the former cavalry officer von Königshofer: 'May salty lightning strike me! I've never seen anything like this! These fellows ride like the devil!' Löwenberg is not quite as impressed, but he also leaves Palestine in a pensive mood, especially at the first signs of renewal that they have seen along the way.

The two eat a festive dinner on the yacht to mark the last night of 1902. While he has given up on the world and on mankind, Kingscourt holds forth in praise of modern technology and predicts that it will be able to make deserts bloom. As they sail south through the Red Sea he evokes Moses and harangues the skeptical Löwenberg:

> Here your old Moses performed his greatest deed ... Just think how poor a time that was, and yet what your old Moses achieved ... And do you know, man, who could show the way? You! You Jews! Just because you're so badly off. You've nothing to lose. You could create the experimental land for humanity. Over yonder, where we were, you could create a new commonwealth. On that ancient soil, Old-New-Land [*Altneuland*]!

But by this time Löwenberg has fallen asleep, under the influence of the wine and rich delicacies they have been eating. The yacht sails on to its distant island destination.

*   *   *

That is the first part of the story. The novel's central narrative takes place however 20 years later, in 1923. Kingscourt and Löwenberg change their plans and decide, despite their original vow, to return to Europe for a brief visit, after two decades of being completely cut off from the world. During those years they have read no newspapers. When they sail up the Red Sea and through the Suez Canal, they learn that the lands around them have utterly changed. The Jews have immigrated en masse to Palestine, which has been transformed into a modern center of business, culture, and technology. The two men decide to take a look at this wonder, and dock at Haifa. When they disembark, they find themselves in a modern and buzzing port city. Mount Carmel is crowned with marvelous buildings and mansions, and Haifa Bay is lined with settlements all the way up to Acre.

At this point the plot splits into two parallel strands. One is a personal story and another the story of the new society that has come into being in Palestine. The personal story is romantic, sentimental, and tackily kitschy. Herzl was a brilliant journalist and essayist but a mediocre playwright and novelist. His narrative is shallow, and with a glaring lack of literary sophistication he arranges his plot such that the two travelers, immediately upon setting foot in Haifa, run into David Litvak, the poor boy from Vienna. David remembers Löwenberg. But the poor boy is no longer poor – he has become one of the leaders of the new society. He brings the two guests to his home – after all, it was Löwenberg's gift that saved the family from ruin. David's sister, Miriam, who was a starving baby when Löwenberg saw her last, is now a blooming and educated young woman. In keeping with the demands of a romantic novel, Miriam and Löwenberg fall in love, and following initial hesitations and delays, they become engaged and win the blessing of Miriam and David's parents, who have also settled in the old-new land. Furthermore, it transpires that the president of this commonwealth is none other than Dr. Eichenstam, the Russian oph-thalmologist whom the two men met in 1902 at the Wailing Wall.

These men are not the only ones to have moved to Palestine. The nouveau riche Viennese Jews that Löwenberg found so intolerable also made their way to *Altneuland*. Their lives are no less shallow and cyn-ical than before. Löwenberg even encounters his former beloved, the woman who rejected him in favor of the crude merchant. She is now a widow, and her beauty has almost vanished – but not her vulgarity. This is one of those parts of the book that, thanks to Herzl's weakness as a writer of fiction, most readers have a hard time getting through.

But in the end it is not this storyline that is central to the book. The important part is Herzl's description of the new Jewish society as it reveals itself through encounters with the inhabitants of Pales-tine and during an election campaign that serves as the focus of the novel's political narrative. Kingscourt and Löwenberg come to know a modern Jewish commonwealth, a society that has adopted the best European and American technology. Elevated trains serve the cities and a system of rapid transit links every part of the country. The cities are the product of advanced urban planning, and a canal stretching from the Mediterranean to the Dead Sea provides electricity not just for the Jewish land but for the entire Middle East. Cars, telephones, telegraphs, and electric record players are in wide use. Herzl was clearly fascinated by science and futurism. But the most salient element of Palestine in 1923 is its social, economic, and political arrangements. It is the account of these that constitutes the book's central message, the political program that Herzl wanted to use the book to promote.

The new society portrayed in the novel is based on a principle that Herzl calls Mutualism, a third way between capitalism and socialism. In learned discourses, David Litvak and other characters expound Herzl's social ideology. The founders of this new society are well aware of the scarcity and poverty that were the products of industrialization in Western capitalist societies. Yet they are also wary of basing their society on revolutionary socialism. They instead opt for Mutualism, which combines capitalism's freedom and individual initiative with socialism's goal of equality and justice. It is 'the middle way between individualism and collectivism. The individual is not deprived of the stimulus and pleasures of private property while, at the same time, he is able, through union with his fellows, to resist capitalist domination.' The result is a society in which 'the individual is neither ground between the millstones of capitalism nor decapitated by socialistic leveling.' As the leaders explain patiently to their guests, 'Our new society does not embrace egalitarianism. Everyone receives a wage according to his labor. We have not abolished competition, but we have leveled the playing field for all.'

There is no private ownership of land. Land belongs to society as a whole, and when mass settlement of Palestine commenced, parcels of land were leased for 49-year periods to those who wished to become farmers and to others who wanted to build a house or a factory. This obviously is a conscious echo of the biblical law of the jubilee year, which prevented the accumulation of inherited wealth. In addition, industry and commerce are based on partnerships and cooperatives. Factory workers hold shares in the factory; the same is true of the workers at large stores that resemble the new European department stores. Associations of manufacturers and consumers operate in accordance with cooperative experiments in Europe (the Rochdale Society, a consumer cooperative founded in England in 1844, is discussed at length). Since everything in the new country has been constructed from scratch, its founders explain, they have been able to adopt innovative technology and social arrangements that were already extant in Europe but which had encountered hostility. The newcomers to Palestine are able to start everything from the beginning, taking the best the West has to offer, the leaders of the new society explain to the two astonished travelers, who are dumbfounded by the advancement they see.

These cooperative methods, based on various kinds of public ownership, also put an end to the characteristic strong Jewish presence in retail business. According to Herzl's book, small-scale merchants and storekeepers have suffered from difficulties in obtaining credit and from competition from large emporia, dooming them to poverty and insufficiency. Neither are the new country's newspapers privately owned – the press is run by joint stock companies, the stock being held by subscribers. Newspaper readers choose their editors and correspondents. Here Herzl allows himself a jab at the owners of the *Neue*

Freie Presse, who banned him – their star correspondent and editor – of even reporting about the Zionist movement he founded and was heading.

Another principle of the new society is social solidarity, providing for individuals when they come on hard times. Furthermore, education is free, from kindergarten through university. Comprehensive government-run social programs provide medical care, hospitalization, and care for the elderly, providing an extensive social safety net that was quite ahead of its time for 1902. Herzl adds an original aspect to this: the former cavalry officer Kingscourt is astonished to learn that the new society needs no army. But that does not mean that its young people are not required to serve their country – teachers, nurses, social workers, and caregivers, among others, are provided by a system of national service. 'All members of the new society, men and women alike, have to give two years of service to the community, usually between the ages of eighteen and twenty, after completing their studies,' the visitors are told. These institutions are funded with public money as well as from donations (because 'Jews have always contributed to charitable institutions').

The founding of what we would today call a welfare state was a cornerstone of Herzl's thinking. It was not sufficient to remove the Jews from European society, where their status was precarious as a result of modernization and the emergence of extreme nationalist movements, and merely bring them to Palestine. According to Herzl, it was necessary also to reconstruct Jewish society, but neither along capitalist nor collectivist lines. The market economy in Europe had produced social polarization, and the new Jewish national society was not to repeat the mistakes of capitalist industrialization. Society would have to be founded on the principle that its members are each responsible for the welfare of all others. Such a system of solidarity would enable every person to realize his full potential – a goal that would bring far-reaching political consequences.

Another important aspect of the new society would be equality for women: 'They have active and passive suffrage as a matter of course. They worked faithfully beside us during the reconstruction period. Their enthusiasm lent wings to the men's courage. It would have been the worst ingratitude if we had relegated them to the kitchen or the bedroom.' In this Herzl followed the decision of the Second Zionist Congress, which granted women equal voting rights, something quite revolutionary for his epoch.

The background to all this was, of course, the plight of the Jews at the end of the nineteenth century. Herzl has David Litvak offer the most comprehensive diagnosis of the social circumstances of post-Emancipation Europe, Austria-Hungary and Germany in particular:

> The persecutions were social and economic. Jewish merchants were boycotted, Jewish workingmen starved out, Jewish professional men proscribed – not to mention the subtle moral suffering to which a sensitive Jew was exposed at the turn of the century. Jew-hatred employed its newest as well as its oldest devices. The blood libel was revived, and at the same time the Jews were accused of poisoning the press, just as in the Middle Ages they had been accused of poisoning the wells. As workingmen, the Jews were hated by their Christian fellows for undercutting wages. As businessmen, they were denounced as profiteers. Whether Jews were rich or poor or middle-class, they were hated just the same. They were criticized for enriching themselves, and they were criticized for spending money. They were neither to produce nor to consume. They were forced out of government posts. The law courts were prejudiced against them . . . It became clear that, under these circumstances, they must either become the deadly enemies of society that was so unjust to them, or seek out a refuge for themselves. The latter course was taken, and here we are. We have saved ourselves.

The founders of the new society do not forget to mention to the travelers that the flourishing agriculture that has so altered the countryside had been based to a large extent on the experience of 'German Protestants,' that is the Templer sect from Württemberg, who had been the first to bring modern farming methods to Palestine.

During the guests' first day in Haifa, while visiting David Litvak's luxurious mansion on Mount Carmel, Kingscourt and Löwenberg meet an Arab from Haifa, a personal friend of the Litvaks. The question of the status of the Arabs (and of other non-Jews, such as Greeks, Armenians, and so on) immediately arises. The Arab friend, Rashid Bey, turns out to have studied engineering in Berlin (he speaks German 'with a slight northern accent'). He testifies to the fact that he is an equal citizen in the new society. Through him, Herzl presents his vision of a society devoid of discrimination and in which religious, racial, and gender equality prevails. The fact that Arabs are equal citizens is stated several times in *Altneuland*. Rashid Bey holds forth on the benefits the Jews have brought to the country. A surprised Kingscourt asks him: 'Were not the older inhabitants of Palestine ruined by the Jewish immigration? And didn't they have to leave the country?'

Rashid Bey's reply reflects the essence of Herzl's liberal faith. It may seem naïve today, but it is important that he wrote it. In a speech that sounds as if it were lifted from a latter-day Zionist pamphlet, Rashid Bey explains how the Arabs have profited from the Jewish immigration. The first beneficiaries were landowners, he says, who sold their land for its full value to the Jewish settlement society, as he and his father did. Afterward,

> Those who had nothing stood to lose nothing and could only gain. And they did gain: opportunities to work, means of livelihood, prosperity. Nothing could have been more wretched than an Arab village at the end of the nineteenth century. The peasants' clay hovels were unfit for stables . . . Now everything is different. They benefited from the progressive measures of the new society whether they wanted to or not . . .

On a drive through the blooming Jezreel Valley, Rashid Bey adds:

> It was a swamp in my boyhood. The new society bought up this tract rather cheaply, and turned it into the best soil in the country . . . This is a Muslim village – you can tell by the mosque. These people are better off than at any time in the past . . . [The Jews] dwell among us like brothers. Why should we not love them?

Yet the tone of this somewhat embarrassing paean to the Jews nevertheless does not overlook the complexity of the problem. When one of the spokesmen for the new society, who is a bit loquacious, says, 'We Jews introduced cultivation here,' Rashid Bey retorts 'with a friendly smile': 'Pardon me, sir! . . . But this sort of thing was here before you came – at least there were signs of it. My father planted oranges extensively.' Furthermore, when Kingscourt praises Rashid Bey for his tolerance, assuming that he has acquired this quality in Europe, he adds that he doubts if simple village and city Arabs share it. Rashid Bey objects: 'You must excuse my saying so, but I did not learn tolerance in the Occident. We Muslims have always had better relations with the Jews than you Christians.'

Undoubtedly, Herzl can be criticized today for his naïve liberalism and for not anticipating the birth of a Palestinian Arab national consciousness that would oppose Jewish immigration. But it is important to keep in mind that when the book was published, in 1902, there was no Arab national movement, neither in Palestine nor elsewhere in the Middle East. If the sparks of nationalism had appeared here and there (for example, in the Young Syria movement at the end of the nineteenth century), it was directed largely against the Ottoman Empire. Moreover, Herzl should not be seen, as some have maintained, primarily as a patronizing colonialist bringing European culture to the backward Orient. After all, the French colonists in Algeria did not grant equal political and economic rights to the Arabs of that territory, and the British imperialists in India were not prepared to confer on the natives there equal rights and suffrage. Herzl did not regard the existing population of Palestine only as objects to be used for and by the Jews; he viewed them as equals, partners in citizenship who would vote and be elected to the public institutions of the society established on what Rashid Bey terms 'our ancestral fatherland, common to us and you.' This is, then, real equality, not colonial domination.

But there is more. Herzl's profound commitment to equal rights and non-discrimination grows stronger as the novel's political plot progresses. As it happens, the two travelers find themselves visiting

Palestine during a highly charged election campaign for the new society's Congress. A new party is contesting the election, headed by a rabbi named Dr. Geyer.* Rabbi Geyer, initially an opponent of Herzl and Zionism, changed his mind and immigrated to the new country, where he founded a party devoted to the principle that the Land of Israel is solely for the Jews. According to the party's platform, non-Jews should be excluded from citizenship rights and should not be allowed to vote and be elected to the institutions of the new society. Two central chapters of the novel focus on the election campaign and on Geyer's racist doctrine, which challenges the liberal viewpoint on which the new society was founded. In his first conversation with Kingscourt, Litvak asserts: 'My colleagues and I make no distinctions between one man and another. We do not ask to what race or religion a man belongs. If he is a human being, that is enough for us.' But he admits that not everyone in the new society agrees: 'There are other views among us as well,' he says, hinting at the appearance of Geyer.

Geyer worries both Rashid Bey and Litvak. While Litvak generally avoids political controversy, he enlists in the campaign against Geyer's party. The seminal political event in the novel is a rowdy election meeting in Neudorf ('New Village'), a prosperous settlement on the edge of the Jezreel Valley and the Galilee. The two visitors are received there with Hebrew songs, but the language used in some of the discussions at the rally is Yiddish (and, of course, German). In a speech to the village's inhabitants, Litvak succeeds in turning them against Geyer's ideology, which is presented at the meeting alongside other views. The arguments of Geyer's intolerant followers are clear and unambiguous, growing out of an ethnocentric, racist, and xenophobic world-view, a clear echo of views that were, at the time, becoming common currency in Europe. Litvak, for his part, responds with complex arguments. On the one hand, he supports equality and non-discrimination on general theoretical grounds: 'It would be unethical for us to deny a share in our commonwealth to any man, wherever he might come from, whatever his race or creed . . . Tolerance, utmost tolerance. Our slogan must

---

* In nineteenth-century German, Geyer means vulture, a bird that eats carrion. Herzl's literary imagination is not always his best ally.

be, now and always – "Man, thou art my brother!"' He also quotes the biblical verses 'Thou shalt love thy brother as thyself' and 'Thou should have one law for yourselves and the stranger within thy gates.' But he also evokes another aspect of the new reality in Palestine. Neudorf, like other farming villages in the country, is a cooperative. This is the source of the fears that fire Geyer's supporters. If 'foreigners' join the cooperative, their shares in it will be reduced. Litvak counters this with economic arguments, maintaining that new members will bring growth. But his most important argument goes back to the socialist origins of the cooperative structure of the new Jewish villages in Palestine. Unlike Geyer and his supporters, who seek to preserve the 'Jewish character' of the new society, Litvak invokes the roots of the cooperative idea that has enabled the flourishing of Jewish society in Palestine – socialist experiments in Europe and North America. He refers to Rochdale in England, to Ralahine in Ireland, and to cooperative communities in the United States. He also cites the 'romantic' Theodor Hertzka, and Edward Bellamy's portrayal of a 'noble Communist society.' In short, as Litvak puts it: 'Actually, Neudorf was not built in Palestine but elsewhere. It was built in England, in America, in France, and in Germany. It has emerged out of experiments, books, and dreams.' But these utopian dreams lacked solid grounding in reality. It is this, Litvak states, that the new society in Palestine has discovered, the solidarity of Jews willing to come to the new land, to build a cooperative society against the background of their own troubles. Herzl has Litvak argue the obligation of the members of the new society to adhere to universal values of equality and social justice.

It goes without saying, following Litvak's impassioned speech (and the somewhat less successful addresses of other leaders of the new society), that on 'That day Dr. Geyer lost the votes of Neudorf.' Toward the end of the book, the liberals win a landslide victory, soundly defeating Geyer and his racist followers. Herzl adds a melodramatic touch to his story. The elderly President, Dr. Eichenstam, dies just a few days after the elections and, in a complex parliamentary maneuver (probably based on Herzl's reportage from the French National Assembly), Litvak is, of course, chosen as President. His dying mother hears the news just a moment before she passes away.

The detailed account of the election campaign, with its contest between the liberal views of the founders of the new society and the racist ideology of Geyer's party, does more than give Herzl an opportunity to present his political philosophy. There is also a tacit political subtext here, with a message directed at Herzl's contemporaries and fellow Viennese. Herzl depicts Geyer clearly as a mirror image of Vienna's racist and anti-Semitic Mayor Dr. Luëger. They were both university trained ('doctors'); the latter had built his populist career on exploiting the fears of Vienna's ethnic Germans regarding 'foreigners' (meaning primarily Czechs and Jews); Dr. Geyer does much the same, in reverse. Racism and xenophobia are the same throughout the world; no society is free of it, Herzl was saying. In this context, Herzl's utopia differed notably from others of the genre. The society it described was far from perfect; on the contrary, it had flaws and included ugly figures like Geyer, who garnered many supporters who threatened to undermine the liberal framework of the new society. Herzl had no doubt that racism was a universal phenomenon and that it could infect Jews as well.

Nevertheless, Herzl emphasized the fundamental difference between Vienna and his vision of the Land of Israel. A racist populist could win, in democratic elections, the mayor's seat of Vienna, the capital of Austria-Hungary, with its decades of liberal and tolerant traditions. But in the land of the Jews another version of that same ideology, a Jewish racist, was defeated decisively. The Jews, rescued from the jaws of the rising racist xenophobia of Europe, have instituted in their land the liberal and egalitarian society that failed in Europe. On the shores of the Mediterranean they have created a just and equal society. The noble social utopias that had failed in Europe and America have been realized in Palestine, where a Jewish society that disregards differences of religion and race has come into being. Vienna's failure has become Zion's victory.

This tolerance and pluralism, which we would today call multiculturalism, was also evident in Herzl's depiction of a Passover Seder ceremony led by the elder Litvak that the travelers attend in Tiberias. The night's ritual involved telling the tale of the Exodus from Egypt, but the celebrants also speak of their own new redemption and deliverance, listening to long speeches on a phonograph that offer concrete accounts of the steps that led to the establishment of the Jewish polity. Tiberias, on the Lake of Galilee, is described as an international tourist destination where the guests see 'impressive mosques, churches with Latin and Greek crosses, [and] magnificent stone synagogues.' The modern Seder combines traditional rituals and texts with stories about the new Exodus. Not only Jews participate. For Kingscourt, it is his first experience of Jewish religious ceremonies, and he is moved. Other participants include Rashid Bey; the abbot of the Franciscan monastery in Tiberias, originally from Cologne in Germany; a Russian Orthodox priest from the church at Sepphoris; and an Anglican priest with his wife. Such is the new Jewish society – it brings everyone, Jews and non-Jews, into all its holidays. Just as the Jews in the Diaspora have learned to live according to the European Christian calendar, so the non-Jews in the land of the Jews learn to live in a society organized around the Jewish holidays and calendar. This is the transformation that takes place in the new Jewish society, which has become a product of broadmindedness and acceptance of the other.

A major issue addressed in *Altneuland* was the international legal status of the Jewish polity. Herzl answers this question gradually and carefully as he recounts the Seder night's narration of the founding of the new society. Up to this point in the book, everything indicates that the Jewish commonwealth is an independent country. It has unique social institutions, laws and a governmental structure, a parliament building and elections, citizenship, property laws, national service, clear civic rights and obligations and a model economic and social policy. But all these are accompanied by a kind of ambiguity and political prudence that the Zionist movement had to demonstrate as it sought to gain legal standing in Ottoman Palestine.

While Herzl had called his groundbreaking pamphlet *The Jewish State*, the Basel Program was deliberately more ambiguous, speaking of a 'homeland' (*Heimstätte*) for the Jewish people, guaranteed by public law. The Zionists realized that any attempt to gain a foothold in Palestine would have to take into account the political reality of Ottoman rule. The movement's, like Herzl's, efforts were thus directed at obtaining a political-legal formula that would grant the Zionist

Organization a status that did not trespass on Turkish sovereignty – a Charter. In addition, Herzl from time to time – in *Altneuland*, for example – refers to the ambivalent status of Egypt at the time. On the one hand, that land officially fell under Ottoman sovereignty, but the government of the Khedive (Viceroy) of Egypt had enjoyed broad *de facto* autonomy since the beginning of the nineteenth century, an autonomy that resembled independence in everything but name. (Another complication was the British imperial presence, but it, too, acknowledged the formal sovereignty of the Ottoman Empire.)

In *Altneuland*, Herzl clearly stated the Zionist movement's very real and potent political aspiration, yet avoided portraying the movement as seeking an entirely independent polity, thus hoping to avoid confrontation with the Ottoman Empire. He carefully portrayed the political and legal actions involved in setting up the new society in Palestine in fine detail during the Seder scene. At first the Jews establish a New Society for the Settlement of Palestine, the name Herzl gave the Zionist Organization in his novel. This body signed an agreement with the Turkish government under which the Society would remit to the Ottoman authorities a one-time payment of £2 million and further annual payments of £15,000, as well as a quarter of the New Society's annual income. The contract's term is for 30 years, after which its income would be split evenly between the Society and the Turkish government. Alternatively, the latter could opt to receive a fixed annual sum, the amount to be agreed on, based on average income during the previous ten years. In the novel, Joe Levy, the official responsible for carrying out the program and for assembling the necessary sum from bank loans and contributions from Jews around the world, explains that, in exchange for these payments, 'we received autonomous rights to the regions which we were to settle.' He stresses that this is 'with the ultimate sovereignty reserved to His Majesty the Sultan.' This formulation enables the New Society to determine to all intents and purposes the form that the government would take, its laws, and immigration arrangements while respecting Ottoman authority.

This less-than-a-state format gives Herzl the occasional opportunity to extol the voluntary nature of this kind of political organization. Some readers of the novel have overstressed this ostensibly inflated ideological innovation, as if Herzl had sought to create a 'non-state society' in Palestine, based on voluntary cooperative structures. But there is no support for this. Herzl clearly chose vague sovereignty enshrined in a Charter because of existing political constraints. The polity depicted in the novel is a country to every intent and purpose (although one lacking an army, since it does not need one). Its organized ways of planning immigration, settlement, land distribution, and grants of credit are the kind that states pursue. Practically, nothing remains of Turkish rule in *Altneuland*. The two visitors do not encounter any manifestation of an Ottoman political or administrative presence, the sole exception being that Rashid Bey and Litvak occasionally converse in Turkish.

Interestingly, while Joe Levy speaks of 'the special regions to be settled' granted in the Charter, he does not lay out their borders – in fact, there is no reference to borders at all in the novel. This ambiguity is clearly deliberate – the book draws no precise map of the new Jewish land. Nonetheless, it offers a fairly clear picture of its territory by its account of the visitors' travels through it and from comments made here and there during the narrative. It is not confined to Palestine west of the Jordan River but stretches north to Tyre, Sidon, and Beirut. There is a train line to Damascus and, while the reference is vague, it sounds as if that city is also included in the territory of the Charter. There is even an indication that Palmyra, the ancient Tadmor, 'has been revived.' Both sides of the Jordan are described as fertile and an integral part of the New Society. New villages have been established on both sides of the Jordan Valley. The Golan Heights are the country's breadbasket, and Herzl offered a detailed account of a visit to the area to see the plans for its cultivation. The region is irrigated, exploiting the sources of the Jordan and innovative technology.

Herzl was obviously viewing the map of the region as a whole from the perspective of his period, not in the context of the specific and smaller area that would later constitute the British Mandate of Palestine – after all, the entire Levant was ruled by the Turks then. As already seen, when Herzl met the German Emperor in Constantinople, he spoke of a Jewish Land Society for 'Syria and Palestine.' Like the entire Zionist movement during its early stages, Herzl was

studiously hazy with regard to the extent of the future Jewish homeland, just as he made use of creative and constructive ambiguity in
searching for ways (such as a Charter) to constitute the political status
of the entity he hoped to bring about. Explicit and clear-cut political goals and borders crystallized in Zionist consciousness and policy
only later, largely in reaction to the new regional order established by
World War I. Herzl's novel is devoid of theological or historiosophical
claims based on divine promises. Viewing the region in the context
of the Ottoman Empire, Herzl would obviously see no reason to view
Haifa and the land west of the Jordan River as inside Palestine, with
Sidon and the East Bank clearly outside. Today, of course, the picture
is entirely different.

In Herzl's story, the New Society respects all religions and the sa-
credness of their holy sites, in both Jerusalem and the Galilee. Some
have taken this to mean that Herzl advocated an extra-territorial
status for Jerusalem. But such readers have overlooked the fact that the
Jewish homeland depicted in *Altneuland* does not have the status of an
independent state and does not enjoy unquestionable sovereignty in
terms of international law. The notion of extra-territoriality does not
make sense in such an ambiguous context. Herzl nevertheless made a
point of noting that the Jewish polity, whatever its precise legal status,
would guarantee freedom of religious practice for all faiths, and that it
would allow them to administer their own sites. This was, in fact, the
approach that took form in liberal Europe in the nineteenth century.
But the holy sites in the novel have no extra-territorial standing – they
are only protected from government takeover. Herzl pointed out that
Christian holy places had already been under non-Christian – Muslim
– rule for several centuries, and that since the disappearance of the
Crusader Kingdom of Jerusalem this had been accepted by the European powers. That being the case, in Herzl's view, it should not be a
problem for these sites to fall under Jewish rule (except perhaps in the
minds of a few Jews). The status quo, Herzl argued, was the best possible situation for the Christians, and it would continue when the Holy
Land passed from the Ottoman Empire to effective Jewish control.

At this point Herzl has Joe Levy relate the practical steps that have
led to the creation of the New Society, the organization of immigrants

at their points of origin, the import of the raw materials needed to provide housing for the Jews who arrived in the mass immigration, and the creation of a credit system. In short, he lays out the entire organizational, political, and economic plan that turned the vision into a reality. To a large extent, Levy's account accords with the working plans that Herzl drafted and which were brought in one form or another before the Zionist Congresses; some were carried out, others could not be realized due to political and financial constraints. But *Altneuland* offers a detailed account of the Zionist organizations around the world and provides a map of the places from which most of the immigrants would come: 'These instructions were also sent to the Zionist district groups in Russia, Romania, Galicia, and Algeria.' Herzl had no doubt, in the wake of his historical analysis of the crisis of emancipation, that the largest pool of immigrants was to be found in those countries with high densities of oppressed and impoverished Jewish communities, especially in Eastern Europe and in North Africa.

The day after the very long Seder night, the two visitors tour the irrigation and agricultural projects in the Golan Heights and on both sides of the Jordan Valley ('The plains on both sides of the river, famed since ancient times for their fertility, were more luxuriantly planted than ever before'). They visit an experimental farm founded, among other reasons, to enable the development of modern agriculture in sub-Saharan Africa, so as to advance the inhabitants of that continent economically and socially. One part of this project is the eradication of malaria. The director of the scientific research center tells his guests: 'There is still one problem of general misfortune that remains unsolved. Only a Jew can comprehend the depth of that problem, in all its horror. I mean the Negro problem.'

The novel's climax is the travelers' visit to Jerusalem. Jerusalem is the capital of the Jewish homeland, its political and symbolic center, while Haifa is its economic and social capital. The Presidential Palace (which 'reminded them of the palazzi of the Genoese patricians') is located in Jerusalem, and the city is the seat of the New Society's legislative body – the Congress. It is the home to the Jewish Academy and a Peace Palace, set up to serve as a mediator in international disputes. The Temple has also been rebuilt in Jerusalem.

Herzl let his imagination run free in his portrait of Jerusalem as the capital of the Jewish homeland. All the frustrations and disappointments that he experienced when he saw shabby Jerusalem up close during his visit in 1898 burst forth here. He offered a view of a blooming, flourishing capital refurbished as a modern city, an international cultural center that integrates Jerusalem's historical significance with Jewish renewal on the basis of advanced urban planning. Much of his description of the New Jerusalem follows the notes he wrote to himself during his visit to the city regarding its potential for revival. The contrast between this future, which is a present reality in *Altneuland*, and its dilapidated past stands out in particular in the first sentences of Book Five of the novel, which is devoted to Jerusalem. The travelers recall their first visit to the city on their way to Polynesia:

> Then, Kingscourt and Friedrich had entered Jerusalem by night and from the West [just as Herzl did when he visited the city]. Now they came by day, approaching from the east.* Then she had been a gloomy, dilapidated city; now she was risen in splendor, rejuvenated, alert, risen from death to life ... Jerusalem and her hills were still sacred to all mankind, still bore the tokens of reverence bestowed on her through the ages. But something had been added: new, vigorous, joyous life.

The renewal of the Old City accords with the proposals that Herzl recorded in his diary in 1898. It is, according to *Altneuland*:

> Now freed of the filth, noise, and vile odors that had so often revolted devout pilgrims of all creeds when, after long and trying journeys, they reached their goal. In the old days they had had to endure many

---

* We do not know if Herzl was aware that, according to Jewish tradition, the Messiah would enter Jerusalem from the east. It may well be that no great significance should be read into this topographic detail. But given that *Altneuland*'s portrait of the new Jewish homeland, and of Jerusalem in particular, is so full of nuances, the possibility cannot be dismissed entirely. This quasi-messianic tone also appears in the passage in which Herzl describes the opera that the travelers attend in Haifa. The name of that work is *Shabbetai Tsevi*, the self-proclaimed messiah of the seventeenth century, sometimes viewed as a precursor of Zionism.

disgusting sights before they could reach their shrines. All was different now. There were no longer private dwellings in the Old City; the alleys and the streets were beautifully paved and cared for. All the buildings were devoted to religious and charitable purposes – hospices for pilgrims of all denominations. Muslim, Jewish, and Christian welfare institutions, hospitals, and clinics stood side by side.

All the expectations that had, in 1898, shattered on the rocks of the city's derelict reality find expression here, as does Herzl's profound love for Jerusalem and his hope for its rehabilitation. Alongside the rehabilitated Old City, Herzl envisioned a planned new city rising on the Judean hills: 'Modern neighborhoods intersected by electric tramways; wide, tree-bordered streets; homes, gardens, boulevards, parks; schools, hospitals, government buildings, leisure resorts . . . Jerusalem was now a twentieth-century metropolis . . . The Old City and the new neighborhood are resplendent with numerous synagogues, devoted to the invisible God whose presence has accompanied the exiled Jewish people for thousands of years.'

This religious element in this portrayal of Jerusalem in *Altneuland* requires explanation. After all, the book describes a largely secular, modern society, and its author was not, fundamentally, a religious man. Herzl did not, on a personal level, feel obligated by Jewish religious tradition as he felt much closer to Spinoza and the Enlightenment tradition. But as a nineteenth-century liberal committed to a tradition of tolerance, he recognized the status of religion in the public sphere. He opposed religious coercion but did not see this position as mandating a confrontational form of atheism. On the contrary, religion, and certainly the Jewish religion, was to be respected in the future Jewish state. Religion was an important force for social cohesion on the symbolic level. It was not, as Protestant tradition would have it, only a matter of inner personal faith. This took on dual meaning given Herzl's view that the Jews were 'a nation according to religion.' In other words, while religion to Herzl was not the substance of Jewish national experience, it demarcated the boundaries of Jewish identity.

Finally, *Altneuland* was written with an ideological and

promotional intent. Herzl knew that the largest pools of potential Jewish immigrants to Palestine, the places that could provide the massive numbers of Jews that he envisioned bringing to the Jewish homeland, lay in Eastern Europe and the Middle East. To bring these huge and largely traditional publics into his camp, to turn them into Zionists, he had to paint them a picture of a reborn Land of Israel in which they would feel at home. Hence the complexity of *Altneuland*'s portrayal of religion in the New Society's life and, especially, its representation of Jerusalem. The complexity is already evident in the Seder night in Tiberias, which is attended by non-Jews as well. Herzl offers a fascinating and bold balance between secular values and religion, one that would not fully satisfy either observant Jews or crusading atheists. But its aim was to create a new Jewish polity that would be a fabric woven from both old and new – hence *Altneuland*.

Just as Herzl had arrived in Jerusalem on a Friday in 1898, so do the visitors in his novel. But in the case of the latter, their first encounter with the city is suffused with the special atmosphere of the Sabbath Eve:

> The streets that at noon had been alive with traffic were now suddenly becoming silent. Very few motor cars were to be seen; all the shops were closed. Slowly and peacefully the Sabbath fell upon the bustling city. Throngs of faithful worshipers wended their way to the Temple and to the many synagogues ... [T]he quiet throngs exchanged Sabbath greetings as they passed. The Sabbath dwelt in people's hearts.

Note that not everyone streamed to the synagogues – only 'faithful worshipers.' Litvak, however, invites the guests to a Friday night service – held in the Temple.

Many readers might be surprised that Herzl chose to make the rebuilding of the Temple a part of his vision. Secularists would not be enamored by this, and religious Jews of many kinds would have reservations, often contradictory ones. Yet Herzl went into great detail about the rebuilt Temple. It needs to be stressed from the start that *Altneuland*'s Temple is not built on the site of the Muslim holy places on the Temple Mount, or on top of their ruins. One of the first sights the visitors see as they arrive in Jerusalem from the east, from the peak of the Mount of Olives, is the Old City, which 'as far as they could see from the mountaintop, had altered least. The Holy Sepulcher, the Mosque of Omar, and other domes and towers had remained the same.' Herzl did not specify precisely where the Temple would stand, nor is it clear whether it is located inside or outside the Old City walls. But he was unequivocal about the fact that it was rebuilt, using language clearly echoing the biblical description of Solomon's Temple:

> Once more it had been erected with quadrangular blocks of stone hewn from nearby quarries and hardened by the action of the atmosphere. Once more the pillars of bronze stood before Israel's Holiest of Holy Places – the left pillar called Boaz and the right one named Yachin. In the forecourt was a mighty bronze altar, with an enormous basin called the Molten Sea – as in the olden days, when King Solomon ruled the land.

Yet there is no indication that animal sacrifices are practiced in the new Temple, nor should one misinterpret the meaning of the word 'altar.' Although Herzl used the German word for 'altar,' which indeed originally meant a sacrificial platform, in contemporary terms the word meant the raised dais at the front of a church. The same word was used to indicate the raised section in Central and Western European synagogues, the place more commonly now called the *bimah*.

When Litvak takes his guests to the Temple on Friday night, it transpires that the sublime welcoming-the-Sabbath ritual they encounter there resembles that of the modern synagogues that Herzl knew in Europe. In fact, Herzl's use of the German word *Tempel* is carefully considered and shrewd – the word applied to both the historic Holy Temple in Jerusalem and modern synagogues. When the guests and their party enter the sanctuary, the women proceed to the women's gallery, 'and then singing voices and string instruments were heard in the magnificent sanctuary.' Music, but not the organ that was the typical instrument of churches (and Reform synagogues), but, rather, instruments recalling David's harp.

Herzl describes how the service moves Löwenberg, who has so little previous connection with Jewish life. Tears come to his eyes, not from remembering the ancient Temple but because it had been so long since he had heard Heine's beautiful poem 'Princess Sabbath,' which for many of Herzl's generation and position was the exemplar of nostalgic Jewish memory, a poem that portrayed for them the spiritual grandeur of the Jewish people dwelling among foreigners:

> The music recalled to Friedrich [Löwenberg] far-off things in his own life, and turned his thoughts to other days in the history of Israel. The worshipers were crooning and murmuring the words of the ritual, but Friedrich thought of Heine's *Hebrew Melodies*. The Princess Sabbath, she that is called the 'serene princess,' was at home here. The choristers chanted a hymn that had stirred yearnings for their own land in the hearts of a homeless people for hundreds of years . . . It was the hymn written by the noble poet, Solomon Halevy [Alkabetz], sung in innumerable synagogues around the world: '*Lecho Daudi, likras kalle!*' ('Come, Beloved, to meet the bride!').

A rebuilt Temple and Heine! That should not be surprising – Löwenberg's deep feelings reflect those of Herzl himself, who goes on to write: 'Heine was indeed a true poet, profoundly immersed in the romance of his own tribe.' He had written the most deeply felt German songs, but this did not hinder him from recognizing the beauty of the Hebrew melodies. Herzl, who had once defined himself as a 'German writer from Hungary,' here signaled his profound identification with the greatest German romantic poet. Here, Herzl echoes many educated Jews throughout the German cultural sphere who loved Heine and identified with him more than the Germans themselves did. Heine was a man of the world, a German poet, a radical revolutionary, a friend of Marx and Engels – who at the same time published a collection of his poems under the title *Hebräische Melodien*. No poem better expresses the interweaving of his European and Jewish identity than 'Princess Sabbath,' marked by an unforgettable blend of romantic sensibility and irony. The poem recounts how a poor, downtrodden Jew, who lives like a dog all week, is transformed into a noble personage with the onset of the holy Sabbath. Here 'Don Jehudah Halevy' is presented as a troubadour; *cholent*, the slow-cooked stew traditionally eaten on the Sabbath is described, taking a page from a poem by Schiller, as a 'divine spark,' a 'kosher ambrosia' (*koscheres Ambrosia*), the secret recipe for which was taught by God to Moses on Mount Sinai as part of the giving of the Torah. And then, the words *Lecho Daudi, likras kalle* appear, in Ashkenazi-accented Hebrew, in the midst of a magical German ballad.

Moreover: we may presume that Herzl was aware that there is a whiff of yearning for the Land of Israel in the poem, when Heine describes how the Jew relaxes in his armchair after a sumptuous Sabbath meal, so notably different from the sparseness of his weekday fare. As his stomach rumbles he asks himself:

> Are not these the waves of Jordan
> That I hear – the flushing foundations
> In the palmy trees of Beth-El
> Where the camels lie at rest?
> Are not these the sheep-bells ringing
> Of the fat and thriving lambs
> That the shepherds drive at evening
> Down Mount Gilead from the pastures?

Herzl's paean to Heine, integrated so naturally into his depiction of the welcoming of the Sabbath service in the rebuilt Temple, is a singular combination. There can be no doubt that it inspired many of those who read the novel in its original language and who were, in one way or another, integrated into German culture while being deeply aware of their Jewish identity.

These associations also provided Herzl with an opportunity to explain the Temple's symbolic significance and thus the reason it had to be rebuilt in the new Jewish homeland:

Suddenly, as Friedrich listened to the music inspired by [Heine's] *Hebrew Melodies*, he meditated on the significance of the Temple. In the days of King Solomon, it had been a gorgeous symbol, adorned with gold and precious stones, attesting to the might and pride of Israel . . . Yet, however splendid it might have been, the Jews could not have grieved for it eighteen centuries long. They could not have mourned merely for ruined masonry . . . No, they sighed for an invisible something of which the stones had been a symbol. It had come back to rest in the rebuilt Temple, where now stood the home-returning sons of Israel who lifted up their souls to the invisible God . . . The words of Solomon glowed with a new vitality: 'The Lord hath said that He would dwell in the thick darkness. I have surely built Thee to dwell in, a settled place for Thee to abide in forever.'

Then Herzl added:

Jews had prayed in many temples, splendid and simple in all the languages of the Diaspora. The invisible God, the Omnipresent, must have been equally near to them everywhere. Yet only here was the true Temple. Why?

Because only here had the Jews built up a free commonwealth in which they could strive for the loftiest human aims . . . Freedom and a sense of solidarity were both needed. Only then could the Jews erect a House to the Almighty God Whom children envision in one way and wise men in another, but Who is everywhere present as the Will Toward the Good.

This pantheistic image, with its obvious foundation in Spinoza, concludes the depiction of the Temple. It also makes clear that, despite the obvious religious and historical reasons for rebuilding it, the impetus for doing so was not merely religious. It was certainly not just aimed at re-establishing the ancient rite. Its importance was political – just as the destruction of the Temple was not only a religious catastrophe but also marked the end of the Judean realm, so its reconstruction symbolizes the Jewish people's re-entry into political freedom: 'Because only here had the Jews built up a free commonwealth.' In the Diaspora, the Jewish people could preserve its identity and existence through prayer and faith, but only in its own land could it return to being a free and independent political nation. The term 'political Zionism' is often used to label Herzl's outlook. Here he paradoxically expressed that outlook by invoking a religious motif that was, in fact, fundamentally political.

After this depiction of the Temple, the remaining chapters of Book Five of *Altneuland*, all of which discuss Jerusalem, are less dramatic. But they were part of Herzl's detailed program. He saw the re-established Jewish society in Palestine not only as a solution to the plight of the Jews but also as the way into a better world. Prominent in Jerusalem's landscape is the Peace Palace, the first modern building that the travelers see as they stand on the Mount of Olives. It is a 'magnificent and glorious new edifice' erected thanks to funds donated by a wealthy Jew from France. It houses an institution that provides aid and charity to the Jewish homeland and its inhabitants, as well as to distant peoples and lands. To a contemporary reader it sounds like a combination of the UN and some of its international agencies, such as the World Health Organization, the World Food Program, and UNESCO:

> When a disaster occurs anywhere in the world – fire, flood, famine, epidemic – it is reported here at once. Large sums of cash are always available here for emergency relief... Inventors, artists, and scholars also turn to the Peace Palace for encouragement. They are attracted by the motto over its portals: *'Nil humani a me alienum puto,'* 'Let nothing human be alien to me.'

The Peace Palace also works for the peaceful resolution of international disputes.

The establishment in the New Jerusalem of an institution for solving international, social, economic, and political problems was the reflection of work for these goals undertaken at the end of the nineteenth century. That period saw international conferences and humanitarian and philanthropic undertakings aimed at finding solutions to both old and new troubles. The globalization process that was an outcome of the development of new means of transport and communications meant that distant humanitarian disasters and wars came far more quickly and saliently into the public eye and thus took on much greater urgency. Aid and peace initiatives included Congresses for Peace in Bern (1891), Antwerp (1894), and Hamburg (1897), manifestations of the apprehensions about war during that peaceful time.

Herzl knew these efforts up close because one of the founders of the Congresses for Peace was Baroness Bertha von Suttner of Austria, a woman who was also a leading crusader against anti-Semitism in Vienna and one of the first non-Jews to support the Zionist movement. Herzl maintained close relations with her and she made several unsuccessful attempts to arrange him an audience with the Czar. Baroness von Suttner was a unique figure, the first woman who was not a member of a royal family to play an active role in international politics. In 1889 she published her first pacifist manifesto in the *Neue Freie Presse*, and in 1897 she submitted to Emperor Franz Joseph a memorandum calling for the establishment of an international court for arbitration between countries in conflict. In 1899 she was one of the organizers of an International Peace Conference held in The Hague. This conference led to the drafting of several international humanitarian treaties that later became known as the Hague Conventions. In 1905, a year after Herzl's death, she became the first woman to be awarded the Nobel Peace Prize.

Suttner's long correspondence with Herzl is notable for their exchange of views on the humanitarian implications of a political solution to the Jewish question. They both believed that it would reduce hostilities and tensions in Europe. It seems certain that in his inclusion of the Peace Palace in his imagined New Jerusalem, Herzl was paying a moral debt to his friend and expressing his support for her claim that an institutional mechanism was needed to address problems that transcended the sovereignty of individual states. The situating of this institution in Jerusalem was intended by Herzl to underline the claim that the future Jewish state would be able to contribute to the solution of general humanitarian problems, not just Jewish ones.

In *Altneuland*, a similar mandate is given to the Jewish Academy, also situated in Jerusalem. This institution, like the Peace Palace, does not restrict itself to Jewish issues. Its mission is 'to seek out the meritorious persons who work for the good of humanity. This duty was obviously not limited by the boundaries of Palestine.' The Jewish

Academy has 40 members who are also members of the Jewish Legion of Honor. This latter order is modeled explicitly on the French Légion d'honneur. Herzl's sensibility and love of symbols of historical significance was evident here as well. He used language reminiscent of his diary entries of 1898. The order's badge is a yellow lapel ribbon, because 'the color recalls evil times in our national history, and reminds us to be humble in the midst of our prosperity. We have taken the yellow badge of shame that our unhappy revered ancestors were compelled to wear, and made of it a badge of honor.' The Jewish Academy, like every national academy, sponsors international conferences and meetings, and seeks in particular to promote technological innovations that ameliorate human life, raise the standard of living, and contribute to individual and collective happiness.

But the New Society also holds other international gatherings that bring the best minds in science, literature, and art to the Jewish homeland. This 'knowledge tourism' will be the basis for a series of publications called *The New Platonic Dialogues*, in which 'the noblest minds of the period' write about subjects of importance: 'the establishment of a truly modern commonwealth, education through art, land reform, charity organization, social welfare for working men, the role of women in civilized society, the progress of applied science, and many other topics.'

On this and many other subjects, Herzl integrates the land of the Jews with world culture. The particular and universal are always interwoven. The Jews will not be a nation that dwells alone, nor will their homeland be a new ghetto on the Mediterranean. Rather, it will be an old-new land, conscious of its identity, tradition, and history, but at the same time part of the family of nations, a partner in its scientific and technological achievements and in its quest to end human suffering.

The double denouement of *Altneuland* is Löwenberg's marriage to Miriam Litvak and David Litvak's election to the Presidency. Löwenberg, the deracinated Jew who, in despair, had chosen to bury himself alive on a Pacific island, now chooses to join the New Society. The staunch misanthrope Kingscourt does the same – after all, the New Society also welcomes non-Jewish members. Kingscourt's induction has a melodramatic aspect. Throughout his visit he has been amazed time and again by what the Jews are capable of doing (he's constantly exclaiming *Donnerwetter!*). But he also is utterly captivated by the Litvaks' infant son, and the child requites his love. When the boy falls dangerously ill, it is Kingscourt's cavalry songs that return him to health. Love works in inscrutable ways.

But these events are all marginal to the novel's political message. The book ends with harmony between the romantic and the real. Miriam Litvak has a fine voice, and toward the end of the book Löwenberg listens to her sing 'songs by Schumann, Rubinstein, Wagner, Verdi, Gounod.' Then 'Miriam began the wistful aria from [the opera] *Mignon* that he had always loved, "Know'st Thou Not That Fair Land?" He whispered to himself, "*This* is the land!"'

The words of this wonderful song of longing come from the book that had been the inspiration for the opera, Goethe's *Wilhelm Meister's Apprenticeship*. Mignon, the novel's female protagonist, expresses the magic spell that draws northerners to the sunny south:

> Know'st thou that Land where the fair citron grows,
> Where the bright orange midst the foliage glows
> Where soft winds greet us from azure skies,
> Where silent myrtles, stately laurels rise? . . .
> 'Tis there, 'tis there,
> Our paths lie, O Father,
> Thither let us repair!

Having been stirred by Heine, Löwenberg is now roused by Goethe. The most Greek and Mediterranean of all great German poets tells him where his land truly is. Yet, in the final passage of *Altneuland*, Herzl frees his vision of the land of the Jews from the spell of the classic German romanticism that was so close to his heart and returns it to the firm ground of Jewish experience. Löwenberg, who has finally found his place in the world, asks those around him: 'We see a new and happy form of human society here . . . What created it?' The answer is given by each one, in accordance with his character, profession, and world-view:

'Necessity!'

'The reunited people!'

'The new means of transportation!'

'Knowledge!'

'Willpower!'

'The forces of nature!'

'Mutual tolerance!'

'Self-confidence!'

'Love and suffering!'

But the venerable Rabbi Samuel arose and proclaimed: 'God!'

And with that the book ends.

There could have been no better conclusion to the book's complexity and intellectual richness than this chorus of opinions. Herzl, after all, had sought to merge old with new, science and faith, equality and solidarity. He foresaw a society in which capitalism and socialism would be bound together. He anticipated a country in which Jews and Arabs would live side by side with equal rights and mutual respect, and together, as Rashid Bey put it, make 'our common fatherland' bloom. Herzl stressed, over and over again, that there was nothing new in *Altneuland*. But it was not just another utopian dream composed of uplifting ideas that could never be put into practice. All the elements of this new society already existed then. Herzl believed that he was presenting a realistic plan. It required, of course, political will and the ability of masses of Jews to take action, as well as navigate a far from simple international political system, but it was doable.

The New Society had its flaws, but it was able to overcome them. One of these was the appearance of a racist political party and a yellow press, fed by false information and trumped-up charges about the ostensible corruption of the New Society's leaders. Nevertheless, Herzl believed that it was not far-fetched for the plight of modern Jews to give birth to a well-ordered society. Altneuland was not, like Cabet's Icaria, the land of Icarus, who flew too close to the sun and consequently perished. It was a draft of a realistic and practical plan that could answer, here and now, in the earthly Jerusalem, the yearnings of the Jewish nation, a nation without a homeland.

So Herzl saw it in 1902, a vision he thought might be realizable by 1923. But, despite all his awareness of the fragility of the Austro-Hungarian Empire and of the impending threats to Europe's long peace, he could not foresee the pivotal event that occurred between 1902 and 1923 – the assassination of Archduke Franz Ferdinand in Sarajevo. That murder, which ended one international order and gave birth to another, very different one, would worsen the plight of the Jews by an order of magnitude in those lands that rose from the ruins of the Habsburg, Russian, and German Empires. The assassination would turn out to be the corridor that led to the Holocaust of World War II. Yet the outcome of the horrifying war that befell Europe in 1914 would also open a gateway of hope for the Jewish people. The dissolution of the Ottoman Empire, the Balfour Declaration, and the writ of the Mandate over Palestine issued by the League of Nations would grant the Zionist movement the historic opportunity that Herzl had sought but did not find in his lifetime. History works in strange ways.

CHAPTER EIGHT

EL-ARISH – KISHINEV – UGANDA: FROM DESERT MIRAGE TO HARSH REALITIES

Herzl sent copies of *Altneuland* to leading statesmen and other important figures, among them Turkish officials in Constantinople. He continued to pursue his labyrinthine contacts with the Sultan's court, tempting them with promises of a large international loan to Turkey, guaranteed by Jewish bankers (Britain's Lord Rothschild had agreed to this, with reservations). He also lavished personal gifts on courtiers there. His exertions at first seemed to bear fruit – the Turkish Ambassador in London asked him to submit a detailed memorandum on the objectives of Jewish settlement in Palestine and on the ways it would be funded. At the end of July 1902, Herzl again set out for Constantinople, hoping to be received once more by the Sultan. He hoped he would receive the Charter he had been lobbying for, the Zionist Organization's foremost political goal.

But his offer of a loan to Turkey ran into complications – it turned out that there was a French offer as well. Herzl's diary entries from this period are laden with complex financial planning that displayed about equal parts of acumen and fantasy. Dozens of letters, memoranda, reports, and even drafts of letters of credit from banks, specifying quite respectable sums, went back and forth between the Zionist leadership and a number of court officials. But, in the end, Herzl left Constantinople disheartened. He had managed to meet several top courtiers, among them Grand Vizier Said Pasha, the protocol chief, and other cabinet ministers, but the promised audience with the Sultan did not materialize. The expensive gifts had no effect – Herzl realized now that nothing would come of this initiative. The cabinet ministers told him, often employing tortuous phrasing ('Byzantine,' in Herzl's words), and sometimes point-blank, that the Sultan would consent to scattered Jewish settlements throughout the Ottoman Empire that could boost agricultural and economic development, but not to concentrated settlement in any specific region, such as Palestine. Certainly the Sultan would not approve a Charter granting territorial autonomy. The Ottoman government clearly understood, despite all Herzl's efforts to reassure it, that a territorial Charter would ultimately lead to an entity with something close to sovereign status. The Ottoman Empire had lost large parts of the Balkans during the nineteenth century, not to mention its control of Egypt, which the British now effectively governed in all but name. The Empire's rulers thus had no interest in an enterprise that would, to all intents and purposes, remove yet another territory from their dominion.

Soon after his earlier disappointment in his contacts with Constantinople, Herzl had written in his diary: 'Thus closes this book of my political novel.' He now wrote the same sentence once again as he left the Ottoman capital. This time, when he learned that the Turks had pursued some of the negotiations with the Zionists with the object of pumping up the proposal they had received from French investors, he added, in bitterness and anger: 'I have left the cave of Ali Baba and the 40 thieves.'

But, ever the optimist, Herzl continued to hope that the Ottoman Empire's financial position would keep on eroding and that the government would turn to him. He also, with some justice, took comfort in the fact that, despite his failure, the Ottoman authorities continued to see him and the Zionist movement as serious players who could be negotiating partners. In another place in the diary he noted that it could well be that the time was not yet ripe and that the Zionists would have to await the dissolution of the Ottoman Empire – perhaps only when that happened would a window of opportunity open for the Zionist movement. Here Herzl had a rare moment of prescience, foreseeing through the mists of time the political context that would, in 1917, produce the Balfour Declaration.

Herzl thus pursued other alternatives. If he could not achieve settlement in Palestine itself, perhaps the Jews could go to a nearby location, one under British rule, which could serve as a jumping-off point for Palestine? During his visit to London in July 1902, a short time prior to his trip to Constantinople, members of the Rothschild family who sympathized with him tried to arrange him a meeting with the British Colonial Secretary, Joseph Chamberlain, to talk about the 'Sinai Peninsula, Egyptian Palestine [*das Ägyptisches Palästina*].' But the matter was left hanging.

Following the acute disappointment in Constantinople, Herzl returned to his attempt to attract the interest of the British. The timing seemed politically favourable – more and more refugees were taking advantage of England's open immigration policies to flee there from Russia's Pale of Settlement. As a result, London's East End was turning into a largely Jewish neighborhood. Confronted with massive Jewish immigration from Russia, the British government appointed a Royal Commission on Alien Immigration to draft a more restrictive immigration law and seek an alternative destination for the refugees. Even Jewish leaders in England were apprehensive about the 'flood' of poor Jews without skills surging into the country. They worried that the newcomers would undercut the status of the Jews already established in the country and that they might set off a groundswell of anti-Semitism. In July Herzl had managed to obtain an invitation to appear before the commission in order to present to it, and through it to the British public, the Zionist alternative to mass immigration to the West. He accordingly returned to London in October 1902 and met with Chamberlain.

By this time he was experienced both at sitting down with statesmen and being disappointed by them. Yet the occasion without a doubt boosted his confidence that he was on the right track. He would meet Chamberlain not as a conventional Jewish supplicant but as the acknowledged representative of a political movement – a weak one, perhaps, but one being gradually recognized by the nations of the world as representing the Jewish people. His diaries clearly show that he sensed he had achieved a breakthrough. He wrote a lengthy account of the meeting, which took place at Downing Street on October 22, 1902. He was well aware of the importance of this session with 'the famous master of England.' Chamberlain was a rising star in British politics and avidly pursued a policy of strengthening the British Empire's economy. Herzl was not shy about admitting: 'Unfortunately, my voice trembled at first ... After a few minutes, however, things improved and I talked calmly and incisively, to the extent that my rough-and-ready English permits it.' In further meetings, Herzl confided to his diary, he would speak French, 'so that the advantage will be mine.'

Herzl opened by saying that he wished to help solve the worldwide problem caused by Jewish refugees fleeing czarist Russia. He reported to Chamberlain that he was pursuing negotiations with the Sultan over Palestine, adding:

> But you know what Turkish negotiations are. If you want to buy a carpet, first you must drink half a dozen cups of coffee and smoke a hundred cigarettes; then you discuss family matters, and from time to time you again make reference to the carpet. Now, I have time to negotiate, but my people do not. They are starving in the Pale of Settlement.

Herzl's wry comment on the Turkish style of negotiation must have tickled the Colonial Secretary – it broke the ice and Herzl could move on to his proposal. He asked that the British government enter into discussions with him about granting the Jews territories in areas under its control – Cyprus or the El-Arish region in northern Sinai.

Chamberlain quickly responded that, as Colonial Secretary, he could speak only of Cyprus. Egypt fell under the purview of the Foreign Office because of the indirect nature of British rule in that land. As for Cyprus, Chamberlain said,

> Greeks and Muslims lived there, and he could not crowd them out for the sake of new immigrants. Rather, it was his duty to stand by them. If the Greeks – perhaps with the support of Greece and Russia – were to resist Jewish immigration, there would be real difficulties.

But, Herzl reported, Chamberlain added that 'if I [Herzl] could show him a spot in the English possessions where there were yet no white people, we could talk about that.' This was the first oblique allusion to Uganda, an idea that would become explicit only later in their talks, in the wake of several dramatic events. Chamberlain stressed his sympathy for the Jews and said he would be proud to have Jewish blood in his veins, but that 'he didn't have a drop.' The English public was upset about the Jewish influx into the East End not because they were anti-Semites, he said, but because the trade unions feared competition with cheap labor.

While Herzl understood that Cyprus was not a real option, he returned to it in another context. He hoped, he said, that he could obtain a permit for Jewish settlement in Sinai and El-Arish. As part of this, if a Jewish Settlement Society capitalized at £5 million were to be established, perhaps 'the Cypriots will begin to want that golden rain on their island, too. The Muslims will move away, the Greeks will gladly sell their lands at a good price and move to Athens or Crete.' Chamberlain made no response to this blatant maneuver, and repeated that with regard to El-Arish and Sinai the proper address was the Foreign Office. Encouraged by the friendly atmosphere, Herzl dared to ask Chamberlain to help him arrange a meeting with the Foreign Secretary, Lord Lansdowne. Herzl had to leave London two days later and the matter was urgent, he said. His audacity paid off: 'After he thought it over . . .' Herzl wrote, Chamberlain asked him to return to his office in a few hours, at which time he would be able to see the Foreign Secretary. When Herzl returned to Downing Street at the appointed time, Chamberlain received him jovially and told him that Lansdowne would receive him that same day at 4:30. He told Herzl: 'Present the whole matter to him, but do not mention Cyprus. The Cyprus part is *my* affair. Tell him in particular that your proposed colony is not a *jumping-off place* aimed at the Sultan's possessions.' Herzl promised, but it sounds as if the two winked at each other. It was the beginning of one of the most fascinating episodes in Zionist history – the El-Arish plan.

Before his session with the Foreign Secretary, Herzl found time to jot down some impressions of his meeting with the Colonial Secretary. He learned from their conversation that Chamberlain did not know exactly where El-Arish was. Herzl drew a map of the Sinai

Peninsula on a scrap of paper he found on Chamberlain's desk, 'and added my Haifa hinterland idea ... Only now did he understand me completely, my desire to obtain a rallying point for the Jewish people in the vicinity of Palestine.' When Chamberlain said that he expected difficulties with the Egyptians, Herzl responded: 'We will not go to Egypt. We have been there already.' Both men laughed.

The atmosphere was excellent, but Herzl noted to himself the deficiencies of his interlocutor:

> Chamberlain does not give the impression of being brilliant. He is not a man of imagination, but a sober screw manufacturer who wants to expand his business. A mind without literary or artistic resources, a businessman, but an absolutely clear, unclouded head. The most striking thing about the interview was that he didn't have a very detailed knowledge of the British possessions which are undoubtedly at his command now.

Before departing, Herzl permitted himself to press Chamberlain one more time, even though the Colonial Secretary had already told him twice that Egypt was not in his bailiwick. Would he personally agree, Herzl asked, to the establishment of 'a Jewish colony in the Sinai Peninsula?' Chamberlain answered cautiously, but encouragingly: 'If Lord Cromer recommends it.' Cromer was the *de facto* British governor of Egypt.

On the train back to Vienna, Herzl summed up briefly his subsequent appointment with Lord Lansdowne. In this meeting, too, one of the most important ones he would have, he did not feel comfortable with his English and switched to French, 'whereupon *l'affaire marchait sur des roulettes* [things rolled along].' He repeated the main points he had made with Chamberlain, but did not bring up Cyprus, as the Colonial Secretary had instructed. Lansdowne asked him to put his proposal in writing so that he could bring it before the cabinet, and so that he could obtain Lord Cromer's opinion. Herzl asked for permission to send, in the meantime, one of his British contacts, Leopold Greenberg, to Egypt to make some exploratory inquiries. Lansdowne approved and gave Herzl a letter of recommendation for Greenberg's mission, addressed to Lord Cromer.

It should hardly be surprising that, in reflecting in his diary, Herzl hardly exaggerated when he wrote, 'Yesterday was, I believe, a great day in Jewish history.' For the first time, two cabinet ministers of the mightiest empire in the world had lent a sympathetic ear to Herzl and the Zionist cause. Herzl understood very well that England's fear of being overrun by Jewish refugees had prompted the two men to listen to him. Furthermore, their prime concern was augmenting the British presence in the Middle East. But facts were facts: after the utter failure of his years of negotiations in Constantinople, a possibility had opened for Jewish settlement in a territory adjacent to Palestine. Herzl acknowledged to himself at this point that this was but a toehold that, perhaps, would lead to an expansion of settlement, maybe with Turkish support, into a part of the littoral of Palestine. It was with this in mind that he continually referred to the El-Arish salient as 'Egyptian Palestine.'

Herzl took special care in drafting his memorandum to the Foreign Secretary. He sent a copy of it to Chamberlain, adding a letter thanking the Colonial Secretary for arranging the meeting with Lansdowne. Herzl began the memorandum by addressing British concern about the surge of Jewish refugees – one obviously tinged with anti-Semitic feelings. But Herzl turned it to his advantage:

> The stimulus for the British government to occupy itself with this question is supplied by the immigration to the East End of London. True, this is still no calamity worth mentioning, and I hope it will never become one to the extent that England would have to break with the glorious principle of free asylum. But the fact that a Royal Commission was appointed for the matter will make it sufficiently plausible in the eyes of the world if the British government considers itself impelled to open up a special territory for the Jews, who are oppressed everywhere and thus gravitate to England.

Herzl intertwined his tribute to British liberalism with a warning about what might happen if England did not attend to his proposal.

It would either be inundated with Jews, in which case anti-Semitism would burgeon, or it could end its laissez-faire immigration policy, which had given it such a sterling reputation around the world.

After this opening, Herzl reported on his lengthy and exhausting negotiations with the Turkish government. In the best case, he said, it would be long before these talks produced results. But more and more Jewish refugees were leaving Russia and a solution had to be found in the meantime. He thus proposed that the British government consider granting a concession for organized Jewish settlement in Sinai:

> In the southeast of the Mediterranean England has a possession which at present is worthless and almost uninhabited. It is the coastal area of El-Arish and the Sinai Peninsula. This area could be made the place of refuge, the home, of hard-pressed Jews from all over the world, if England permits the establishment of a Jewish colony there.

Herzl then enumerated the resources that the Zionist Organization was prepared to put at the disposal of this project, including leasing fees. A Jewish Eastern Company, with capital of £5 million, would be chartered to oversee the resettlement. 'A staff of technicians and agricultural experts will immediately be sent there,' Herzl wrote, 'to plan the construction of roads, railroads, and harbors, survey the land, and divide it for allotment.' To prove to the Foreign Secretary that he had a solid organization behind him, Herzl named the Zionist Federations and their leaders in Britain, South Africa, and Canada, adding with some hyperbole, 'We have several thousand Zionist associations all over the world. These are grouped into federations in each country.' He stressed how important it was that the concession apply to a specific territory, and that it not allow individual settlement there, independent of the official Zionist project. Granting these rights would create

> a tremendous attraction for the poor and unfortunate Jewish people. Not only the hungry people of Eastern Europe will move where they find work. People with some capital, too, will establish enterprises . . . Even some very rich people from Russia will go along. All these

are facts which I know in detail and for which confidential proof is available. In a few short years the Empire will be expanded by a rich colony . . . Human beings are the wealth of a country, and England can make an enormous acquisition of human beings, which will be a huge conquest.

Herzl highlighted the global benefits that would accrue to Britain if it helped the Jews, and dropped Bismarck's name to hint that the Jews might have other options. Consider, he wrote,

[N]ot only the hundreds of thousands who will immigrate within a few years . . . all other Jews in the world, too, will come into England's fold at one stroke – if not politically, then at least morally. This is one of those imponderables that Bismarck had such an appreciation of.

There are, at conservative estimate, ten million Jews in the whole world. Not everywhere will they be allowed to wear the colors of England openly; but they will all wear England in their hearts if through such a deed it becomes the protecting power of the Jewish people. At a stroke England will get ten million secret but loyal subjects active in all walks of life all over the world . . . [T]hey are also wholesale merchants, industrialists, stockbrokers, scholars, and artists and newspapermen and other things. As at a signal, all of them will place themselves at the service of the magnanimous nation that brings long-desired help. England will get ten million agents for her greatness and her influence . . . It is surely no exaggeration to say that a Jew would rather purchase and propagate the products of a country that has rendered the Jewish people a benefaction than those of a country in which the Jews are badly off.

This document, which Herzl labored over long and hard with the help of British friends and supporters, displays many of the features of the Zionist diplomacy that would, in the years to come, lead to the Balfour Declaration and the United Nations partition decision of November 29, 1947. He plucked the chords of Jewish affliction, and noted the Jews' international influence; he emphasized humanitarianism while pointing as well to geopolitical facts and British imperial interests. He then wrapped it all up with a set of commercial arguments. Herzl's political maturity, forged in failure but also inspired by his extensive diplomatic experience, was clearly on display in the complexity and variety of the case he made.

The memorandum was submitted to Lord Lansdowne on November 12. Chamberlain, having received his copy, set out in the meantime on a tour of Africa, including a stop in Egypt where he discussed Herzl's proposal with Lord Cromer. On December 22, Herzl received a reply from the Foreign Secretary via the Foreign Office's Permanent Under-Secretary. He joyfully wrote in his diary that it was 'a historic document. Lord Cromer reports that the Sinai Peninsula project will be feasible – if the Commission finds that the actual conditions permit it. The Egyptian government would demand only Ottoman citizenship and a yearly contribution for the preservation of internal and external order.' He replied that same day to the Secretary and Under-Secretary that he would make a trip to England following the New Year. In the meantime he started preparations for sending a delegation to conduct a survey of the territory in question – the first time the Zionist movement had, in its short history, actually set up a group of experts to consider the feasibility of a specific territory for large-scale Jewish habitation.

In retrospect, it turned out that Herzl's hopes for the El-Arish plan were too high and that Cromer's reply had been cooler than Herzl understood. Cromer seems to have been unenthusiastic about the plan from the start. But, seeing that it had been positively received in London, he realized, as an experienced politician, that the best way to undermine the idea was to set up a committee to study it. The committee, he presumed, would find insurmountable problems that would prevent implementation, as it indeed, once constituted, proceeded to do. Herzl also seems to have been misled by overly optimistic dispatches from Greenberg, his delegate in Cairo.

Nevertheless, Herzl's enthusiasm was easy to understand. After the failure of his contacts with the German Emperor, and following months of Byzantine negotiations with Ottoman courtiers and a clutch of Levantine go-betweens whose motives were sometimes suspect, he now found himself conducting serious diplomatic negotiations along the European lines that he knew – no need for bribes and no Oriental obsequiousness – with two top members of the cabinet of an Empire that ruled territory adjacent to Palestine. Furthermore, progress in negotiations with Britain would help advance possible future approaches to Constantinople.

Herzl infected his supporters with his zeal. It took just a few weeks to put together a seven-man delegation, despite the jockeying egos and the exaggerated demands raised by some of the participants. The delegation included hydro engineers, architects, an agronomist, and a military man, from England, Austria, Belgium, South Africa, and Palestine. The Zionist movement had had no previous experience with such an operation. Herzl himself negotiated with the Thomas Cook travel agency to organize and equip a delegation being sent to an unfamiliar land. Money for the trip came from Zionist Organization funds and from the British branch of the Rothschild family (after all, their government was behind the idea). It was an irony of history that the first comprehensive survey delegation on behalf of the Zionist Organization was sent to Sinai rather than Palestine. But this was a product of political circumstances – the British were willing to consider the idea if the survey produced positive results. The delegation's findings, not a program drafted in advance, would determine the future of the settlement proposal.

The delegation's work is amply documented in Zionist Organization files, memoirs, and Herzl's diaries, and these provide material fascinating enough for a historical novel. In Herzl's mind, the delegation would have a dual purpose. First, it was to study the feasibility of settlement in the north of the Sinai Peninsula and El-Arish, including the possibility of building a deep-water port at Lake Bardawil and a pipeline – running above or below the Suez Canal – from the Nile to provide this arid region with water for farming. Second, assuming that the results of the study were positive on these issues, the committee's work would lead to negotiations for a Charter for the El-Arish region.

Herzl knew very well that he had to proceed with great caution because of Egypt's ambiguous diplomatic and international legal status. Officially, it remained part of the Ottoman Empire and under its sovereignty, even though the country had, since Muhammad Ali assumed control at the beginning of the century, been to all intents and purposes an autonomous territory ruled by a Khedive (Viceroy). But a series of events following the opening of the Suez Canal, including the bankruptcy of the Egyptian government and the repression of a rebellion led by Ahmed Orabi Pasha in 1882, made the English the effective rulers of the land. As noted, the British unofficial governor of Egypt was its Consul-General, Lord Cromer. Herzl summed up the three layers of the Egyptian regime as follows: 'Ownership is in the hands of the Egyptian government, power in the hands of England, the legal rights in the hands of Turkey.' This complex situation, of course, made it awkward to conduct negotiations and to obtain a Charter. Herzl would also discover, to his chagrin, that he would have to negotiate not just with the British. He had to include the Egyptians, which returned him to a milieu not unlike that of the Ottoman court in Constantinople. In the meantime, he was carrying on his contacts with the Ottomans through the Turkish Ambassador in Vienna, to whom he submitted another proposal for Jewish settlement, without a Charter, restricted to the Haifa-Acre region. He reported these moves to the Austro-Hungarian Foreign Minister, Count Gołuchowski, and tried, without success, to gain an audience with the Czar.

From Vienna, Herzl tried to steer the delegation in various ways, sometimes using coded telegrams to conceal their contents from the British and Egyptian authorities. During the delegation's stay in Sinai, which lasted several weeks, and its preparation of a report, it transpired that the Egyptian government would not agree to a Charter and that it would be necessary to make do with a 'concession.' Herzl agreed, but was concerned – he was receiving contradictory reports from Egypt and began to lose confidence in Greenberg, his closest associate there. Greenberg was sending him cables with the salutation 'Mazzeltov' and reporting that the Egyptian government had agreed to Herzl's terms. And Greenberg had in fact obtained a letter from the Egyptian Foreign Minister, Boutros Ghali Pasha, but it obscured more than it revealed – and it did not mention the Zionist movement or Herzl at all. Herzl was so concerned that he decided, after much hesitation, to set out himself for Egypt to clear things up. On March

18, 1903, he proceeded from Vienna to Trieste, and sailed from that port on the *Semiramis* to Alexandria. He arrived in Cairo on March 23 and installed himself, like all visiting European dignitaries, at the Shepheard Hotel.

This hasty trip to Egypt, his second and last visit to the Middle East, was instigated by the same motives that led to his first, to Palestine, four years previously: he hoped to obtain a dramatic breakthrough. Then the expectations he had had of Kaiser Wilhelm II in 1898 proved unfounded; this time, too, his high hopes were dashed. Herzl did not realize this immediately, perhaps because he did not fully comprehend the intricacies of British diplomacy in the region, and perhaps because he repressed the initial signs of failure and carried on as if all were going well.

On March 25, Herzl was received by Lord Cromer – who made a very bad impression. 'Lord Cromer is the most disagreeable Englishman I have ever met,' Herzl wrote in his diary, adding that the British Consul-General behaved like a despot. Their conversation proceeded pleasantly enough, but every time Herzl made a proposal, including an offer to brief Cromer on the delegation's positive preliminary findings, Cromer replied noncommittally, 'We'll talk about that later' and 'We shall see.' Herzl soon learned that Cromer's principal reservation about the proposal was the issue of water for the cultivation of Sinai. When Herzl asked him whether he was to see the Egyptian Foreign Minister, Cromer answered in the affirmative, saying: 'I already told him this morning that you were here.' Clearly the two men were coordinating their positions.

Later that day Herzl was received by the Foreign Minister, Boutros Ghali Pasha. He was well aware of how unimportant his host really was. 'An Egyptian Ministry in which the Egyptians can't give any orders,' he noted in his diary, characterizing Boutros Ghali as 'an old, seedy-looking, obese man, a Copt.' Their meeting consisted largely of an exchange of pleasantries. The only practical question Ghali asked was 'Where are you going to get the water from?' It was obvious to Herzl that Ghali had been prompted by Cromer to ask this question. The two men sipped coffee and the meeting ended because the Austrian Consul was waiting to be received.

Herzl sensed that his initiative had hit a sandbar. He tried to reassure himself that the problem might lie in one or another minor detail. Perhaps he should have spoken French with Cromer, or maybe he should first have sounded out the man's secretary before meeting him. The members of the delegation, who had in the meantime returned to Cairo from Sinai with a largely positive assessment, proposed that they send their report directly to the sympathetic Foreign Secretary Lansdowne rather than to the apparently hostile Cromer. Herzl ruled this out on the grounds that in the end it would be Cromer who would determine the future of the plan: there was no point in trying to circumvent and thus risk insulting him. On March 28, Herzl and the delegation met with the Consul-General, who received them 'briskly but not in an unfriendly way.' After reading the report he said that the next step was requesting a concession from the Egyptian government. He referred them to the British legal counsel to the Egyptian government, who was to draft a contract with them. Intimating that he could not be bypassed, now or in the future, Cromer told the delegation that 'the matter would be settled here and not in London.'

Some of the members of the delegation came out feeling that the meeting had been a positive one, but Herzl had his doubts. Together they decided to retain the services of a Belgian attorney resident in Egypt, a man versed in the local legal system, to help draw up the concession contract. Herzl remained in Egypt until April 9, repeatedly meeting with the legal counsel and with other officials, accompanied by the lawyer the delegation had hired. The draft contract that Herzl proposed was too broad for the tastes of local British officials, who indicated that the Zionists were trying to insert provisions of a political Charter into what was meant to be merely a concession, a purely commercial document. This matter remained unresolved when Herzl had to return to Vienna to carry out his obligations to his newspaper. He left some members of the delegation behind in Cairo to attempt to conclude the negotiations with the help of the attorney. Herzl seems to have understood, deep down, that the initiative was moribund, yet he continued a steady correspondence from Vienna with the members of the delegation, and to pursue his goals in other channels. On May 12 he was notified from Cairo that the negotiations had collapsed.

There were a number of reasons. One was that the quantity of water required for any sort of agricultural program in Sinai was five times greater than the delegation had estimated. Another reason was that the construction of a pipeline from the Nile, over the Suez Canal, would interfere with navigation in that waterway for many long weeks and thus was not feasible.

What had seemed, for a moment, to offer the Zionist movement a toehold on the edge of Palestine had now dissipated into the desert mist. On May 14, two days after receiving the news that the negotiations had led nowhere, Herzl admitted in his diary that, initially, he had been absolutely certain that his scheme would succeed. 'I thought that the Sinai plan was such a sure thing that I no longer wanted to buy a family plot in the Döbling cemetery, where my father is provisionally laid to rest,' Herzl wrote. 'Now the debacle seems so complete that I have already been to the District Court and am acquiring plot no. 28.'

Herzl had spent three weeks in Cairo in nearly non-stop meetings and discussions. Nevertheless, he found the time to see some sights, and this at a time when romantic European 'Egyptomania' was at its peak. One of his stops was, of course, the pyramids. Notably, when he wrote of the trip in his diary, he focused more on the poor Egyptians he saw on the way than on the monumental structures: 'In the evening, a drive to the pyramids . . . The misery of the *fellahin* by the road is indescribable. I resolve to think of the *fellahin*, too, once I have the power.' The thought could have occurred to any sensitive observer, but it may have had greater force in the mind of a man who thought that he would some day wield state power – after all, Herzl was then in the midst of negotiations to obtain control of a territory where *fellahin* lived, even if their numbers in Sinai were minuscule. The implications for Palestine and its Arab peasant population were clear.

But Herzl took in and considered the future of not only Egypt's poor but also its growing educated class. Conspicuously, his views on the subjects of colonial regimes ran counter to those prevailing in Europe at the time. One evening he attended a talk by Sir William Wilcox, the designer of the first Aswan Dam and an authority on waterworks in Mesopotamia. Herzl's interest was sparked by the importance of water for his El-Arish project, but while listening to the lecture ('tedious,' he wrote) he also noticed something else that he made a point of noting in his journal:

> What interested me most was the striking number of intelligent looking young Egyptians who packed the hall. They are the coming masters. It is incredible that the English don't see this. They think they are going to deal with *fellahin* forever. Today their 18,000 troops suffice for this large country. But how much longer? . . . What the English are doing is splendid. They are cleaning up the Orient, letting light and air into the filthy corners, toppling old tyrannies, and doing away with abuses. But along with freedom and progress, they are also teaching the *fellahin* how to revolt. I believe that the English example in the colonies will either destroy England's colonial empire or lay the foundation for England's world domination . . . It makes one feel like coming back in 50 years to see how it has turned out.

Almost fifty years to the day after Herzl wrote this, the Free Officers Movement, led by Muhammad Naguib and Gamal Abdel Nasser, overthrew what remained of British imperial power in Egypt. Few Europeans were as astute as Herzl in understanding the dialectical implications of the modernization that colonial rule brought to Asia and Africa. One of the handful of Westerners who saw what Herzl saw was Karl Marx, who half a century earlier had offered a similar analysis of what British rule in India would eventually bring in its wake, but few other nineteenth-century Europeans even considered such a possibility. Herzl's comment about the future of British power in Egypt demonstrates not only how sharp his perceptions were but also his fundamental understanding that Western imperialism was not permanent and that it would, sooner or later, be cut short.

*   *   *

Herzl was still collecting himself after the failure of the El-Arish plan when an event occurred that had far-reaching consequences for Zionist and Jewish history and thinking. A massive pogrom broke out on

Easter 1903 in Kishinev, in what was then the west Russian province of Bessarabia. By the end of the pogrom, which lasted for three days, close to 50 Jews had been murdered, about 100 were severely injured, and hundreds of Jewish homes and stores had been burned and looted.

The pogrom stunned and outraged the Zionist movement and Jews all over the world because, since 1882, there had hardly been any violent outbursts against Russian Jews. The shock was all the more intense because this was the first pogrom of the twentieth century, a century that had begun with optimism produced by many years of European peace. Furthermore, Kishinev's proximity to Russia's western border enabled news of the pogrom to spread quickly through the West, by way of new technologies such as telegraph communications. Thanks to the new art of photography, Jews and non-Jews around the world could view graphic pictures of the aftermath of the riots, and the rail network that now connected the continent enabled refugees and witnesses to bring their stories to communities outside Russia. Horrifying pictures of mangled bodies and torched houses were widely circulated, and detailed first-hand reports appeared in newspapers around the world, many of which – including the *New York Times* and *The Times* of London – devoted considerable space to the pogrom. Journalists and writers from all over the world rushed to Kishinev, and leading Russian literary figures, such as Leo Tolstoy and Maxim Gorky, fiercely condemned the attacks. Jewish organizations sent delegations to investigate. The most famous of these arrived from Odessa and had as one of its members the Hebrew poet Chaim Nachman Bialik. After seeing the disaster wreaked by the rioters and speaking to the survivors, he wrote one of his most famous, shocking, and influential poems, 'In the City of Slaughter.'

No other pogrom in history had had such reverberations. The previous wave of deadly anti-Jewish riots in Russia, in 1882, had lasted for weeks, occurred over a much larger area, and claimed thousands of victims, but they aroused little international outcry. By 1903, though, the international community was scandalized that such a horrifying event could occur in a Russian city so close to the West. The pogrom prompted a series of broader questions about the very nature of the czarist regime and its future, and whether the pogrom did not demonstrate that Europe's image of itself at the dawn of the new century as a continent of progress and humanity was not an illusion. The fact that the attacks on the Jews had raged for three days also suggested that the Russian authorities had not acted as they should have to stop the killings. This passivity led to rumors – some of them doubtful, others probably true – that local or national officials had connived in the killings. One person who specifically came under attack was Russia's arch-conservative Interior Minister, Vyacheslav von Plehve, who had previously served as chief of the Russian political police, the Okhrana, and was considered the epitome of czarist authoritarianism. Some saw him as being personally responsible for the pogrom, or at least blamed him for not taking steps to end the violence. At the time, Russia was in the midst of negotiations with Western investment banks about an international loan, and Jewish banking circles now called for a credit ban against the country. For the first time, a pogrom had international repercussions going beyond how to deal with murderous attacks on Jews – it became an international issue that impacted global finance. It also posed an unprecedented challenge to Herzl and the Zionist movement.

Initially, Herzl was a bit late in reacting, in part because he was still preoccupied with the El-Arish initiative and also because he did not immediately comprehend the extent of the pogrom's repercussions. But once he grasped its enormity and the implications of the wave of Jewish refugees now pouring into the West, what had happened in Kishinev became central to his work over the months that followed. This activity compensated to a certain extent for his disappointment over El-Arish. While here and there Herzl tried to restart the El-Arish initiative, the Zionist movement's priorities had changed. With Herzl in its lead, it now acted on two fronts.

First, Herzl saw an opportunity to reverse his unsuccessful attempts to establish contacts with the Russian authorities. Russia's leadership was in a vise – it stood accused by world public opinion of complicity in the killings just as the country was desperately seeking an infusion of foreign funds. Herzl saw that this could help him prevail in getting Russian officials to talk to the Zionists. Second, following the failure of his contacts with Constantinople and Cairo, Herzl realized that if the Zionist movement did not quickly produce a solution for the plight of the Jews, it might become irrelevant. As things stood, the Zionist movement had up until then failed to provide a haven for Jewish refugees fleeing from Russia in the wake of Kishinev. Palestine, at least for the time being, could not serve that purpose, so Herzl began searching for other alternatives, and it was in this context that the possibility of a Jewish refuge in East Africa, in the territory the British then called Uganda, came to be seen by him as a serious alternative. He had previously rejected this idea out of hand, when El-Arish seemed a real possibility. But here was a proposal that had British support, if only because of that country's interest in preventing more Jewish refugees from settling in England. These two projects – an attempt to open channels to Russia and a possible Jewish settlement in Uganda – would produce the two major initiatives of the final year of Herzl's life. He would enter into one of his most impressive diplomatic undertakings, with the Russian government; and he would make his biggest political blunder, by agreeing to consider Uganda as a refuge for the Jews, even if only a temporary one.

Herzl's previous direct and indirect approaches to members of the Russian government had gone nowhere. Now, in the aftermath of Kishinev, he succeeded. On May 19, 1903, he wrote to Interior Minister Plehve, modestly introducing himself: 'My name may perhaps be known to Your Excellency as that of the leader of the Zionist movement.' But he immediately deployed the political weaponry at his disposal. In despair, he warned, most of Russia's young Jews would join revolutionary movements. Only Zionism, and a mass exodus of Jews from Russia, could prevent this. In other words, in his approach to a cabinet minister known for his distaste for Jews, Herzl did not make just a humanitarian plea. Rather, he appealed directly and bluntly to the common interests of the Zionists and the Russian government: to help Jews get out of Russia. Herzl asked that the Czar, whom he had petitioned indirectly in the past to no effect, receive him. 'This fact alone would have an immediate calming effect,' Herzl advised, 'even if not a word about the course of the conversation should be made known.'

That same day, Herzl sent a copy of his letter to Plehve to Konstantin

Pobedonostsyev, who had served for years as the government overseer of the Russian Orthodox Church. Pobedonostsyev's voice was decisive in the government on issues relating to the Jews (he was credited with saying that 'a third of the Jews will be killed, a third will convert, and a third will emigrate'). At the same time Herzl managed to persuade his old friend, the humanitarian activist Baroness Bertha von Suttner, to write directly to the Czar asking him to grant Herzl an audience. She should present him, he told her, as 'an outstanding writer and a courageous champion of all humanitarian movements,' who had been of much assistance to her at the Peace Conference at The Hague in 1899. She added to this that Herzl had already met the sovereigns of Turkey and Germany, 'and now, if he were received by the Emperor of Russia, he would be able to promote the peace of the Empire and of mankind.' An audience would calm the frightened Jewish masses, she advised: 'One does not leave seven million wretched people in fear of being murdered.'

Herzl did not stop there. From the Alt-Aussee resort (his health was growing increasingly precarious as he exhausted himself with unceasing activity, his internal struggles within the Zionist movement, and his diplomatic disappointments), he wrote on July 8 to another old friend, the Polish poet Paulina Korwin-Piotrowska, who lived in St. Petersburg at the time and had good connections with Plehve. As a Polish national poet, she supported the Zionist movement and had composed a Jewish national poem that was read at the opening of the Second Zionist Congress. Herzl now asked her, in the wake of the Kishinev pogrom, to intercede on his behalf. He briefed her on how his requests to the Czar, Plehve, and others had failed to produce results. He entreated her to explain to Plehve that he, Herzl, had a practical program of 'organized emigration without the right of re-entry,' and expressed his hope that she would be able to persuade the Interior Minister that this was a manifestly Russian interest. Korwin-Piotrowska succeeded – on July 23, Herzl wrote in his diary that she had arranged a meeting with Plehve. The phrase 'emigration without the right of re-entry' had apparently sparked the desired response. Plehve suggested a date late in August, but Herzl asked for an earlier one because he would be busy with preparations for the Sixth

Zionist Congress, which was scheduled to begin on August 23. Plehve agreed.

On August 7, following a flurry of preparations (such as obtaining a Russian visa), and after a short stop in Warsaw, Herzl arrived in St. Petersburg. Together with two of his Russian Zionist supporters, he checked into the Europa Hotel on Nevsky Prospect. Ironically, none of his letters and inquiries over the years had been able to gain him an entrée into the Russian leadership the way the Kishinev pogrom had, but the international furor over Russian treatment of the Jews had worsened the czarist regime's dire political and financial straits.

Not everyone liked the fact that Herzl was going to see Plehve. Many Jews viewed the Russian Interior Minister as the archetypical anti-Semite, and the Russian revolutionary movement saw him as the Czar's hangman. No few Russian Zionists thought the meeting (which none of them could have managed to arrange by themselves) would be a historic mistake. Many members of the Bund, the anti-Zionist Jewish socialist party that was the largest workers' association in the czarist empire, viewed the meeting with Plehve as further proof of the reactionary nature of Herzl's movement. Herzl disregarded this criticism. He would be seeing Russian officials whom no Jewish leader before him had managed to speak to, and this following years of refusal on the part of the Russian leadership. He first met with Korwin-Piotrowska to thank her for facilitating the meetings. She told him she had been assisted by a number of Russian intellectuals and officials. As he had done on visits to other capitals, Herzl also made local contacts to help him understand the workings of this foreign locale.

The day after his arrival he was received by Plehve for a session that lasted an hour and a half. It and a subsequent meeting were among the highlights of Herzl's diplomatic career and his full political maturity was on display. His diary makes no mention of the unequal standing of the two, on the one hand one of the most powerful statesmen in Europe, on the other the leader of a small group of Jews. Even discounting the overstatement that Herzl was sometimes prone to in his diary, a reader cannot help being impressed by the ambience that prevailed at the encounter. His account makes it sound like a complex game of chess between two statesmen parrying their opposing interests to see if they reach a basis for an agreement. In this and other meetings he had in the Russian capital, Herzl negotiated as if he were the Foreign Minister of a Jewish state – despite the fact that his state did not yet exist.

Herzl understood why Plehve had agreed to meet with him: he wished to avoid another embarrassment for Russia by heading off a frontal assault on Russia at the Sixth Zionist Congress later that month. True, the Zionist movement was hardly a great power, but Russia wanted to prevent another wave of condemnations of its policies in the world press, which would be reporting on the Congress. Such newspaper accounts would impact on Russia's chances of obtaining credit from international banks, many of which were headed and owned by Jews. This confluence of Jewish hardship in Eastern Europe with the power wielded by Jewish financiers in the West was Herzl's principal strategic asset in the negotiations.

Herzl consequently opened by presenting Plehve with a memorandum, constituting a draft of a statement he proposed that the Russian government issue following the audience. It was a bold move – the Zionist movement was presenting the Czar's government with a draft statement on which it was asked to sign off. If the Russians agreed to the document, an appropriate notice would be presented to the Zionist Congress, and 'Your Excellency will decide to what extent and in what way this would be made public.'

The memorandum, written in French (the language in which the meetings with Plehve were conducted) opened with the preamble: 'The Imperial Russian Government, intending to resolve the Jewish Question in a humane manner, out of consideration for the demands of the Russian state as much as for the needs of the Jewish people, has judged it useful to give aid to the Zionist movement, whose loyal intentions are recognized.' The give-and-take of this sentence is crystal-clear – Russia would assist the Zionist movement, and would recognize the organization's legitimacy ('loyal'). In exchange, it would receive Zionist endorsement of the claim that the Russian government sought to solve the Jewish problem in a 'humanitarian' way. Following the Kishinev pogrom and the consequent deterioration of Russia's image in the West, this amounted to a Zionist endorsement of Russia and perhaps of Plehve himself, who was perceived as the 'evil genius' of the czarist regime and its anti-Semitic policies. According to the memorandum, the Russian government's support of the Zionist movement would manifest itself in a number of ways, including:

- 'Effective intervention with His Imperial Majesty the Sultan,' so as to obtain a Charter for settlement in Palestine that would preserve Constantinople's titular status in the country but place actual administration in the hands of the Jewish Settlement Society.
- Financial assistance from the Russian government for Jewish emigration to Palestine, from funds taken at least in part from taxes on Jewish individuals and institutions.
- Russian government sanction of overt and 'loyal' activity by Zionist associations throughout the Empire.

It was, without a doubt, an ambitious program. Herzl knew very well that the Czar's government would not accept all its provisions. But never before had such an unequivocal memorandum been submitted by any Jewish individual or organization to any government in the world.

Plehve began with pleasantries, saying that he had agreed to the meeting 'in order to come to an understanding with you about the Zionist movement, of which you are the leader. The relationship which will be established between the Imperial Government and Zionism – and which can become, I will not say amicable, but in the nature of an understanding – will depend on you.' He maintained that the Jewish question 'is not a vital question for us,' but then stressed that the issue of the Jewish population throughout the Empire constituted a difficult problem for the Czar's government, one without a solution. On the one hand, the Interior Minister said, 'The Russian state is bound to desire homogeneity of its population' (although he immediately acknowledged the need to preserve Finland's autonomy and special arrangements). On the other hand, 'what we must demand of all the peoples in our Empire, and therefore also of the Jews, is that they take a patriotic view of the Russian state. We want to assimilate them.' How could that be done? Through 'higher education and economic advancement.' Those who, through this process, would come to support the existing order would be 'given full civil rights.' Yet, he asserted, 'this assimilation that we desire is a very slow process.'

The cat was out of the bag – after an opening that ostensibly offered Russia's Jews tolerance and integration (although, clearly, only at the cost of giving up their own national identity and culture), Plehve acknowledged just how profound the problem was: 'To be sure, we can confer the benefits of a higher education upon only a limited number of Jews, because otherwise we would soon run out of posts for Christians.' The Jews, according to the Interior Minister, were being drawn into revolutionary movements. The limits England would soon impose on immigration from Russia would cause Russia difficulties; hence, the Czar's government was 'sympathetic' to the Zionist movement. Herzl heard the distress that Plehve was voicing – the *numerus clausus*, the quota limiting the number of Jews who could study in Russian universities and academic high schools, was pushing them into the revolutionary camp. Here the opposing positions of the czarist government and the Zionist movement coalesced – both were interested in getting the Jews out of Russia.

At this point, Plehve surprised Herzl by showing that he was well informed about the internal affairs of the Russian Zionist movement. (He pointed to a thick dossier on his desk, containing the reports of the political police on Zionist activity.) The Czar's government, he said, was indeed sympathetic to Zionism 'so long as it works toward emigration.' But 'ever since the Minsk conference we have noticed we have seen a change in the leadership. There is less talk now of Palestinian Zionism than there is about culture, organization, and Jewish nationalism. This doesn't suit us.'

Plehve put Herzl in a difficult position. The conference of Russian Zionists that had convened in Minsk in September 1902 was the first such meeting to be held with the approval of the authorities. The major voice at the conference was that of Ahad Ha'am, a writer and essayist who was the leader of 'cultural Zionism,' which downplayed the attempt at a political solution to the Jewish problem and which thus stood opposed to Herzl's approach. As a result, the conference had focused for the most part on Jewish culture and identity. The debate between Herzl and Ahad Ha'am was of great moment for the Zionist movement; it was a dispute about what the movement's priorities should be. But to the Russian authorities it looked as if the Russian Zionists were not as interested in emigration as in fostering a distinct Jewish culture *within* the Russian Empire. At a time when other minorities within the Empire, such as the Poles and Ukrainians, were also seeking to promote their separate national identities and demanding the recognition of their language and other cultural national rights, Plehve and his colleagues viewed the emergence of Jewish national consciousness within Russia as a threat to the Empire. The government would respond to such a Jewish national movement the same way it responded to other national movements – with repression.

Herzl was obviously not at ease carrying on his disputation with Ahad Ha'am in the office of the Russian Interior Minister, all the more so given just how up-to-date Plehve had showed himself to be about the internal debates within the Zionist movement. Plehve ticked off the names of Russian Zionists who, according to his intelligence, did not support Herzl's emigration program but, rather, sought to further Jewish culture in Russia. Herzl did his best to downplay the importance of this internal Zionist debate, but he drew the obvious conclusion. To keep the Russian authorities from persecuting the Zionist movement, it would have to state unambiguously that it sought emigration as its solution to the plight of Jews in Russia. For this reason, Russian Zionist support for the Palestine program was essential. Obviously Herzl would rather not have been confronted with this dilemma by the Russian authorities, but he reiterated that the sole goal of Zionism was resettling the Jews in Palestine. But giving this promise would cause Herzl future difficulties with some Russian 'cultural Zionists' who were more focused on developing Hebrew culture within Russia than on emigration to Palestine.

Herzl asked Plehve to recommend him to Finance Minister Count Sergei Witte for a meeting. Witte, like Plehve, was a member of the Baltic German nobility that held a prominent place in the czarist bureaucracy. He was Plehve's chief rival and adversary in the government, so the Interior Minister was hesitant. Herzl explained that such a meeting was vital because the Finance Ministry had forbidden the sale of shares in the Jewish Colonial Trust company, the institution assigned to capitalize a Zionist bank. In the end, Plehve told Herzl that they should meet again after he had studied the memorandum Herzl had submitted. Prior to that second meeting Herzl met with the Finance Minister as well as with Baron Nicholas Hartwig, director of the Foreign Ministry's Asia Department. Hartwig also served as president of the Russian Imperial Palestine Society, responsible for Russian Orthodox Church sites in the Holy Land – among them the Russian Compound in Jerusalem, as well as sites in Nazareth and Jaffa.

On August 12, Plehve sent Herzl a letter in which he summed up their first meeting. Eventually, Herzl would publish the letter in advance of the Sixth Zionist Congress. Following the letter, the two men met again. Herzl wrote in his diary that the atmosphere was friendly and that the meeting 'went much more favorably than the first, by far.' It was evident that they appreciated each other and enjoyed the diplomatic chess game that they played. In one gambit, Plehve apologized for the delay in sending his letter and in holding the second meeting, but explained that he could not issue an official document without receiving the personal approval of the Czar who was 'the overlord of the country, the head of the government, and *le souverain autocrate*.' Since the subject was the government's support for the Zionist emigration program, Plehve reiterated to Herzl how deeply the Czar had been insulted by the personal attacks on him, especially following the Kishinev pogrom. The complexity of the Russian position and the bind in which its government found itself were palpable. Plehve condemned what he viewed as the hypocrisy of the Western governments – it was easy for them to criticize Russia when they didn't have many Jews themselves:

At this opportunity [when the Czar approved the letter], His Majesty the Emperor also took the occasion to express himself about the attacks to which Russia has recently been subjected on account of the Jews. He was extremely hurt that anyone should have dared to assert that the Russian government had participated in arranging these excesses or had even passively tolerated them. As head of state, His Majesty is equally favorably disposed to all his subjects, and in his well-known great kindness he is particularly grieved at being thought capable of any inhumanity. It is easy enough for foreign governments and for public opinion abroad to adopt a magnanimous attitude and reproach us with the way we treat our Jews. But if it were a question of letting 2–3 million poor Jews into their countries, they would sing a different tune. Such an admission is out of the question, and they leave it to us to cope with this problem. Now, I certainly don't want to deny that the situation of the Jews in the Russian Empire is not a happy one. In fact, if I were a Jew, I too would probably be an enemy of the government.

Then he added: 'However, things being what they are, we have no other choice but to act the way we have acted up to now, and therefore the creation of an independent Jewish state, capable of absorbing several million Jews, would suit us best of all.'

Herzl clearly discerned Plehve's defensiveness (although he said that Russia did not want to lose 'all the Jews' and would like to keep some of the educated and wealthy ones). Herzl wanted to strike while the iron was hot. He stressed to Plehve how important it was that the Russian government exert its full influence in Constantinople at the highest level: 'Everything depends on the energy with which the Russian government intercedes on our behalf in Constantinople.' He maintained that it was not sufficient for this to be done on the level of foreign ministries. 'The most effective thing,' he said, 'would be the Czar's personal intercession with the Sultan.' He once again asked that Plehve arrange him a personal audience with the Czar, but the Interior Minister's response was chilly and Herzl understood that it was not on the cards. In the letter he sent Plehve after the meeting, however, Herzl again called for assertive and immediate intercession in Constantinople: 'There has not been such an auspicious moment for a long time; and who knows when similarly favorable circumstances will present themselves again.' When Plehve said that Russia nevertheless wanted Jews 'of superior intelligence' to remain, Herzl took the opportunity to ask him to ease the existing restrictions on Jews:

But in the meantime, Your Excellency, it might still be a good idea if you did a little more for those Jews of yours who are still in Russia. It would greatly facilitate my work of reconciliation if, for example, you extended the right of settlement to Courland and Riga, or if within the present Pale of Settlement you permitted the Jews to acquire up to ten *dessiatines* [about 27 acres] for agricultural purposes.

Plehve was inclined to agree to a right of settlement in Courland, a Baltic region inhabited largely by Germans and Latvians. 'We have absolutely no objections to admitting Jews to such places where they do not outclass the local population economically.' As for permitting the Jewish purchase of land in the Pale of Settlement, Plehve told Herzl that he had previously sought to permit Jews to purchase land up to a certain limit in the Pale, 'but when I published this intention in the newspapers, a storm of protest rose from the Russians – I was trying to Judaize the land, etc. So I had to give up the plan.' He added that he was, in any case, a friend of the Jews. He had, he related, grown up in Warsaw, and 'there I played with Jewish children exclusively. My boyhood friends were Jews. So you will notice a certain predisposition in me to do something for the Jews.' Herzl, of course, made no response to these statements, not even in his diary, simply recording Plehve's own words. Plehve doubted whether he could again raise the idea of Jews purchasing land as private individuals, but if the Jews wished to organize on a community basis for agricultural settlement, he saw that as a possibility. Herzl said that he was encouraged by this, but repeated that the most important thing was the Czar's intervention with the Sultan.

Herzl's meetings with Plehve were the most politically significant ones he had had with any statesman. Here Herzl acted on all the principles according to which Zionist diplomacy would be conducted from here on out. He did not restrict himself to meeting just with friends of the Jews, who in many cases lacked political influence; he was not deterred from meeting hostile leaders and even explicit anti-Semites to seek a basis of mutual interests; he understood that humanitarian arguments would never suffice to achieve Zionism's goals. The experience of the national movements of Europe's peoples – Greeks, Serbs,

Romanians, and Bulgarians – taught Herzl that only a confluence of interests could produce effective policy. For example, the support the European powers lent to Balkan Christians was not a product simply of sympathy for the suffering of fellow believers living under Ottoman-Muslim rule, or of purely humanitarian sentiments. Britain and Russia, whose larger interests were opposed, nevertheless found a common cause in their desire to push back Ottoman rule. The beneficiaries were the weak Balkan nations. Had the powers no realpolitik interests to pursue there, the Balkan Christians would have continued to suffer under the Turkish yoke. Herzl sought to apply this insight to the efforts of the Zionist movement, but not all his followers agreed with him. He knew that it was easier to shout '*Gevald!*' and present the Jews as victims than to conduct complex negotiations with a man like the Russian Interior Minister, especially when you had so little real power.

Herzl met Finance Minister Witte on August 9, in his summer residence on an island at the mouth of the Neva River, just before the point where it empties into the Gulf of Finland. It was not a pleasant encounter – Herzl termed Witte 'not at all amiable.' He noted in his diary, with a bit of condescension, that Witte's French was weak and unpolished. The Finance Minister enumerated a number of reasons for anti-Semitism, and four types of anti-Semite, adding, 'It must be admitted that the Jews do provide reason enough for hostility.' In contrast with the diplomatic acumen displayed by Plehve, who knew how to cast his personal feelings in the language of interests, Witte made no effort to curb his language. Herzl was impressed, at least, with his candor. Plehve had tried to cast the Russian government's dilemma regarding the Jews in logical terms. Witte put it bluntly: 'While there are only 7 million Jews among our total population of 136 million, their share in the membership of revolutionary parties is about 50 per cent.' He refused to acknowledge that Jews might have reasons that impelled them to join the revolutionaries. But he grudgingly admitted that 'we oppress the Jews too much.' He added that he once told the late Czar Alexander III: 'Your Majesty, if it were possible to drown our 6 or 7 million Jews in the Black Sea, I have absolutely no objection to it. But if it isn't possible, we must let them live.'

Herzl had a hard time finding a common idiom with a man who spoke this way, especially given that Witte told him 'Russia is much more resilient than people abroad realize.' He intimated that external pressure would have no effect on his country's policies. In other words, he displayed none of the sensitivity to the international condemnations of Russia's treatment of the Jews that had been evident with Plehve and which Plehve had said the Czar shared. As for the Zionist program, Witte repeated the hoary joke about the Austrian Jew who claimed that he supported Zionism because he wanted to be the first Jewish ambassador in Vienna.

Despite the Finance Minister's sour attitude, Herzl managed to get in the request that was the purpose of the meeting – that the Russian treasury revoke its ban on the promotion and sale of shares of the Jewish Colonial Trust. Witte surprised him with his answer: he was willing to consider the request favorably on condition that the company open a registered branch office in Russia, 'so that [its] transactions could be supervised.' Herzl agreed to this condition because, 'after all, this disagreeable man had actually promised me what I wanted.'

Herzl had another, shorter meeting with Hartwig, director of the Asia Department. Here, too, he was given to understand that the Russian government was thoroughly up-to-date about developments in the Zionist movement. Hartwig showed him a file of reports on the Congresses in Basel, composed each year by the Russian Envoy in Bern, who 'hadn't much to do.' Herzl was pleased, noting that, despite the Zionist movement's small size, it had gotten the attention of Europe's diplomatic class. Hartwig was concerned about what the status of Christian holy sites would be in the Jewish state, if it were established, a subject that had also come up with Witte. Herzl did his best to assure his interlocutor that the holy sites would be granted extra-territorial status. 'At that moment,' Herzl wrote, 'his face unfroze.' He repeated the request he had made of Plehve – that the Russian Foreign Minister instruct the Russian Ambassador in Constantinople to intercede with the Sultan. Hartwig asked Herzl for a comprehensive document to be submitted to the Foreign Minister. Herzl emerged from the meeting feeling that it had been good to have even a noncommittal conversation with an official who, while of middle rank, held the relevant regional portfolio in the Foreign Ministry.

During his two-week stay in St. Petersburg, some unexpected political developments looked as if they might impinge on his mission. Herzl noted them in his diary, but unforeseen events are not rare in politics and Herzl had encountered such things before. A Turkish soldier had murdered the Russian Consul in Monastir, Macedonia, a Balkan province of the Ottoman Empire, and this of course led to tensions between the two countries. One effect was that Russia's Foreign Minister, Count Vladimir Lamsdorff, refused to receive Herzl. Herzl wrote in his diary that it would be best to wait until the situation had calmed, but that he would not let this discourage him.

When he left St. Petersburg, he sent a letter to Lord Rothschild reporting on the positive responses he had received from the Russian authorities, adding; 'It would be greatly helpful if the newspapers that are friendly to the Jews would stop expressing such a hostile attitude toward Russia.' As Herzl's diplomatic efforts were based on the uncomfortable position Russia found itself in after the Kishinev pogrom, he did all he could to take advantage of this situation, and was prepared to deliver to Russia a quid pro quo. One example came at a ball that had been sponsored in his honor by St. Petersburg's leading Zionists on August 12, between his two meetings with Plehve. Herzl knew that whatever he said there would be reported to the political police and Plehve himself. So he declared in his speech that now was not the time for social issues (meaning socialism) to enter into internal Jewish discourse. When the Jews had their own state in Palestine, they could debate political ideologies, he said: such debates would have a place in the future Jewish commonwealth, not in Russia. He further warned Russia's Jews not to repeat the mistake made by Western Jews – they should not get involved in the politics of the countries in which they resided. Such activity had not helped the Jews of the West – it had only caused them harm.

Herzl wrote to Plehve in the same spirit just before he left the capital. On the one hand he entreated him once more to give a firm message to the Sultan, but he also left it to his judgment as to what would be the best steps for Russia to take:

I intend to work at the task of reconciliation with all my resources, even before the Congress. I am leaving tomorrow, Saturday evening, and on Sunday I plan to stop in Vilna, between two trains, to make a speech. I am told that some demonstrations hostile to me may take place, but this does not frighten me; in fact, the very reason I am going there is to straighten out misguided people, if there are any there.

This was the payback for the letter Plehve had given to Herzl. The letter was to be published, in its French original, in *Die Welt* on August 25, 1903, during the Sixth Zionist Congress. It was the most explicit document that the Zionist movement had ever obtained from any government up to that point and Herzl went ahead with its publication despite the opposition of most of the Russian members of the Zionist Executive, who continued to be skeptical about the negotiations with Plehve. The opening paragraph stated as follows:

> If the meaning of Zionism is the wish to create an independent state in Palestine and promote the emigration from Russia of a certain number of our Jewish subjects, then the Russian Government will be willing to view it favorably ... In this case [Zionism] can count on the moral and material support of the Russian Government.

The letter also included a promise that the Russian government would support Zionist representatives in their contacts with the Ottoman authorities. It would permit the activity within Russia of Zionist organizations dealing with Jewish emigration, and would support them financially through taxes that would be levied on the Jewish population. The letter further committed the Russian government to broadening the right of Jews to live beyond the Pale of Settlement, and to taking steps directed at improving the overall status of Jews in the Russian Empire, alongside the encouragement of emigration.

But these promises came with restrictive conditions that would exacerbate tensions between Herzl and the Russian Zionists. This friction explains, in part, the resentment against Herzl when, at the Congress, he raised the possibility of negotiating with the British over the Uganda proposal. 'But the moment this central aim of Zionism,' Plehve's letter warned, 'is replaced by mere propaganda for Jewish national unity within Russia, it would only be natural for the Government not to tolerate such a new Zionist path.' The firmness of the Russian position resulted from the fear, on the part of the Czar's government, of encouraging separate national movements within the Empire's territory 'which are inimical to the patriotic feelings that are the foundation of the strength of every country.'

It was clear that Herzl's political achievement, the first declaration by any European government of support for the establishment of an independent Jewish state in Palestine, came at a high cost – limiting Jewish national cultural activities within Russia, as well as worsening divisions between Herzl and the supporters of Ahad Ha'am, who viewed international politics and diplomacy as trivial and of secondary importance. But Herzl continued to pursue his channel with Plehve through the mail, even during the Uganda debate. He pressed Korwin-Piotrowska to lobby Plehve to meet him once again, and reiterated to Plehve his request to be received by the Czar. In a letter dated October 24, 1903, Herzl stressed that, in opposition to rumors that had been spreading, 'not one of the Russian delegates to the Congress has neglected his moral and legal duties as a Russian subject. As in every parliament, he told the Interior Minister, there were different opinions among the deputies in the Congress, but he could promise that the Russian Zionists were loyal to their country, 'the loyalty of true Zionists, even those who oppose me.'

On December 6, Plehve wrote to Herzl that, following consultations with Foreign Minister Lamsdorff, the Russian Ambassador in Constantinople, Ivan Zinoviev, had been instructed to inform the Ottoman authorities that Russia took a favorable view of the Jewish plan to return to Palestine, and that Turkish agreement to this would be taken by Russia as evidence of improving relations between the two countries. On December 11 Herzl thanked Plehve for his letter and for the approach to Constantinople, but noted that, given the Turkish style of diplomacy with which they were both well acquainted, a routine diplomatic request on ambassadorial level would not suffice. 'The only effective way to make His Imperial Majesty the Sultan take the matter seriously,' Herzl emphasized, 'would be a personal act of His Majesty the Emperor of Russia, either in a letter to the Sultan or in an audience granted to me, which I would be authorized to make public.' Plehve received an emissary of Herzl's, and, in a letter dated December 27, Herzl thanked him and provided him with a list of the proposed board members of the Russian branch of the Jewish Colonial Trust ('All are honorable people and deserving of absolute confidence,' he assured Plehve). This correspondence took place during the Christmas season, and Herzl, who was well aware of what was troubling the Russian government, added a diplomatic but quite firm warning:

> May I also be permitted to direct Your Excellency's attention to a piece of news which is obviously a fabrication, but is now making the rounds of the European press. The rumor is being circulated that there will be more massacres at Kishinev on the occasion of the Russian Christmas [which was to be celebrated according to the Gregorian calendar on January 7, 1904]. To me, this is an abominable falsehood; but I think it is my duty to advise you of it, now that I am acquainted with your very humanitarian views.

On January 4, 1904, Herzl once again reported to Plehve that he had heard from people in Constantinople that if the Russian approach were not made at the highest level (that is, by the Czar himself), there would be no breakthrough.

A month later, in February 1904, the Russo-Japanese war broke out. Herzl knew that Russia desperately needed credit and made a final attempt to spur Plehve to take more concerted action regarding Constantinople. Herzl's final letter to Plehve was written on May 13 from the spa at Franzensbad he had gone to after a further decline in his health. He wrote that he could inform Plehve that an American banker (Jacob Schiff, of Kuhn, Loeb & Co.) would be prepared to negotiate a loan 'provided that something were done for the Jews in Russia.' He asked Plehve to meet with his personal emissary to discuss this. Herzl reported to Schiff on his talks with Plehve and the detailed proposals he had made in his memorandum to the Interior Minister – only some of which were mentioned in the letter from Plehve that had been published in *Die Welt*. These contacts did not bring about the breakthrough Herzl hoped for, and on July 15, 1904, Plehve was assassinated while riding in his carriage in the streets of St. Petersburg. The assassin was a member of the Russian Social-Revolutionary Party.

But we have gotten ahead of ourselves.

*   *   *

As Herzl told Plehve he planned to do, he stopped in Vilna on the way home to Vienna. His meeting with that city's Jews was one of the most exhilarating experiences of his life and to no small extent established him as the leader among Eastern European Jews. The visit was widely publicized. Some of his Russian Zionist friends had advised him not to go to Vilna, which was a stronghold of the Bund, because that movement's partisans were likely to make trouble: they were furious with Herzl for meeting Plehve and for his condemnation of revolutionary activity in his speech at the event held in his honor in the Russian capital.

But the brief stop in Vilna succeeded beyond anyone's wildest imagination and remained etched in Herzl's memory. The Russian police, who feared riots (whether by the Zionists or the Bund), forbade public assemblies during Herzl's time in the city, nor would they permit him to visit a synagogue or tour the city. Despite the ban, 'I did drive through tumultuous Jewish streets to the offices of the Jewish community, where the officials and deputations awaited me in packed throngs.' This was Herzl's first encounter with Eastern European Jews on their home territory. It was a new experience for him to encounter masses of Jews who acted as a cohesive public and who constituted such a large part of a city's population, as was the case in Vilna. Herzl was moved by the speeches made in his honor, and as a journalist he was also aware of the political significance of the scene. He wrote in his diary: 'There was a note in their greeting that moved me so deeply that only the thought of the newspaper reports enabled me to restrain my tears. In the numerous addresses I was enormously overpraised, but the unhappiness of these sorely oppressed people was genuine.'

He was invited to a dinner in a distant suburb, about an hour's drive from the city, in an area where 'Jews are ordinarily not allowed to reside.' One of the city's merchants, a Zionist activist, had nevertheless managed to rent a summerhouse there despite the law. Herzl was not particularly impressed by some aspects of the dinner, to which some 50 people had been invited (it was, he said, a 'ghetto, with good ghetto-talk'). But his host received him with 'a fine, stately speech of welcome, one of real old-Jewish nobility.' But what moved him to the bottom of his soul, he wrote, was the sight, outside the house, of scores of 'poor youths and girls from Vilna who had come all the way out there (about a two-hours' walk) to see me at table.' Among those who welcomed him was a worker in a blue shirt whom Herzl originally took to be a Bundist. But he surprised Herzl by toasting 'the day when *Ha-Melekh* [King] Herzl would reign. And outside, cheers of *Hedad!* [Hurrah! in Hebrew] rang.' At midnight his party set out for the train station. 'The town was awake, awaiting my departure,' Herzl wrote. Again the Hebrew cheer sounded. 'The people stood and walked in the streets through which we had to pass, shouting *Hedad!* as soon as they recognized me. The same from the balconies.' The police tried to keep the crowds out of the train station, but masses of Jews pressed forward as a chain of policemen tried to repel them. A group of about 50 of Herzl's supporters managed to make their way into the station, where Herzl conversed with them as the police watched from a distance. Herzl was perplexed by the behavior of the police. 'Was this to be attributed to an order from St. Petersburg to protect me,' he wondered, 'or to the police officers' secret fear of the crowd?' When his train reached the station at the border crossing with Germany, another group of Zionists from a nearby town awaited him with 'one more speech, and a bouquet.'

This outpouring of emotion, so foreign to Herzl, brought home to him for the first time both the vitality and the anguish of Eastern Europe's Jews. Up until then he had met only Zionist activists from that region or students from there who were studying in Vienna. All these Jews had adopted the reserve that was inherent in Western manners. Now he saw the Jewish masses face to face, in all their emotionality, pain, and despair. And he felt he could see the hope that he brought them – this may have been the point when he truly realized who it was that he represented. It was hardly surprising, then, that he concluded his exhaustive and poignant diary entry on his visit to Vilna with the words 'That was Russia.' Russia was Plehve and Witte, but it was also the Pale of Settlement and its huge Jewish population. It was these Jews, not the Jews of Vienna, who saw him as King Herzl. Obviously this flattered him and may even have turned his head a bit, but the enthusiasm and the anguish may have also led him to perhaps the most momentously misguided decision of his life – to consider the Uganda option that was emerging at that very time. It was his new first-hand knowledge of just how precarious life was for Eastern Europe's Jews and his seeing how stirred they were by the idea of a Jewish state that impelled him to grab at a lifeboat, as it were, that, he thought, might serve as a 'night refuge' for these millions of Jews. Few of history's great political miscalculations have had such noble motives.

*   *   *

In the days leading up to the Sixth Zionist Congress in Basel on August 23–28, 1903, Herzl had to choose between several alternative paths. Each one had its advocates and detractors and would not only lock him into a mode of action but also had the potential to cause the deepest fissure the Zionist movement had yet experienced. On the one hand, Herzl learned that his diplomatic initiatives of the previous year had failed. His long efforts over many years to gain Turkish agreement to Zionist plans had come to naught; Cyprus was not on the agenda; and, despite his hard work, high hopes, and the initial positive report from the Sinai exploratory delegation, the El-Arish plan had gone nowhere. The Kishinev pogrom created a new crisis among Russian Jews, and Britain was making further Jewish immigration more difficult. These Russian Jews were now banging on the doors of the Habsburg Empire, to the displeasure of its rulers. Nor were Austria-Hungary's Jews enthusiastic about welcoming masses of *Ostjuden*, the Jews of the East, into their midst.

On the plus side, his Russian trip had produced Plehve's letter declaring the Russian government's support for the establishment of a Jewish state in Palestine and for encouraging Jewish emigration from Russia (with its caveat about Jewish national and cultural activity within the Empire's borders). Despite this achievement, Herzl had to face up to the fact that his diplomatic initiatives had all failed, as Zionism still could not offer a territorial refuge at a time when the plight of the Jews was growing ever more acute. At most he could offer a glimmer of hope that the Russian government would support Zionism. True, the Zionist enterprise had never enjoyed calm sailing and Herzl had always been aware of the dire distress of many Jews, but now, sailing into a storm, it was being tossed in a whirlwind.

Under these circumstances, the vague offer the British had made earlier regarding Uganda appeared in a new light. The idea had first been raised by Colonial Secretary Chamberlain during his third meeting with Herzl, on April 23, 1903, after returning from his tour of Britain's African colonies. 'I have seen a land for you on my travels . . .' he told Herzl, 'and that's Uganda . . . the climate is excellent, even for Europeans. You can raise sugar and cotton there. And I thought to myself, that would be a land for Dr. Herzl. But of course he wants to go only to Palestine or its vicinity.' Herzl confirmed this: 'Yes, I have to . . . Our base must be in or near Palestine. Later on we could also settle in Uganda, for we have masses of people ready to emigrate. But we have to build on a national foundation, and this is why we must have the political attraction offered by El-Arish.'

He reiterated to the Colonial Secretary just how important the El-Arish plan would be (even though by this time it already appeared that there was little chance of it going forward) in the power game in the Middle East. 'Once we are at El-Arish under the Union Jack,' he said, 'then Palestine too will fall into the British sphere of influence.'

When it became clear that the El-Arish plan had no future, and after he had comprehended the full import of the Kishinev pogrom, Herzl wrote to Lord Rothschild on May 30, indicating that, despite his failures, his spirits remained high. 'I already have another plan,' he confided. 'Kishinev is not over. The effects are yet to come. According to my information, a terrible fear has taken hold of the Jews of Russia. The immediate consequence will be a new emigration movement. Where? To America? To England?' In his despair Herzl was putting out feelers to the Portuguese Ambassador regarding its African colonies, but without results.

At the same time, England's Zionists, who had initiated the contacts with Chamberlain, continued to press Herzl not to say no to Uganda. It would be a bad idea thus to close channels to the British government and to Chamberlain himself, who seemed, in his own way, better able than any other British leader, to understand the plight of the Jews and to want to help them. Herzl was uncertain, although his correspondence with Nordau shows he thought that, perhaps, British support for Jewish settlement in Africa might impel the Turks to agree to at least limited Jewish settlement in the Acre district if nowhere else – a scaled-down proposal that Herzl had tried to push the Turks to accept. But when Herzl realized that the El-Arish initiative was dead, and in the wake of his moving visit to Vilna, where he became sharply aware of the sense of crisis among Eastern Europe's Jews, he for the first time seemed ready to grab at the proffered straw. On August 14, a day after Plehve sent his letter of support, Sir Clement Hill, Superintendent of African Protectorates in the British Foreign Office, sent a letter to Leopold Greenberg, the Zionist liaison with the British government. In it, Hill expressed his readiness – with reservations, in the best tradition of British diplomacy – to consider the possibility of Jewish settlement in East Africa.

Since Hill's letter would be the basis for the Uganda proposal submitted to the Sixth Zionist Congress, it is worth taking a close look at how it was worded. Hill wrote that, in response to an inquiry by Colonial Secretary Chamberlain, Foreign Secretary Lansdowne had studied the idea. He had not had the time to go into all the details (which had also not yet been discussed by the full cabinet), but there was willingness to agree to the dispatch of a survey delegation to the East African Protectorate that could determine whether there was 'vacant land' appropriate for settlement purposes. Hill stated further:

> If an area will be found which the Jewish Colonial Trust and H.M.'s Commissioner will find appropriate, and if H.M.G. [His Majesty's Government] will agree to it, Lord Lansdowne will be willing to entertain favorably proposals for the founding of a colony or a Jewish

settlement under conditions which would allow the colonists to maintain their national customs.

If such an area were found, then, subject to further consultations, the Foreign Secretary would be willing to consider the plan in detail, including the possibility, the letter went on to say, of 'the appointment of a Jewish official as head of local administration, allowing the colony a free hand with regards to municipal legislation and the administration of religious and internal affairs, with this local autonomy being dependent on the right of H.M.G. to maintain general control.'

Clearly what was on the table here was a minimal concession with bureaucratic and political conditions that would have to be decided in the future, all this dependent on the report issued by the exploratory committee. But at a time of crisis it looked like a ray of hope, and Herzl decided to publish Hill's letter in *Die Welt*, just as he had previously done with that of Plehve. The letter appeared in the issue of August 29. The fact that Herzl wrote little about the proceedings of the Sixth Zionist Congress in his diary was due not to a lack of time during the wearying and charged debate. In the past he had shown himself capable of recording detailed accounts even under pressure. Clearly his frustration had made it difficult for him to report on what was happening. To a certain extent, Herzl simply did not understand what an ideological and personal minefield he had gotten himself into when he brought up the Uganda proposal for discussion.

Warning signs of the coming storm were evident at a meeting of the Zionist Executive, held just before the Congress on August 21. Herzl reported on the failure of the El-Arish initiative, the results of his trip to Russia, and the British East Africa proposal, which he asked to bring before the Congress. Most of the Russian members of the Executive were skeptical of Plehve's promises, and they received the British proposal coolly. Herzl seems not to have comprehended just how intense the opposition was. He disregarded the recommendation of a few of the Russian members – that he present the British proposal as an impressive achievement but not ask the Congress to ask for a formal decision about it. Such a procedural maneuver might have defused the impending crisis.

In his opening speech to the Congress on August 23, Herzl announced that all his diplomacy with respect to Constantinople had failed, and that the El-Arish proposal was not practical because of the water issue. He reported that he had an offer from several British cabinet ministers (he was careful not to say that it was an official British initiative) to discuss the possibility of allotting a territory for an autonomous Jewish settlement in East Africa. 'This is not Zion, it could never be,' Herzl added, but he pointed out that an African settlement could provide the Jews with valuable experience that they would later be able to put to good use in Palestine. He proposed establishing a subcommittee to look further into the East Africa suggestion. The next day Nordau, in his speech, also advocated examining the British proposal. It was he who first termed an East African Jewish settlement a 'night refuge,' implying that it would be simply a way station on the road to eventual settlement in Palestine. He seconded Herzl's suggestion that the Zionists could learn important administrative and political lessons from such an experience.

From this point onward the Congress proceedings deteriorated into a rancorous dispute revolving around ideas, culture, and personalities. The Russian delegates to the Congress held a special caucus and decided by majority vote to express their gratitude toward the British government for its proposal but to inform it that a *Zionist* Congress could not take up the subject of Jewish settlement in East Africa. The days that followed were filled with complex parliamentary maneuvers and attempts at compromise, but to no avail. Herzl insisted that the appointment of a subcommittee was not a sufficient response and that an explicit resolution to send an exploratory delegation to Africa needed to be brought before the Congress for a vote. Following a tempestuous debate in the Zionist Executive, a draft was put before the full body. The resolution passed – 295 delegates voted in favor, 178 against, and 99 abstained. Some of the opponents walked out of the hall in protest after the vote. Most of the opponents were Russian Zionists, the exceptions being the religious Mizrahi movement, whose delegates were open to considering the Uganda idea for pragmatic reasons. But for the non-religious Russian delegates, giving up Zion for even an hour seemed like a severe and elemental ideological heresy.

Despite the formal acceptance of Herzl's proposal, it was a Pyrrhic victory. It was only later that he grasped how utterly he had been defeated. But first he had to overcome his feeling that he had been treated ungratefully – after all, he had worked long and hard over many months negotiating with Russia and Britain. 'I deserved a word, or at least a smile, of thanks,' he wrote bitterly in his diary. Instead, he found himself under attack. At the end of the Congress, after he was re-elected President and the subcommittee was charged with studying the Uganda proposal and putting together the survey delegation, he cried out in Hebrew before the delegates '*Im eshkachech Yerushalayim, tishkach yemini!*' ('If I forget thee, O Jerusalem, may my right hand forget her cunning!' [*Psalms* 137:5]). But this did not appease his opponents. Before his eyes he saw the Zionist Congress on the verge of fracture. The dispute would cast a pall over the months that followed, which turned out to be the last months of Herzl's life. This came to a head with an attempt at a *de facto* putsch against his leadership at the Russian Zionist conference held at Kharkov in November 1903, which explicitly distanced itself from the decisions of the Sixth Congress. At a Zionist Hanukah ball held on December 19, 1903, in Paris, a Russian Jewish student, Zelig Luban, fired two shots at Nordau, shouting 'Death to the African Nordau!' Nordau was only scratched but it was the movement's first experience of an attempt at an ideologically motivated assassination. Russian revolutionary violence had found its way into Zionism.

Yet Herzl remained oblivious to the fissure, if not the rupture, that had shaken the foundations of the movement he had founded. The long months he had spent traveling and conducting a wide range of diplomatic negotiations seemed to him, with a good deal of justification, to have produced despite everything impressive achievements for the movement by drawing political, diplomatic and public attention to it. He had met several times with the British Foreign and Colonial Secretaries, with the effective British governor of Egypt, with representatives of the Sultan, and with the Russian Interior and Finance Ministers, thus achieving legitimacy for the Zionist Organization as the recognized representative of the Jewish people. The governments of Russia and Britain had conveyed to him policy proposals that, even if they did not fulfill all Zionist hopes, could further bolster its standing. The movement had become a player in international politics. No Jewish person before him had attained this status. He had presented the Uganda plan as a 'night refuge,' an immediate and practical solution, in the wake of the Kishinev pogrom, to the growing danger to Russian Jewry. Did any of his critics have a better answer?

The Russian Zionists, most of whom came from the Hovevei Zion movement, which had decades of experience in settling Palestine, viewed settlement there and the promotion of Hebrew culture in Russia as their central goals. Living under the repressive czarist regime, political action seemed foreign to them. Who of them had ever met a government minister or any other policy maker, in Russia or in the West? It was hardly surprising that Herzl's frenetic diplomatic activity did not appeal to them. To a certain extent, they looked askance at what seemed to them largely no more than an ego trip for Herzl. For his part, Herzl, in his diary, characterized Menachem Ussishkin, his leading Russian opponent, as a provincial who had no idea how the world worked. Herzl's low opinion of Ussishkin was evident in the dismissive way he treated the man in public, which surely did not contribute to good relations between the two camps.

Herzl's talks with Plehve, in which he showed himself willing to curtail Jewish cultural activity inside Russia, seemed to many of the Russian Zionists as tantamount to treason. The 'Uganda deviation' was the last straw for them. And Russia's Zionists, unlike those in the West, were not accustomed to the parliamentary tradition of accepting majority rule. They refused to submit to the Congress's decision on Uganda and did all they could to subvert it.* Each side in the Uganda controversy operated within its own political and cultural environment. This brought to the fore internal contradictions anchored in the different traditions from which the members of the Zionist movement

---

* Russia's Social Democratic Party ran into similar problems at about that time – it proved unable to find a *modus vivendi* between its majority faction, the Bolsheviks, and minority faction, the Mensheviks. Party infighting preoccupied its members for years, causing animosity and repeated rifts that severely weakened the movement. In contrast, most Western social-democratic movements managed to live with ideological pluralism and differences of opinion.

came. Those in the leadership, too, had very different political identities and cultural backgrounds. It is simply wrong to claim, as some have, that the debate between the 'Zionists of Zion' and the supporters of the Uganda plan was solely the product of Eastern European Jews' intimate and direct experience of *Yiddishkeit* – Jewish tradition, community, and culture – versus the more alienated backgrounds of people like Herzl and Nordau.

The Uganda plan never came even remotely close to realization for a number of reasons. The British government did not take a consistent stand on it, especially after Chamberlain resigned from it in 1903, a short time after the Sixth Zionist Congress. Other figures in London did not like the idea, nor was it ever clear precisely what territory was under discussion. Herzl made several attempts at reconciliation inside the Zionist movement, especially at a special meeting of the Zionist Executive, which convened in Vienna on April 11–12, 1904. At that time he redirected the movement's immediate activity toward Palestine and declared emotionally, 'for us a solution can only be found in Palestine.' The meeting, which received the name 'the reconciliation conference,' approved a resolution by the Russian Zionists to carry on buying land in Palestine even in the absence of a political agreement. Herzl and Ussishkin met to patch up their differences, and both sides acknowledged that the dispute had gone beyond what was proper.

While a split in the movement was averted, the fissures remained, both among Zionists and within their hearts. Later, the Seventh Zionist Congress, which convened in 1905, after Herzl's death, would officially take the Uganda proposal off the agenda. In response, some of Herzl's oldest supporters, among them the Anglo-Jewish writer Israel Zangwill (who, it will be recalled, considered the Jews a race, a position Herzl profoundly rejected), walked out of the Zionist Organization and founded the Jewish Territorial Organization, which lasted, without achieving anything, until the Balfour Declaration.

Even after the April reconciliation much bad feeling remained. Herzl's leadership, which had been unchallenged up until then, was severely weakened. Nevertheless, as the internal struggle played out, Herzl continued his diplomatic efforts to gain an agreement about Palestine. When riots broke out in September 1903 between Christians and Muslims in Beirut, Herzl wrote to his old friend Prince Philip von Eulenburg, the German Ambassador in Vienna, asking him whether, 'after the incidents in Beirut, perhaps the Great Powers will finally decide to help orderliness and modern civilization make a breakthrough in this region?' He reminded von Eulenburg, citing Plehve's letter, that Russia 'has publicly declared itself in favor of our being given Palestine.' Perhaps it was time to approach the German government again?

On December 23, Herzl again tried his luck with the Turks, this time through that country's military attaché in Vienna, Shukri Pasha, the son of the Ottoman Minister of War. Herzl handed him a memorandum for his father in which he reiterated the minimalist proposal he had already made in the past – not a Charter for all of Palestine but a right of settlement in the Sanjak of Acre, in exchange for an annual payment of 100,000 Turkish pounds and guarantees for a comprehensive international loan for Turkey. As already noted, he also carried on his correspondence with Plehve and his other contacts in the Russian court in order to spur the Czar's government to carry out its promise of support by having the Czar make a personal appeal to the Sultan. He also sent a long memorandum to Hartwig, the head of the Russian Foreign Ministry's Asian Department, in which he reiterated his proposal to grant extra-territorial status to the holy sites. Concerned that the Uganda proposal would diminish Russia's possible willingness to intervene with the Sultan on the issue of Palestine, he added:

> But the only country in the world that irresistibly attracts almost all Russian Jews, with the exception of a tiny minority, is Palestine. All other countries attract only the lost children of Judaism. Only the Promised Land, the land of their ancestors, calls to all of them, the faithful.

Ussishkin and his associates may have doubted Herzl's loyalty to Zion, but they had no way of talking with the Russian leadership and explaining to it the centrality of Zion to the Zionist movement.

As in the past, none of these efforts came to anything, but Herzl did not give up. Through contacts that he continued to build, he set out in January 1904 for a meeting in Rome with the King of Italy. During this trip he also obtained an unplanned audience with the Pope.

In parallel, Herzl carried on his editorial work at the *Neue Freie Presse*. On top of that, during the Sixth Zionist Congress, the Berlin Royal Theater premiered his new play, *Solon in Lydia*. In a letter written at the beginning of September to his friend General Alexander Kiriyev in St. Petersburg, to which he attached a copy of the play, Herzl related that he had not attended the premiere because he had been too busy with the Congress. But the acrimony the Congress had left him with was evident in his comment that 'I much prefer literature to politics.' The play was based on a *feuilleton* that Herzl had written for his newspaper in April 1900. He dramatized that prose piece a year and a half later while waiting for a reply to one of his petitions to the Sultan, but its staging was delayed for various reasons.

The play is difficult to place in the wider context of Herzl's thinking. Its plot comes from a Greek legend according to which Solon, the Athenian lawmaker, spends time in the court of the Lydian King Croesus, a king who is unable to achieve happiness despite his celebrated wealth. Herzl added a twist to the traditional story. A young man appears in the King's court, claiming that he has found an effortless way to produce flour. This will enable him to supply sustenance to all of humankind and spare them their labors. Everyone enthusiastically accepts this solution to human suffering, but Herzl – speaking through his character Solon – is skeptical. If people do not need to work, they will become soft and lazy and cultural progress will cease. After all, it is need that goads them to try and invent new things. And, in fact, when free flour is distributed to the population riots and revolutions break out. In the end, everyone agrees with Solon that the young man should be done away with.

The idea that want is the engine of human cultural development was not original, but it ran counter to many streams in nineteenth-century romanticism. The melodramatic way in which Herzl presented the idea was shallow and unpersuasive. Nor was he the first to say that the purpose of human existence is not the search for happiness but self-fulfillment through work. So it is not clear why Herzl chose this subject for a drama. That the play was not a success should not be a surprise. It is also hard to see a connection between the play's theme and any of the important insights Herzl had about the Jewish question. The play does show sympathy for the hungry masses and criticizes grain speculators, so some of Herzl's commitment to social justice seems to resonate in some of the scenes. But all this pales in comparison with the play's central message, that human beings would be worse off if they were able to get all they needed easily. Some have viewed the play as Herzl's way of casting doubt on social utopias; we have seen that *Altneuland* was a work that sought, despite its adoption of the utopian genre, to avoid offering utopian solutions. Whatever the case, during its run the play was far from the center of Herzl's attention. He focused instead on trying to find more ways to gain a Jewish homeland in Palestine. It was with this purpose that he traveled to Rome, just a few months before his death.

CHAPTER NINE

TOWARD THE END:
ROME AND JERUSALEM

WHEN HE WROTE *The Jewish State*, Herzl was unaware of Moses Hess's *Rome and Jerusalem*, published in 1862. Hess, a close friend and collaborator of Karl Marx, wrote his book under the impact of Italian unification and the thinking of Giuseppe Mazzini, calling for the establishment of a Jewish commonwealth in Palestine as a solution to the 'Last Nationalities Question,' the subtitle of his book. We do not know who brought the book, largely forgotten by the end of the nineteenth century, to Herzl's attention. But when he founded *Die Welt*, Herzl asked one of his associates, Leon Kellner, to write a series of articles on 'writers who supported Zionism: Disraeli, George Eliot, Moses Hess.' On his forty-first birthday, May 2, 1901, he wrote in his diary that he had taken Hess's book on his journey to Jerusalem in 1898, 'but had never been able to finish it properly in the rush of those years.' Now, having finally read it, he wrote,

> I was enraptured and inspired by him. What an exalted, noble spirit! Everything we have tried is already in his book. The only bothersome thing is his Hegelian terminology. Wonderful, the Spinozistic-Jewish and national elements. Since Spinoza, Jewry has brought forth no greater spirit than this forgotten, faded Moses Hess!

In January 1904, Herzl traveled to Rome for an audience with King Victor Emmanuel III of Italy, arranged by a leading Italian Zionist.

Herzl had made his first trip to Rome when he was 27, in February 1887, as part of the *de rigueur* cultural pilgrimage expected of all educated Europeans, to view the glories of Italy. Now, nearly 44 years old and ailing, he was returning on a Jewish national mission. By coincidence he met on the train to Venice a Hungarian painter, Berthold Dominic Lippay, who served as court artist to the Pope and boasted the title of Count conferred on him by the Pontiff. He promised to present Herzl to Pius X. Herzl was skeptical at first, but Lippay ended up being true to his word. Eventually, as Herzl's diary shows, the unplanned meeting with the Pope, despite its disappointing outcome, appeared to him more significant than the meeting with the Italian King.

When Herzl arrived in Rome on January 22, a message was waiting for him in his hotel informing him that the Pope would receive him following a meeting with the Holy See's Secretary of State, Cardinal Rafael Merry del Val. Lippay coached him for the meeting. The artist had been impressed by how Herzl had spoken of Jesus when they met in Venice, saying that 'after all, I consider [him] a Jew.' So he proposed that Herzl tell the Cardinal that his view of Jesus was the Catholic view. Herzl was incensed: 'No sir, this I shall not do!. . . The very idea! After all, I am not going to the Vatican as a convert, but as a political spokesman for my own people.' Lippay offered another suggestion – that Herzl ask the Pope for a protectorate. Herzl demurred – all he would ask would be a statement, in one of the papal encyclicals, that he had no objections to Zionism. By this time it had transpired that Lippay was no altruist. He was angling for a loan from Herzl or one of his donors – or to get a Rothschild or some other Jewish financier to buy his paintings. Lippay agreed with Herzl's approach, again promising him that the audience would indeed take place, and accompanied Herzl to the Vatican. There Herzl was kept waiting a long time but enjoyed watching the comings and goings of the Swiss Guard and the Princes of the Church. 'There was certainly something like the atmosphere of a royal court about it,' he wrote in his diary. He was also deeply impressed by the Raphael paintings in the ante-chamber where he waited. He examined a sculpture of Christ hanging on a wall, a 'crucified figure, pitiful, suffering, the epitome of human misery,' and wondered what Jesus would have thought of the riches so ostentatiously on display before him. 'Would it have made dying easier for him, or harder?' he wistfully asked.

These meditations by a Jew of European upbringing, with all the consequential complexities elicited by thoughts about Jesus the Jew, were interrupted when he was called into the presence of the Spanish Cardinal Merry del Val. Herzl, speaking in French, reiterated the request that Lippay had made to the Secretary of State: 'I ask the good will of the Holy See for our cause.' The Cardinal spoke bluntly, as the Pope, too, would – although in a milder way – expressing the doctrinal position that would characterize the Holy See's stance on Zionism and Israel, until the Vatican established diplomatic relations with Israel in 1993:

> I do not quite see how we can take any initiative in this matter. As long as the Jews deny the divinity of Christ we certainly cannot make a declaration in their favor. Not that we have any ill will toward them. On the contrary, the Church has always protected them. To us they are the indispensible witnesses to the phenomenon of God's term on earth. But they deny the divinity of Christ. How then can we, without abandoning our own highest principles, agree to their being given possession of the Holy Land again?

Herzl asserted that he was not seeking a theological imprimatur. 'We are asking only for the profane earth,' he said, reiterating that holy sites would retain an extra-territorial status. Nor was there any need for the Pope to declare his support of Zionism – all that Herzl was asking him to do was to say that he did not oppose it. 'You could achieve a great moral conquest here,' Herzl maintained. But the Cardinal did not budge:

> [A] Jew who has himself baptized out of conviction is for me the ideal. In such a person I see the corporeal, his descent from the people of Christ, united with the spiritual. A Jew who acknowledges the divinity of Christ – *mais c'est St. Pierre, c'est St. Paul* [this is St. Peter, this is St. Paul].

But Herzl's words seem not to have fallen on deaf ears. The Secretary of State seemed impressed when Herzl showed him Plehve's letter – if for no other reason than that the document had come from the world's greatest Orthodox power, the Vatican's religious rival. Herzl asked that the Cardinal recommend an audience with the Pope, and it looked to Herzl as if the answer would not be negative, despite the fact that the conversation with Merry del Val had been conducted as though it had been two monologues. Herzl turned out to be right. An invitation to the Pope was indeed forthcoming, although it arrived four days later.

In the meantime, following his meeting with the Vatican Secretary of State, Herzl was received by the King of Italy. Herzl was well aware that, as a constitutional monarch, the King did not make policy decisions, but the Italian head of state's meeting with the leader of the Zionist movement was of course significant and could open doors with the offices of the Prime Minister, Foreign Minister, and other officials.

Despite its limited practical significance, in its contents and its ambience this was one of the most pleasant meetings Herzl had had with a head of state. Victor Emmanuel turned out to be even shorter than Herzl expected and quite affable. He was well versed on policy issues and displayed a sometimes astonishing acquaintance with Jewish subjects. It transpired that initially the King thought that Herzl was a rabbi, not just the leader of a Zionist movement, and his error had to be politely corrected. This conversation, too, was conducted in French. At the start the King expressed his justifiable pride in the equal rights enjoyed by Italy's Jews, who, he said, had been able to achieve more in his country than anywhere else in Europe. 'In our country,' he boasted, 'there is no distinction between Jews and Christians. Jews can become anything, and they do. The army, the civil service, even the diplomatic corps – everything is open to them.' He noted that there were eighteen Jews in parliament, even though proportionately, by their share in the population, they might be expected to have only a single member. Jews had participated in every Italian government, he said, mentioning in particular Luigi Luzzati, then serving as Minister of Finance (and who would later become Prime Minister); Giuseppe Ottolenghi, who had been Minister of War in 1902–3; and Leone Wollemberg, a former Finance Minister. He mentioned other names as well, too many for Herzl to write down.

When the subject of Palestine came up, the King said that he knew the country well from his visits there. 'The land is already very Jewish,' he said. 'It will and must become yours; it is only a question of time. Wait till you have half a million Jews there.' Herzl was impressed by the King's sympathetic and secular attitude, so different from the theological dogmatism he had encountered the previous day in the Vatican. He told the King that Jews faced obstacles to settling in Palestine and that the Ottoman Empire was blocking every attempt to get it to agree to grant the Jews a Charter. The King responded that it was all a matter of money – the Turks could always be bought and it was just a matter of determining their price.

Herzl gently repeated that what was needed was diplomatic pressure exerted on the Turks, and showed him Plehve's letter. He asked the Italian King to write to the Sultan, but the King explained that, despite his sympathy for Herzl's cause, he was constitutionally prevented from doing so without first consulting with the Foreign Minister, Tommaso Tittoni. He recommended that Herzl speak to Tittoni.

The conversation, pleasant from the start, gradually took on a truly friendly tone, but without any clear purpose. The King suddenly brought up Shabbetai Tsevi, the false Messiah of the seventeenth century, and related that one of his ancestors, Carlo Emmanuel II, Duke of Savoy, had approached Shabbetai Tsevi and sought to appoint him King of Macedonia (there is no evidence that such an event actually occurred). Jokingly, the King asked if there were still Jews waiting for their Redeemer. Herzl replied guardedly that some religious Jews still did, but that 'Among our own academically trained and enlightened circles, no such thought exists, of course . . . our movement is purely national.' He added that, when he visited Jerusalem, he deliberately avoided riding on a white donkey or horse, lest people take him for the Messiah. The King laughed.

Victor Emmanuel told Herzl that he knew of the existence of Jews in Eritrea, which Italy had recently annexed – they were called Falashas, he said. He also had heard that there were Jews in China. He reminded

Herzl that Napoleon had attempted to re-establish the Sanhedrin, the assembly of sages that served as the supreme Jewish religious and judicial authority in ancient times. The King added that a member of the Ottolenghi family had participated in the attempt. Herzl responded: 'Napoleon had ideas about restoring the Jewish nation, Sire!' But the King begged to differ: 'No, he just wanted to make the Jews, who were scattered all over the world, into his agents.' According to Herzl, the conversation was 'erratic' and he kept trying to steer it back to the subject of Palestine. He referred to the Uganda plan to demonstrate to the King how good his connections with the British were. When, toward the end of the conversation, Herzl remarked, 'the partition of Turkey is bound to come, Your Majesty,' the King agreed but said that it would not happen soon, though 'a people such as yours can wait even a hundred years.'

Whatever the audience's shortcomings, it had results. The King asked Foreign Minister Tittoni to receive Herzl, and the two had a short, businesslike talk. The King had informed Tittoni of Herzl's request that Italy intervene in Constantinople, and Tittoni now promised to instruct the Italian Ambassador in Constantinople 'to proceed jointly with the Russians.' If it went well, it could be that the King would contact the Sultan directly, he said. The Foreign Minister also asked for a comprehensive memorandum laying out the Zionist movement's requests of Turkey, with a focus on the proposal to receive a Charter for the Sanjak of Acre. He added that the fact that Italy did not have a Jewish problem would give its position greater diplomatic weight.

Two days later Herzl had his audience with the Pope. It reflected, both in its substance and the accompanying protocol and ceremony, all the tension and ambivalence of Jewish-Christian relations, and even a non-observant Jew like Herzl could not help feeling uneasy. He was led, along with Lippay, through sumptuous anterooms and halls, 'past the Swiss lackeys, who looked like priests, and priests who looked like lackeys, the Papal officers and chamberlains.' Lippay said that the Pope would expect Herzl to kiss his hand, but Herzl asserted that he would neither kneel nor bow. In his diary, he reported:

He received me standing and held out his hand, which I did not kiss. Lippay had told me that I had to do it, but I didn't. I believe that I incurred his displeasure by this, for everyone who visits him kneels down and at least kisses his hand. This hand kiss had caused me a lot of worry. I was quite glad when it was finally out of the way.

To Herzl, the Spanish Secretary of State had come off as an experienced Curia diplomat. The Pope, in contrast, reminded Herzl of 'a good-natured, corpulent village priest.' Pius X did not know French, so Herzl had to converse with him in Italian, a language he knew well enough but was not fluent in. When he apologized for the meagerness of his Italian, the Pontiff responded magnanimously: '*No, parla molto bene, Signor Commendatore!*' ('No, Knight Commander, you speak it very well!'). In accordance with a piece of advice from Lippay, Herzl had made a point that day of wearing, for the first time in his life, his Order of the Medjidie medal, which he had received from the Sultan, and according to Vatican protocol the Pope addressed him as a knight. This, and the fact that they conversed in Italian, lent their already singular conversation a somewhat surreal air. Popes must have met Jews in the past, but this was the first time the occupant of the Throne of St. Peter had given an audience to a representative of a modern Jewish national movement. Herzl was profoundly aware of this novelty.

Herzl went right to the point, as he had at his meeting with Merry del Val, and asked for the Pope's support. Pius displayed no less alacrity in voicing a refusal cast in the terms of classic Christian theology. In the midst of his German diary entry about the conversation, Herzl recorded the Pope's response in the original Italian:

We cannot give approval to this movement. We cannot prevent the Jews from going to Jerusalem, but we could never sanction it. The soil of Jerusalem, if it was not always sacred, has been sanctified by the life of Jesus Christ. As the Head of the Church I cannot tell you anything different. The Jews have not recognized our Lord, therefore we cannot recognize the Jewish people.

Herzl noted to himself: 'Hence the conflict between Rome, represented by him, and Jerusalem, represented by me, flared up again.' He tried, unsuccessfully, to mitigate the Pope's rebuff by reiterating his commitment to extra-territorial status for Christian holy sites, but this was no more persuasive with the Pope than it had been with the Cardinal. When Herzl was so bold as to ask how the Church managed with the existing situation, the Pope responded: 'I know, it is not pleasant to see the Turks in possession of our Holy Places. We simply have to put up with that. But to support the Jews in the acquisition of the Holy Places, that we cannot do.' Herzl supposed that if he were to stress the humanitarian aspect of Zionism, as a way of addressing the hardships faced by so many Jews, as well as Zionism's nonreligious nature, he might be able in part to circumvent the Church's theological objections. But instead he jumped from the frying pan straight into the fire. The Pope told him:

> There are two possibilities. Either the Jews will cling to their faith and continue to await the Messiah who, for us, has already appeared. In that case they will be denying the divinity of Jesus and we cannot help them. Or else they will go there without any religion, and then we can be even less favorable to them. The Jewish religion was the foundation of our own; but it was superseded by the teachings of Christ, and we cannot concede it any further validity. The Jews, who ought to have been the first to acknowledge Jesus Christ, have not done so to this day.

Herzl tried to hold himself back from replying directly, but could not help remarking, 'Terror and persecution may not have been the right means for enlightening the Jews.' According to Herzl, the Pope's reply was 'magnificent in its simplicity':

> Our Lord came without power. *Era povero* [He was poor]. He came *in pace* [in peace]. He persecuted no one. *He* was persecuted. He was *abbandonato* [forsaken] even by his apostles. Only later did He grow in stature. It took three centuries for the Church to evolve. The Jews therefore had time to acknowledge His divinity without any pressure. But they haven't done so to this day.

Herzl realized it would be fruitless to enter even further into a theological debate, so he returned to the dire circumstances of the persecuted Jews of Eastern Europe who were seeking a refuge. The Pope asked: 'Does it have to be *Gerusalemme*?' Herzl responded that the Jews sought only the terrestrial Palestine. But this made no difference. The Church, the Pope said, was well aware of the plight of the Jews: 'Indeed, we also pray for them: that their minds be enlightened.' He added that the day of their meeting, January 25, was peculiarly appropriate – on the Church calendar it was the Feast of the Conversion of St. Paul, commemorating the epiphany that Paul had experienced on the road to Damascus. On this day Catholics prayed that all unbelievers also see the light that Paul saw. 'And so,' the Pope explained, 'if you come to Palestine and settle your people there, we shall have churches and priests ready to baptize all of you.'

It became increasingly clear that the conversation was going nowhere. The Pope's position remained a dogmatic *non possumus* – 'We cannot.' As the audience approached its end, Lippay joined them. When the Pope dismissed them, Herzl wrote in his diary, 'Lippay spent some time kneeling before him and couldn't seem to get his fill of kissing his hand. Then I realized that the Pope liked this sort of thing. But on parting, too, all I did was to give him a warm hand-squeeze and low bow.' When he emerged from the audience, Herzl noticed a Raphael fresco on the wall of one of the anterooms. It showed Charlemagne kneeling before the Pope who, seated on his throne, placed the crown of the Holy Roman Empire on his head. Herzl wrote in his diary: 'That's the way Rome wants it.'

We have no way of knowing whether Herzl had been reminded, during his audience with the Pope, of his momentary idea, many years before, that the Jews might convert to Christianity en masse (it should be recalled that he imagined that he and the Jewish leadership would not participate). If he did recall it, how distant that moment of despair must have seemed from the present occasion! The head of the Roman Church had sat face to face with the man who saw himself as the leader of the Jewish people, a people returning to identity and to its land. One had power, the other only wishes and hopes. But when they spoke, they had spoken as equals.

Throughout his stay in Rome, Herzl soaked up the city's beauty and historical richness. But he could not help thinking of Jerusalem. As during his visit there in 1898 and when he imagined in *Altneuland* the city as it would look in 1923, he could not avoid juxtaposing the two eternal cities. He recorded in his diary a thought he had had during his carriage ride to his audience with the Italian King at the Quirinal Palace (which had been a papal residence before being expropriated from the Church at the time of Italian unification in 1871):

> On the drive through old-new Rome I had the idea of building a street in Jerusalem to be called Diaspora Road, and there display the architectural styles of all the ages and nations through which we have wandered. Building regulations are to be given for each section of this street, and sites are to be allotted (gratis?) only to people who pledge themselves to build in the style of their particular section. At 11:05 I drew up before the Royal Wing of the Quirinal.

Truly, if I forget thee, O Jerusalem . . .

*   *   *

The final significant political meeting Herzl had before his death was with the Austro-Hungarian Foreign Minister, Count Agenor von Gołuchowski. Like many leading government officials in Vienna, he hailed from the Galician Polish aristocracy. In retrospect, the meeting was tinged by irony. Herzl, an Austro-Hungarian subject who had met heads of state and senior ministers of many European countries, had never conferred with the Foreign Minister of the Habsburg Empire. As previously noted, since 1867 Austria and Hungary had separate governments but a common Foreign Ministry. While Herzl had met over the years with two Austrian Prime Ministers, Count Kasimir Badeni and Ernest von Koerber, who had backed his ideas in principle, they had scant ability to put any pressure on Constantinople. It was this lack of Austrian influence on the Turks that had given him no reason to have met earlier with the Austro-Hungarian Foreign Minister, even though he had had a passing acquaintance with Gołuchowski when the latter was serving as an Austrian diplomat in Paris during Herzl's time there. Now, in the spring of 1904, Herzl asked for a meeting, and one took place on April 30. Herzl wrote in his diary that it had been a 'big and possibly consequential discussion.' While Herzl's evaluation is debatable, it can be taken as a sign of how he was grasping at straws during the final months of his life. His dejection undoubtedly exacerbated his illness.

In his request for the meeting, Herzl noted it was odd that he had never met the Foreign Minister of the 'land of his birth.' At the start of the meeting he told Gołuchowski that he had not wanted to bother him so long as he had nothing concrete to speak of. But now he had that – he showed the Foreign Minister Plehve's letter, which 'he read over twice, with well-concealed astonishment.' The conversation turned to history, beginning with Jewish-Christian relations and ending with the question of whether there could be anti-Semitism in France, when there were so few Jews there. Gołuchowski related that he was well acquainted with the hardships of the Jews from his own family estate: *'Ils crèvant de faim et de misère'* ('They are perishing of hunger and destitution'). Herzl used the same ammunition he had used in St. Petersburg, telling his host that *'Mai avant de mourir . . . ils s'en iront aux parties revolutionnaires'* ('But before they die . . . they will go over to the revolutionary parties').

Gołuchowski agreed that no solution to the Jewish problem could be found in Europe, so he told Herzl that he supported his ideas, adding that it would not be sufficient to encourage the emigration of 100,000–200,000. 'The Great Powers will act,' he said, 'only if we asked Turkey for land and legal rights for 5–6 million Jews.' Herzl was fired up. That being the case, he said, would Gołuchowski agree to take such an initiative? Gołuchowski suggested that Herzl enlist Count István Tisza, the Prime Minister of Hungary, as well. Herzl remarked that no doubt the rich and prominent Jews (*Grossjuden*) of Hungary would oppose the initiative. Herzl and Gołuchowski joked about the fact that the *Neue Freie Presse*, Herzl's own newspaper, did not cover the Zionist movement because the newspaper's Jewish owners maintained that there was no such thing as a Jewish people. Herzl remarked cuttingly that he was frustrated both with his paper's proprietors and with Austria's

Jews in general, who were not prepared to confront the harsh facts of Jewish life in the Austro-Hungarian Empire. As a consequence, he said, they were left without a real homeland, while at the same time denying this. The Foreign Minister asked him if one of the top persons at the *Neue Freie Presse* was a Protestant. Herzl replied: 'No. He belongs to a species which I have never seen: he is an Austrian. I know Germans, Poles, Czechs – but I have never seen an Austrian.'

Gołuchowski agreed that it was important to gain England's support and added that 'He considered the project of leading the Jews to Palestine so praiseworthy that . . . in his opinion, every government ought to support it financially!' The meeting ended with general agreement but without any real commitment to take action.

On July 3, 1904, Herzl died at Edlach, a resort not far from Vienna. His funeral, held in Vienna on July 7, was attended by tens of thousands, among them people who came to the city by train from all parts of the Austro-Hungarian Empire and all of Europe. Vienna, it was said, had never before seen such a funeral.

*   *   *

Herzl's life and work cannot be separated from the history of the Zionist movement. He transformed the idea of a Jewish state from one bandied about by a small coterie of educated but marginal Jews to an item on the international political agenda, a position which it keeps to this day. In founding the World Zionist Organization and its agencies and subsidiaries, he laid the cornerstone for the representative democratic institutions not only of the Zionist movement but of the State of Israel as well. Herzl understood that Zionism was an unusual project: on the face of it, it was just one more national movement, yet it was a unique attempt to restore a people – one that many did not consider a nation – to a land it had not lived in for almost 2,000 years. To do this, he understood he needed the help of the Great Powers and an international constellation conducive to its realization.

Despite his unflagging efforts, Herzl proved unable to persuade the Great Powers that the creation of a Jewish homeland in Palestine was a vital interest not only of the Jews but also of Europe and the world as a whole. And he knew very well that without their support the Zionist idea would remain no more than a dream. But, as he noted on a number of occasions, the fact that he personally had not succeeded did not mean that the Jewish state would not come into being: 'Moses did not bring his people into the Promised Land.' Herzl may not have seen the birth of the Jewish state, but his death, reported in most of the world's newspapers, heralded the return of his people to their own land. Through Herzl's diplomatic efforts, unsuccessful as they were, Europe's educated elite, its royal courts, its Prime Ministers and Foreign Ministers came to know of the existence of the Zionist movement. Consequently, when the right constellation did eventually appear upon the disintegration of the Ottoman Empire after World War I, and then again in 1947, after World War II and the Holocaust, the Zionist movement was able to establish its national home and Jewish state on the ideological, organizational, and diplomatic foundation that Herzl had laid during his nine years at its helm. The many diplomatic failures he suffered are best viewed as glorious failures that nonetheless made a profound impression on Jewish and world history. During the twentieth century other small nations also made their presence known to the international community; in many cases they caught the world's attention primarily by employing terror, murder, and violence. But, as a journalist, Herzl understood that words could speak just as loudly, and realized that the modern world's mass media could give power to the powerless. And he harnessed the power of the word to his goals as no other statesman before him had done.

The truest words ever written about Herzl may be those that he himself wrote in his diary in the bleak days of June 1901, at the time when an internal opposition first emerged within the movement that had not long before come into being largely as a product of his own efforts:

One day, once the Jewish state comes into existence, all this will appear petty and unremarkable. Perhaps a fair-minded historian will find that it was something after all when an impecunious Jewish journalist, in the midst of the deepest degradation of the Jewish people and at a time of the most disgusting anti-Semitism, made a flag out of a rag and turned a miserable rabble into a people rallying around that flag.

What could be a better epitaph?

*   *   *

A saying circulated during the French Revolution: 'How beautiful was the Republic – under the monarchy.' Visions of an ideal future seldom live up to the expectations of the prophets who dream them. Such was the case in the French Revolution, when the ideals of liberty, equality, and fraternity transmogrified into the Jacobin Reign of Terror; the same thing happened with the Enlightenment ideas of the American Founders, who declared that 'all men are created equal' but produced a constitution that protected slavery. Neither would it be hard to make a long list of the disparities between Herzl's vision of his Old-New Land and the realities of Israel. But it is impossible to understand the European cultural and political context out of which Zionism emerged and the enormous energies that went into the Zionist project and the establishment of the Jewish state without considering the phenomenon of Theodor Herzl. His broad intellectual horizons, his tireless energy, his political instincts and insights meant that he, more than any other person, was responsible for turning the Zionist idea from a dream into a dynamic, organized political movement with a solid institutional foundation. Those who seek to close the gap between today's Israel and Herzl's vision, to turn the sometimes flawed terrestrial Israel into a heavenly *Altneuland*, would do well to take to heart Herzl's insistence on human agency in his epigraph: 'If you will it, it is no dream.' But that is a matter for another book.

BIBLIOGRAPHICAL NOTE

HERZL'S WRITINGS are quoted in the book according to the available English translations. Despite their almost canonical standing, in some cases these translations may today sound archaic, as even the spelling 'Theodore' may suggest; hence some modernizing was necessary in several cases:

Theodore Herzl, *The Jewish State: An Attempt at a Modern Solution to the Jewish Question*, trans. Sylvie d'Avigdor, 2nd edition (London, 1934)

Theodore Herzl, *Old-New Land*, trans. Lotta Levensohn (New York, 1960)

Theodore Herzl, *The Complete Diaries*, ed. Raphael Patai, trans. Harry Zohn, 5 vols (New York, 1960). This translation was based on a partial German edition, which suffered from many omissions. In every case I compared this with the full German edition of the *Diaries*, now included as vols II and III of the critical seven-volume Propyläen edition of Herzl's *Briefe und Tagebücher* (Frankfurt-Berlin, 1993–7).

Herzl's reports from Paris for the *Neue Freie Presse* are translated from his collection *Das Palais Bourbon* (Leipzig, 1895). Articles from *Die Welt* and quotes from Herzl's letters are translated from the available German editions.

For further readings on Herzl's life, see the following:

Alex Bein, *Theodor Herzl* (Philadelphia, 1941)
Steven Beller, *Herzl* (London, 1991)
Amos Elon, *Herzl* (New York, 1975)
Jacques Kronberg, *Theodor Herzl – From Assimilation to Zionism* (New York, 1993)
Ernst Pawel, *The Labyrinth of Exile: A Life of Theodor Herzl* (New York, 1989)

INDEX

INDEX

25- 11- 14